# THE   SCISSORS   OF   METER

# The Scissors of Meter

## GRAMMETRICS AND READING

Donald Wesling

ANN ARBOR

THE UNIVERSITY OF MICHIGAN PRESS

Copyright © by the University of Michigan 1996
All rights reserved
Published in the United States of America by
The University of Michigan Press
Manufactured in the United States of America
Ⓢ Printed on acid-free paper
1999   1998   1997   1996      4   3   2   1


A CIP catalog record for this book is available
from the British Library.

Library of Congress Cataloging-in-Publication Data

Wesling, Donald.
        The scissors of meter : grammetrics and reading / Donald Wesling.
            p.   cm.
        ISBN 0-472-10715-1 (cloth : acid-free paper)
            1. Includes index. 2. English language—Versification.
        I. Title.
        PE1505.W47   1996
        821.009—dc20                                            96-9950
                                                                    CIP

*Do not be led astray*
*by the surface of things;*
*in the depths*
*everything becomes law.*

—Rainer Maria Rilke

# Preface

*The Scissors of Meter* is last in a set of three studies of verse technique, whose earlier books are *The Chances of Rhyme* (1980) and *The New Poetries* (1985). Here as in my two earlier books, the discourse is literary, not technical-linguistic; my audience is writers, teachers, students, and all readers fascinated by reading, attentive to their own attention.

This book consists of a critique of modern theories of poetic meter, primarily on the ground that these are unable to relate their formalizing gestures to any adequate exegesis (part 1); and of a proposal that students of poetry might include what I call *sentencing* as part of a notation, so that we might begin to integrate metrical with other types of reading (part 2). In earlier versions of this study, I spoke of "grammetrics and interpretation," but now I more modestly use *reading* because I have come to feel that interpretation is a term we should reserve for historical-ideological accounts of the poem. My other accounts of poetry during the last decade will show that I think no reading is innocent of the historical and ideological dimensions. In the present study, however, such interpretation is absent: it need not, but usually does, *come after* patient, tentacular, elementary reading. (A distinction is possible in logic, if not in time, between exegetical and ideological reading; the distinction is not appropriate or desirable, except in cases like the present book, which aims to reassure readers about their powers of simultaneous processing.) Ideological interpretation is perhaps easier to perform than elementary reading, because we are more conscious of the processes and logics of interpretation; but reading in my title's definition is difficult because it is precisely what is automatic and taken for granted. All I wish to give back to the reader here is what the reader already has. But we need to know more about what, in language, we know, do, and experience. I have ventured into these polemics about reading with one aim: to reinstate metrical study as a branch of cognition, as a part of literary criticism, an essentially humanistic discipline.

My title, *The Scissors of Meter*, summarizes the constructive part of the book's argument, because the ambiguity of English permits me to say that meter is a scissors and is itself scissored, meter is both active and acted upon. Meter is the scissors of sentences, and of their segments; sentences are the scissors of meter. *Scissors* is a plural word for a single instrument; the attempt is to hold metering and sentencing in the same thought.

The commentator who dares to write on all the technical and contentious subjects of meter, grammar, and reading must risk omissions, overstatements; must act on partial knowledge or not at all. Then of course the writer waits to be corrected. Within literary studies, the history of metrical theory offers perhaps the boldest instance of the process of conjecture and refutation. Traditionally the conjectures have been sometimes loony and the refutations nearly always savage. It would be foolish to hope to escape.

Concluding his *Defense of Rime* in the midst of a Renaissance paradigm-dispute between warring ideas of meter, Samuel Daniel wrote very sensibly: "But in these things, I say, I dare not take upon mee to teach that they ought to be so, in respect my selfe holdes them to be so, or that I thinke it right; for indeede there is no right in these things that are continually in a wandring motion, carried with the violence of our uncertaine likings, being but onely the time that gives them their power." Except that we are better able to graph the forms of change in cognition and in history, one can hardly disagree with the tone or direction of that; it holds true now of metrical theory, as it did in 1603.

This book, conceived and drafted in the 1980s, has had many forms. It was shorter when it was a breakaway chapter of my earlier study, *The New Poetries* (1985), and then it grew considerably longer than it is now with a computer-assisted study of the array of fourteen texts, and with endnotes that were the partial record of a running dialogue I have had with Richard D. Cureton of the University of Michigan. The computer study proved inconclusive—worse, contrary to the habits of attention the book itself fosters; but I learned about human mental process by running against the limits of machine, and I have preserved traces of the computer study in the last two chapters. While my friendly contest with Richard D. Cureton engages significant issues, I have decided this book should go forward in streamlined form simply to justify, state, and give examples for my own idea. I remain grateful to Richard D. Cureton for his generous attention.

For help and advice, thanks (but no blame for errors!) to Christa Beran, Eleanor Berry, Dora Sue Besser, Laurence Bogoslaw, Enikö Bollobás, Mark Breitenberg,

T. V. F. Brogan, Matthew Chen, Charles Cooper, Richard D. Cureton, Robert Dilligan, Edwin Fussell, Gregory Hidley, Ronald Langacker, Richard Levy, James K. Lyon, Erika May, Louis Montrose, Alec Ormsby, and Andrew Wright. This book is for them, and for scholars and students, but I should record that this is in the first instance for the poets of America.

Two brief "Grammetrical Readings" from this book were printed in *Sniper Logic* 3 (spring 1995), published by the Creative Writing Program at the University of Colorado, Boulder. My thanks to Jennifer Dorn, the Editor of *Sniper Logic,* for permission to reprint.

*I should like to thank these authors and publishers for their kind permission to reprint the following poems:*

Cid Corman and Potes and Poets Press, Inc., for "The Tortoise" from *Root Song* by Cid Corman. Copyright © 1986 by Cid Corman.

David R. Godine, Inc., for "Fog Burning Off Cape May" from *The Broken Blockhouse Wall* by John Peck. Copyright © 1978 by John Peck.

Edward Dorn and Donald Allen, for "The Rick of Green Wood," from *The Collected Poems of Edward Dorn, 1956–1974.* Copyright © 1975 by Edward Dorn. Reprinted by permission of Edward Dorn and by Donald Allen for the Four Seasons Foundation.

Farrar, Straus & Giroux, and Faber & Faber, for Number 13 from *Berryman's Sonnets* by John Berryman. Copyright © 1952, 1967 by John Berryman. Reprinted by permission of Farrar, Straus & Giroux, Inc. UK and British Commonwealth rights by permission of Faber & Faber, London.

Farrar, Straus & Giroux, and Faber & Faber, for "Man and Wife" from *Life Studies* by Robert Lowell. Copyright © 1956, 1959 by Robert Lowell. Copyright renewed © 1981, 1986, 1987, by Harriet W. Lowell, Caroline Lowell and Sheridan Lowell. Reprinted by permission of Farrar, Straus & Giroux, Inc. UK and British Commonwealth rights by permission of Faber & Faber, London.

Houghton Mifflin Company, for Sonnet 129 from *The Sonnets of William Shakespeare,* from the Quarto of 1609 with Variorum readings and commentary, edited by Raymond Macdonald Alden. Copyright © 1916 by Houghton Mifflin Company.

New Directions Publishing Corporation, for "Anniversary Poem" from *The Collected Poems of George Oppen,* copyright © 1975 by George Oppen, and for original and Roger Fry translation of one four-line stanza from *The Selected Poems of Stéphane Mallarmé,* by Stéphane Mallarmé, copyright © 1951 by New Directions Publishing Corporation, and for "Portrait of a Lady" from *The Collected Poems of William Carlos Williams, 1909–1939,* vol. I, by William Carlos Williams, copyright © 1938 by New Directions Publishing Corporation, and for "The Return" from *Personae* by Ezra Pound, copyright © 1926 by Ezra Pound.

Oxford University Press, for "A Satirical Elegy . . ." from *The Poems of Jonathan Swift,* Harold Williams, ed., copyright © 1958 by Oxford University Press, and for "Oppositions: Debate with Mallarmé," from *The Way of a World* by Charles Tomlinson, copyright © 1969 by Charles Tomlinson, and for Poem VII of *In Memoriam* by Alfred Tennyson, from *In Memoriam,* Susan Shatto and Marian Shaw, eds., copyright © 1982 by Oxford University Press.

The publishers and the Trustees of Amherst College, for Poem 303, "The Soul selects," reprinted by permission of the publishers and the Trustees of Amherst College from *The Poems of Emily Dickinson,* Thomas H. Johnson, ed., Cambridge, MA: The Belknap Press of Harvard University Press, copyright © 1951, 1955, 1979, 1983 by the President and Fellows of Harvard College.

W. W. Norton & Co., for the 38-line Ice Skating episode from *The Prelude,* Book I, by William Wordsworth, from *The Prelude: 1799, 1805, 1850,* Jonathan Wordsworth, M. H. Abrams, and Stephen Gill, eds. Copyright © 1979 by W. W. Norton and Company.

*Every effort has been made to trace the ownership of all copyrighted materials in this book and to obtain permission for its use.*

# Contents

# Part 1

# CRITIQUE OF MODERN METER

# Chapter 1

## The Existing Scholarship

The historical fate of metrics has been to be removed from poetry and thrust to the margins of poetics. Time and again since George Gascoigne and George Puttenham in the sixteenth century, narrowing definitions of poetic form have compelled prosody to turn back into a special science. No branch of literary scholarship has suffered more from the false emulation of the scientific disciplines, from false analogies with nonverbal arts, from lack of agreed-upon definitions and notations, from disproportion between working concepts and the reality of poetry as written, and from unexposed anachronisms. The radical lack of a strong theory of meter, which is the greatest part of prosody and which I take as standing for prosody in this book, has made prosodic scholarship arcane, unfashionable, indeed *impossible* in the sense of offering a place from which theory as such might be ruthlessly criticized.[1] We need to inquire, I propose, whether there can still be a metrics at all, when this field has attained such a high degree of autonomy. Craig La Drière thinks the term *autonomy* is too polite: "possibly more accurate would be to say that this specialized study has, for whatever reasons, been relegated to relative isolation within the main stream of literary scholarship."[2] The result, in practice, is the most bitterly and unproductively contentious of all the literary disciplines.

Robert Bridges once gave the "qualifications of an English prosodist: 1) the educated misunderstanding of Greek and Latin verse; 2) a smattering of modern musical rhythm. His method 1) to satisfy himself in the choice of a few barrel-organ rhythms, and 2) to exert his ingenuity in finding them everywhere." This example, said Bridges, "is not likely to be recommendable to a student."[3] And in fact the technical aspects of poetry are difficult to teach. The teacher—even the teacher who hears more than barrel organ rhythms—has no guarantee that his or her kit of rules matches with the text in any way but suggestively. There may even be an element of bad faith in this attitude toward poetic technique for the purposes of instruction: poetic technique is felt to be arcane, doubtful, imprecise or overprecise, and anyway a subject for obsessive hacks; and at the same time metrics, in measured portions severely limited (because after all it is ornamental to the main study), is felt to be perfectly adequate for ordinary purposes, a whiff of the bracing stuff, nevertheless a diversion from the real study of theme, emotion, cognitive content, meaning. So teaching too suffers from inadequate theory.

And the process of reading through centuries of scholarship in this field is even more sobering. Far more often than patches of continuity and agreement, one finds the lack of logical contact between theories. This passage from 1911 is typical in its ferocity of tone.

> Thus arises the fundamental and hideous error that disfigures M. Verrier's whole work: namely that all English verse is correctly pronounced when it is pronounced in the style of everyday conversation—as the most pedestrian of prose. . . . No one with the least ear or with the slightest feeling for form in verse could possibly, for a single moment, apply the same principles of scansion to . . .

> What fields, or waves, or mountains?
> What shape of sky or plain,

> and . . .

> Suddenly flashed on her a wild desire,

> And yet M. Verrier does so.[4]

After a study of articles on metrics in *PMLA,* one scholar found that "the great disappointment . . . is their lack of relation to each other. No body of accepted fact or even of critical opinion has been built up over the years. Seldom does one scholar refer to the findings of another. The result is a field obscure and uncertain in its various emphases." Karl Shapiro, one of the best modern commentators, has written that perhaps the "most distressing" aspect of this study "is the necessity of beginning with absolute fundamentals and working up through an enormous copia of unscientific scholarship, analyses which have not even premises in common, and the prejudices of the poets, critics, and students of the past three and a half centuries."[5] Recent statements by authorities in the linguistic and the structuralist approach to versification are cautious, as if to suggest that metrics is a practice infinitely delayed:

A metrical theory which is logically sound, linguistically well-informed, and semantically serviceable to literary criticism is a challenging prospect.[6]

In spite of the existence of a very abundant literature (which stretches back 2000 years), essential notions in the realm of versification do not yet possess a rigorous definition. Discoveries of modern linguistics, particularly phonology, have rendered defunct a number of ancient rules and laws, without always replacing them with new ones.[7]

Seymour Chatman, author of the first of these statements, had earlier written a whole book with the title *A Theory of Meter* (1965), but here (1970) he is still affirming that "metrics needs a theory and scansion a rationale." Especially since romanticism in England, poets have expressed the same felt need for, in the words of Edgar Allan Poe, a "Prosody Raisonnée." Coventry Patmore's judgment, in his "Essay on English Metrical Law" (1857), will stand for many: "upon few other subjects has so much been written with so little result."[8] Coleridge, Poe, Patmore, Bridges, Hopkins, Auden, W. C. Williams: the persistent request of the highly conscious postromantic poets of stature has been for a united prosody. They do not want a "science of versification," as Webster's has it, but a nonprescriptive poetics of technique that will aid in the making and reading of poems. The absence of a unified period style and prescriptive rule-system, with the memory that such things existed in a powerful way in Europe in the years between Dryden and Dr. Johnson, makes the expressed need for a workable poetics of technique the more acute. And the less likely.

A poem strictly unprecedented, with its own laws of structure, or rather of growth, the perfect postromantic poem, which does not exist except as a theoretical limit, would have to be described—if it could be described—by perfect case-law. If all poems were of that sort, metrics and prosody would be a disjunctive collection of rule-of-thumb hints: or nothing. Metrics would not exist except as a desperate hope for an unreachable delayed synthesis. It becomes necessary to inquire into the possibility of metrics in an era whose main imperative is to deflate literature as an institution—a period relatively far advanced in the avant-gardist ethos and the attempt to be or seem unprecedented.

Case law empiricism ought to be reduced to the minimum by the action of a powerful generalizing theory. (The problem, as Richard D. Cureton has said, "lies in developing a theory that adequately describes any given use of a norm, not just the norm."[9] That is how power is earned, by showing how unique usages interact with the norm.) We prepare for such a theory by showing the range and explanatory adequacy of existing theories. The need for such a theory is so pressing and has been felt to be so urgent for the whole of the period since the 1790s, that many reductive and unhistorical syntheses have been produced. Though the "accentual-syllabic" theory held from Patmore and Saintsbury through W. K. Wimsatt and George T. Wright has come to dominate, no system has seemed fully authoritative. What Patmore says of the earlier writers still applies to work in this field since the middle of the nineteenth century, with the possible exception of George T. Wright on Shakespeare's meter and Richard D. Cureton on rhythm: "no one of these . . . renders anything like a full and philosophical account of the subject." Parts of the accounts given by Puttenham, Gascoigne, Webbe, Campion, Daniel, Bysshe, Say, Steele, Guest, Patmore, Hopkins, Bridges, Saintsbury, Jespersen, Jakobson, Wimsatt, Paul and Edwin Fussell, Halle and Keyser, Kiparsky, Chatman, Dilligan, Hollander, and Wright have value. Yet in their sphere the theorists of what I shall call the physiology of versification—Walt Whitman and Charles Olson among them—also have value: explaining other facts, facts that those in the first list have not even perceived. W. H. Auden and Robert Graves have said that they think a sort of feudal apprenticeship system, with regular instruction in the arcane meters, would be a workable way of training writers in their craft. Yet more valuable for both writers and readers in this unhistorical system might be: an initial contemporary survey, to see what writing has been done in the recent and receding past, to generalize limits and discover patches of continuity and relationship, and from there to imagine the conditions of possibility for technique in any given period. This might also mean convicting the existing prosodic tradition of anachronisms, and reducing the claims of any "scansion" that excludes many choices of the writer, many responses of the reader.

"That English verse is not properly measurable by the rules of Latin and Greek verse" (Patmore) is perhaps the first axiom to be urged. The second, also a testimony to the force of unworkable previous paradigms, is that English free verse and English prose poems are not properly measurable by the rules of traditional English verse (if those are rules at all). The third axiom is that the more inclusive a new metrics, the more it embodies the facts of history and language, the horizons of both author and reader, the more satisfying will be its usefulness to exegetical and ideological reading. Only then can we extend meter's definition beyond counting out the sound-features of the language; only then may we counteract the sense, here expressed by W. K. Wimsatt, that the term and discipline of prosody have been "pre-empted by modern linguistics . . . to refer to phonetic features."[10] Prosody, as a term subsuming meter, signifies technique in the poem in the broadest sense, from punctuation to the character of syntax and tone in the whole poetic utterance. In this study I do not claim to cover every device and explain its effect; in the practical readings in part 2, I am more concerned to propose certain nonstandard weights and measures than to be comprehensive. Overall, I have tried to show the general historical situation of all prosodic devices in an avant-garde era, and to widen prosodic analysis to take under its aegis the facts of syntax and sentencing.

These definitions make humanistic claims. It is one of my themes that while grammatical and semantic systems can be analyzed as in essence prosodic, ironically the discipline of metrics, so concerned with the sensuous aspects of language, has only begun to account for the sound-system of the poetic text (for example, in the work of Bruce Hayes and Richard D. Cureton). The musical systems invented by Steele, Ruskin, Lanier, Taig, and others, and the numerical system for stress (Trager-Smith) and stress maxima (Halle-Keyser et al.) devised more recently by linguists, formulate only part of the complex scale and have no adequate procedures for getting from metricality to meaning. Thus, in my terms, these accounts are inadequate for the purposes of reading, though of course they do serve the ends of the sort of identification that can lead to meaning. No notation, like that in music, has proven anywhere near effective for performance or for sound-meaning analysis of poetic texts. We need to know, too, where sound fits in the reader's reception of the poem; syntax and grouping, the categories I foreground in this book, are divorced from sound and are arguably more crucial in the economy of attention.

There is not even agreement as to what would constitute adequacy in such a notation: lacking an elaborated prosody, we lack an agreed-upon vocabulary of crucial terms, working distinctions between mental and oral performance, and a definition of what makes for sufficiency in either sort of performance. When, in part 2, I argue that scholarship should subsume and use the category of syntax, I make the explicit choice of a method: with its attendant standards of adequate explanation, which are not those of traditional prosodic theory.

In this I try to invent a theory consonant with the poems themselves of a period that requires the devaluing, deflation, and exposure of technique and of devices of equivalence, and thereby the subversion of formal versification. We need to discover how this situation came into being, and just how far the dynamic of nihilism carries. The formal metrics still persists: triumphant. However, there is a crisis of commentary even among the adherents of the system of rhyme and accentual stress: I think, for instance of the debates that followed Halle and Keyser's "Chaucer and the Study of Prosody" (1966), an article that reformulated English iambic pentameter. Directly pertinent here, too, are all those literary facts of prosodic avant-gardism (sprung rhythm; prose poem; free verse; concrete and talk poetry) that elude the reigning prosody and cannot be countenanced or described. We require, therefore, a reasoned summary of the canonical theory, and a critique, as a way of clearing the ground. Despite the impulse of the nonsyntactic, or language-as-material writers of the 1990s, who obliterate not only formal prosody but also the form of the sentence, there may be something to preserve of the elaborate system evolved for prescriptive and descriptive purposes over hundreds of years. Yet a rethinking of the fundamental purposes of this discipline is long overdue. Poetry of our time demands the reassessment and the inner renovation of all devices and their definitions. It puts under extreme pressure the very concept of a device and the very fact of literature. The call for absolute modernity, now known as postmodernity, requires the rewriting of literary history. It requires the skeptical revaluation of all that stands in the relation of rhetoric to the quintessential, the identity-forming and identity-dispersing poetic.

## Chapter 2

# Accentual–Syllabic Theory: The Reigning System

By far the largest part of the body of poetry in English respects the conventions of accentual-syllabic meter. The metrical theory that describes this majority poetry tries to specify those conventions, and to show how poetry can excite interest within this formal matrix. Not despite, but by means of, somewhat inflexible secondary functions of language, words in the verse-line are so arranged that by and large, and certainly enough to make systems of expectation possible, their stresses compose a pattern. In iambic pentameter, each line typically has ten syllables divided into five feet, with the stress on the even-numbered syllables. There are possible "substitutions" of irregular but pleasing feet. Yvor Winters, W. K. Wimsatt, and Monroe Beardsley have argued that there is more "interplay of syllable-stress meter with various other features of linguistic organization" than in free verse or poems with less predictable stressing, and this is why (so they say) the greatest English poetry has "after all been written in the more artful syllable-stress meter."[1] These are the basic attributes and praise for traditional English meter. Expectation so defined would appear to be retrospective rather than prospective: not expectation at all.

Over many centuries, there are also, copresent, several minority poetries with their own measuring, if not metrical, theories. To try to write the history of these impulses is to make a myth, to conflate things that need to be kept separate, to make a type out of several historical choices. This other type is in each period one or more alternative paradigms, as strong as the historical conditions allow. These represent a markedly different principle, even though at times their methods and rationales are those of classical revival. These measures use stress, also, to constitute the line, but not alternately, not with the predictability of strong-weak. In periods before the 1790s, which (as I argue in the early chapters of *The New Poetries*) is the decade of the break in concepts of poetic form, these prosodies were always alternatives but never posed much of a threat to the majority styles. It is hard to say whether a failure to realize them was necessary or an accident, though one suspects it was necessary: not because their measures go against the grain of the language, but because major poets—Chaucer, Spenser, Shakespeare—wrote in the central tradition in the main dialect and developed technical resources of the majority style in the most profound and influential way. Only after the 1790s do these measures come into more and more prominence, until today, in free verse, they may be called the major alternative way of writing; judging from US and UK anthologies of the past ten years, this constellation of measures may now claim priority over metered poetry, at least in numbers. These measures will not eliminate the traditional mode, which will never lose its historical greatness or contemporary appeal; yet the alternative methods do work outside of traditional metrical theory, and they provoke hybrid forms or deviations toward far other norms than those followed by writers in the rhyme-meter track. Now, they are not so much subversive as modifying, working as they do both inside and outside the traditional schemes—often within the poems of a single writer, as in, say, Robert Creeley.

The theorists of the heavy-stress measures are Steele, Coleridge, Hopkins, Olson. However, lack of an adequate metrical theory has never prevented the writing of poems. Often, in fact, the lack of fit between the reigning theory and actual habits of composition has permitted poetry to flourish; on the other hand, sometimes theory coerces practice. Renaissance writing on prosody, mesmerized by the classics, is comparable to our own postmodern moment of lag, when the poetry outstrips a theory flagrant in its anachronism. When Sidney and Marlowe and others were writing a native syllable-stress meter of increasing sophistication, the earliest English prosodists (Gascoigne, Harvey, Puttenham, Campion) were interpreting English meter in classical terms—confusing the stress their ears heard with the quantity their concepts required. This view saw metrical feet as being based on quantity alone, defined in terms of syllable length, one long syllable equal to two short; meter thus tended to degenerate into syllable arithmetic, and classical rules of quantity became the pattern for interpreting existing works and making new ones.[2] In the period between Dryden and Johnson, poetry and prosodic theory realign, and the classicism of a mathematics of syllables produces culturally central measures. Poets use syllable count and tend to suppress stress; their claim is that earlier eras in poetry are sloppy and unregulated, not "correct." Dryden, Pope, and Swift revolutionized technique by an array of devices to tailor or stretch their phrasing: elision, syncope, apocope, synaloepha, and diaeresis, avoidance of some words and formulaic reliance on others, all to keep the right count. Edward Bysshe and Alexander Pope are the theorists of Enlightenment counting measures.

Paul Fussell has shown the ethical imperatives behind these Augustan techniques, in the poet's hope to fill and regulate the reader's mind.[3] The special mission of Pope and his contemporaries was to submit poetic composition to the test of reason: in Thomas Taig's phrasing, "to demonstrate that form had an intellectual as well as a sense-appeal; their aim was to compose verses, not for the ear alone, but in accordance with the laws of 'numbers' as they understood them," and in consequence metrics became in their era a systematic study for the first time in English literary history.[4] This attempt to rationalize meter, an expression in literature of the will to authority that dominated all the other spheres of life and thought in the moment of Augustan form, made a very distinguished poetry by subordinating the ear to theory. A syllabic prosody gives special pleasure through its learned artifices of contractions and elisions. "The long couplet in the classical tradition, and especially that couplet as it is refined by Pope, is a structure composed of *processed words,* words manipulated into new, momentary phrases—ellipses, compressions, inversions, zeugmas, extraordinary junctures, suspensions."[5] Infinite variety of combination is possible, even within these close limits. Of course all poetry of whatever age or provenance must process words, yet no poetry in English so constrains the poem in the reader's ear, so compels the reader's attention. As the words are manipulated, so is the reader.

Yet within the citadel of this numerical and classicizing metrics there developed poets, like Thomson, who worked in the tradition of Miltonic blank verse, and prosodists, like Samuel Say and Joshua Steele, who recognized the importance of English stress. Say is one of the first (1745) who sets out the premises of an accentual-syllabic prosody in recognizably modern terms, and in so doing he finds it necessary to ridicule the fashionable doctrine of contractions (words with apostrophe to signal a dropped vowel) and to put Milton above the writers of the quantity-based, ten-syllable heroic line.[6] Say represents syllables by musical notes: a procedure that, while it is hardly an adequate representation of metrical form, at least has the merit of recognizing that poetry is made up of reader-recognized, sounded, expanding and contracting durations. These premises refute the quantitative explanations.

That a musical notation tries to account for features of both stress and time (melody and measure) is pronounced in the very subtitle of Joshua Steele's remarkable *Prosodia Rationalis* (1779): *An Essay Towards Establishing the Melody and Measure of Speech, to Be Expressed and Perpetuated by Peculiar Symbol.* Steele uses musical notes to show the intonation pattern of the "To be or not to be" soliloquy in Garrick's version, giving pitch patterns of individual syllables, durations, dynamics. "For the first time in the history of our literature," according to T. S. Omond, "a writer proclaims that verse is essentially a matter of musical

rhythm, and applies musical methods frankly and fully to the notation of me-
ter."[7] The text chosen for analysis is a represented speech-act: dramatic rather
than satiric, Shakespeare rather than Pope, Garrick pretending to be Hamlet:
plainly a countercouplet instance, used to expound and glorify English stress and
to relate actual speech-stress to its literary transformation. Implicit is a general
linguistic theory that contravenes reigning notions of language and of meter.
Despite its sketch at a notation that could be objective, Steele's is, as John
Hollander notes, a "*performative* system of scansion, rather than a truly *descriptive*
one." Yet it does not disguise the more subjective system as the other, and it has
the advantage of boldly displaying the equal importance of a poem's stress fea-
tures and its duration features.[8] Later treatments of verse with the categories of
musical rhythm, for instance in Sidney Lanier, often forget Steele's sensible
reminder that syllabic relations are not as clearly definable as musical notes, and
tend to promote a purely temporal thesis that is not fine-tuned to perceive the
significant variations in temporal extent between prominent and unprominent
syllables. Stress as length, as pitch, as intensity, as energy, as speech act is recog-
nized in Steele, and this is his theory's very great claim to subversive originality.
Steele's theories hollowed out Augustan form from within, and in retrospect we
may see him as a transitional figure, preparing, in the field of meter and metrical
theory, the extreme extension and reversal of premises that was English romanti-
cism. From Bysshe to Dr. Johnson, the idealizing prosodic system was dominant,
though overlapping with the speech stress system of Say and Steele. The artificial
scansion is more challenged by the sense scansion in the 1790s, just at the
moment when general history itself shifts to another distinct view of reality and
of the relationship of poetic language to reality. This dramatic conjuncture is the
best instance we have that, as Paul Fussell Jr. has said in his book on eighteenth-
century prosody, "the history of prosody is . . . inseparable from the history of
ideas." A break occurs that is at once epistemological and prosodic; though this
shift in the ground of poetic discourse has seemed to later historians nearly
invisible, we need only rearrange our information to see its audacity.

     Stress, the broader linguistic term that I have preferred to use here, is not
accent, though after the late eighteenth century the terms are for most prosodists
synonymous. The signature of the new school is stress, and the influential poem
that most radically enacts its premises is written by S. T. Coleridge in the late
1790s. "Christabel," and its famous preface proclaiming a "new principle" for
poetry, "that of counting in each line the accents, not the syllables," is by
traditional consent the work that turns both poetry and prosody toward the
poem in the ear. Writing to Byron about the poem in 1815, Coleridge said: "I
count by Beats or accents instead of syllables,—in the belief that a metre might

be thus produced sufficiently uniform and far more malleable to the Passion and Meaning."[9] There is nothing in Steele that foreshadows this; the idea of a prosody malleable to meaning is extremist, organicist, and avant-garde. But such a prosody is incapable of being actualized in the strict sense, and though others later attempt to write in the beat-counting mode, Coleridge himself does not, despite the claims in his preface. The poem becomes not so much a model as a landmark.

Down into and through the nineteenth century, the general principle of an alternation of stronger and weaker syllables becomes dominant. It is exemplified in the work of Patmore (1857), Mayor (1886), Saintsbury (1910), Lascelles Abercrombie (1923), Paull F. Baum (1922), and others to the present day. This view attempts to give equal weight to both the stressing and the timing aspects of poetic language. When it moves over toward stressing, the theory becomes inclined toward accent as the constitutive feature: Thelwall (1812), a disciple of Steele and friend of Coleridge, offers a case in point, and later we have the instance of Edwin Guest, whose vast *History of English Rhythm* (1838) celebrates "Christabel" and makes a great deal of the stress features of Anglo-Saxon verse. When the theory moves over toward time, isochrony of syllables, pauses, and the like, it is biased toward a musical view of verse structure and offers an account that now seems even less balanced and credible: Ruskin, Poe, Lanier, and Omond (to a degree) are examples, though in all cases this now-discredited purely temporal view produces interesting readings, valid partial descriptions, and necessary reminders about the way poetry takes place in the human time of expectation. As David Crystal remarks, "the broad distinction between temporal and nontemporal theories . . . does seem to be a valid one, and is the most consistent area of disagreement throughout this period."[10] The later time between 1855 and 1910 is one I would call a crisis of versification, because of the wild growth of overlapping and competing paradigms.

With only a little exaggeration one may say that between Whitman and Hopkins and Bridges, anything was possible in practice as in theory. It is in no essential sense different from other postromantic times; only just then the collision of nearly all possible warring schemas looks particularly virulent and conscious. Patmore's "Essay on English Metrical Law" (1857), Bridges's careful study *Milton's Prosody* (1910; 1921), Schipper's *History of English Versification* (Vienna, 1895; London, 1910), Saintsbury's *History of English Prosody* (1906–10), all espouse versions of the traditional strong-weak, alternation-of-syllables view. Yet Patmore salutes Steele and the musical or temporal style of analysis; Bridges's book, in 1910, is bound in with Will Stone's treatise on the possibility of a quantitative metric for English poetry. (Bridges himself writes a Virgil translation and later a whole book of poems in English quantitative measures.)[11] At the same time, Ruskin and Lanier are applying musical notations to English verse structure. Hopkins's sprung rhythm and Whitman's free verse are oddly fraternal attempts to give a line based on emphatic stressing, letting the gabble of syllables in between the stresses take care of itself: trusting the syllables to make a sweet pattern even when they are, within limits, random. The absolute disregard of Hopkins in this time, and the phenomenon of Whitman as a storm center— passionately hated or admired, but not influential in his technique until after 1910—makes of these two writers, from our perspective, indices of the whole moment.

Robert Bridges's whole career has its symbolic summation in his attitude toward the work of Hopkins. His explanation for not printing the poems in his care was, weakly, that Hopkins was too crude and new. Bridges favored experimentation, invention; but wherever he turned he encountered his own fundamental timidity. So the experiments in quantity, in syllabics, in the *Testament of Beauty* line were all doomed to produce curious freaks, craftsmanly and inimitable. Bridges's defenders speak of him as the perfect traditionalist, maintaining forms and standards into the midst of an era of modernist disintegration.[12] But Bridges is instead the perfect poet of crisis. His career shows him wandering among the plurality of styles, searching for prosodic authority, hesitantly bold as he tries to enliven his measures. His major contributions may be described as his services to Hopkins while Hopkins lived, providing an adversary audience; and *Milton's Prosody,* a tough-minded piece of historical theorizing that uses examples brilliantly, and that remains, with Jespersen, one of the foundational essays in modern metrical theory.

George Saintsbury is a contemporary of Bridges; his *History of English Prosody* reflects the same prosodic moment of a subparadigm shift, a moment of both culmination and crisis. The famous three-volume *History,* ending its tale with Swinburne, appears perfectly timed to coincide with Ezra Pound's innovations around the year 1910. Whitman's invention of a new way of writing gets a page in this narrative: a grudging, question-begging page that maintains that while the American poet's "actual medium is often a plum-pudding-stone or conglomerate of metrical fragments," Whitman could write a more or less regular meter when he wanted to. Hopkins is treated under the heading "Some More Dead Poets," as an "anti-foot and pro-stress" author who "never got his notions into thorough writing order." Saintsbury, like T. S. Omond in *English Metrist* (1921), conveys to the reader a sense of English meter's progress to culmination in the late nineteenth century, especially in the capacious achievement of Tennyson; yet this assurance is undermined by awareness of the great nineteenth-century multiplication of meters, of the anomalous existence of alliterative and quantitative revivals, and of hard-to-explain phenomena like sprung rhythm and free verse. "Time will show" where "our rhymelessness, our discord-seeking, our stress-prosodies" belong, writes Saintsbury very sensibly: "But one thing I think we may dare say that even he will not show, and that is any positive and final solution of continuity in the general course of English prosody."[13] The irony is that just when the "foot" is being abandoned in practice by Eliot, Pound, and others, the idea is given its apotheosis in Saintsbury's massive work.

The metrical foot is Saintsbury's quintessential building block of English verse. The foot is the traditional combination of weak and strong in the usual patterns. Here is his theory in a sentence: English verse works by the system of stress plus time, in combination; with possible substitutions of irregular feet for certain planned effects, and usually with rhyme at the line ends. With this loose and conventional set of notions, Saintsbury makes a valuable map of the forms of English poetry; the immense body of quotation, speculation, prejudice, and charming commentary is lifted in a way nobody would like changed. But this is not a theory. The work itself, as Omond rightly comments, "seems to have been planned as a history rather of our verse itself than of what critics have said of it," and his doctrine of "equivalence" and of "long" and "short syllables" is never explained as a working assumption: "His scansions are a glorious higgledy-piggledy of iambs and trochees, or dactyls and anapests, without any clue given as to how these can be interchangeable."[14] The physical length of the survey and the reiterated claim to be presenting a fundamental fact of verse structure in the foot have led to a belief in some quarters that Saintsbury is definitive of a certain kind of prosodic position. In its 1972 survey of modern poets' attitudes toward technique, the journal *Agenda* asked whether writers used "the traditional Saintsbury type of system"; most avoided the question or said they had never heard of Saintsbury.[15]

In a sense Saintsbury is the last gasp of an older paradigm, the final restatement of traditional theory. Of course, people will be reinventing him anew in every generation, so long as his assumptions seem to apply to past production in syllable-stress poetry and fit some fraction of the poetry being produced—yet in strict historical perspective Saintsbury's book comes up against an edge. In 1910 there is a subparadigm "break," this time one thoroughly within the mode or enclave of the romantic tradition. Modernism is the logical working out or acceleration of romanticist premises in themes as in prosodies. *Prosodies* is now in the plural; from here on, there is no single assumed system of versification, but several, with one dominant. The minority prosody has forced the majority to concede at least this.

First the reigning prosody is broken down in imagism, an Anglo-American project; then when the image, and indeed the very syllable, is isolated into the lobes of the poetic line, imagist practice is enriched: image and discourse, in the writing of Stevens, Eliot, Williams, find a new form of seamless combination. Yet it was Eliot, a writer in free verse, who argued in his "Reflections on *Vers Libre*" (1917) that this is not a genuine kind of poetry because it can only be defined negatively, by the three absences of pattern, meter, and rhyme. Though Eliot, like Milton before him, thinks the freeing of rhyme perhaps a welcome development, he finds the absence of meter unforgivable. Apparently Eliot disagrees with Saintsbury's more relaxed sense that prosody "quietly defeats the efforts, of the willful ones who are hers, to escape her jurisdiction."[16] For Eliot, as for most of the Anglo-American New Critics, meter formally defined is nothing less than the poem's principle of authority; without some reference to meter the poem is not a poem, but is prose and uninstructed ego. The issue as between Eliot and rival modern poets in the Whitman tradition in modern writing is not (as they seem to have thought) between metric and no metric, but between existing metric and a radically new metric.

After Saintsbury others develop the traditional view of prosody with various emphases. Verrier (1911), Brander Matthews (1911), T. S. Omond (1921), Paull F. Baum (1922), Lascelles Abercrombie (1923), George R. Stewart Jr. (1930), and Pallister Barkas (1934) all present descriptive classification systems for poetic structure and for theories of that structure. At one time or another, all emphasize the importance of both stress and time as prosodic variables. Like Saintsbury, they achieve basically mixed systems and take meter as, for their purposes, synecdochically for nearly the whole of prosody—thus scamping consideration of such features as rhyme, image, grammar, sentencing, and tonal structures. Omond in 1921 had concluded that "the upshot of the whole matter" was "that we have as yet no established system of prosody. Much analytic inquiry has yielded no synthesis authoritative and generally accepted."[17] This did not keep Omond himself from proposing a system basically temporal, though his two books also acknowledge the role of stress. A generation later, there are fewer doubts about the progress of scholarship, and the New Critics like John Crowe Ransom tend to speak with more assurance, as if major matters had been settled. Metrics indeed achieves a twentieth-century form of authority, based on scaling down its assumptions and purifying its methods. John Crowe Ransom's division of the poem into an executive *structure* and a more affective *texture,* his placing of meters as repertoires in the category of structure, is typical in the way New Criticism separates off and reifies the meter.[18] So considered, meter becomes a field for positivist investigation: identification of metrical schemas as architectural frameworks. Thus W. K. Wimsatt and Monroe Beardsley: "We hold that [meter] inheres in aspects of the language that can be abstracted with considerable precision, isolated, and even preserved in the appearance of an essence— mummified or dummified."[19] This kind of thinking leads to the use of physical analogies for metrical effects: quart bottles, picket fences, milestones (all from Wimsatt). Meter seems, here, virtually a physical entity; yet to scan the poem we must perform what Wimsatt and Beardsley call "an exercise in abstraction." This position is at once too concrete and too idealized, the result of a confusion of levels. What it misses is the ontological status of meter as a phenomenon bound up inseparably with the whole poem as a structure of intention.

The state of metrical theory in Saintsbury's work may be shown by his hearty idealist affirmation that "in English, by the grace of God and the Muses, the poetry makes the rules, not the rules the poetry." Attitudes toward the way poetry is a rule-governed activity are the best clue to the writer's understanding of the relationship between identification and, in the sense of my book's title, *reading*. If Saintsbury claims too much and actually explains very little by his implicit belief that all in prosody is case law, Wimsatt and Beardsley have conducted their metrical purification to the point where meter has little bearing on meaning. It is possible to feel sympathy for the quandary of the student they describe in their article:

> A student in a seminar presided over by one of the present writers was stumped . . . in scanning in a line at the blackboard and refused to put the next stress mark anywhere at all. "I don't see how to show the interaction between the meter and the sense." As if by scanning he *could* show the interaction. As if anybody expected him to. As if the meter itself could be the interaction between itself and something else.[20]

This student, straining against the scansion, attempting to get from meter identification to a reading hypothesis, is essentially a surrogate for the poet. The postromantic poet, such is the theme of the present book, wants to enliven rhetoric and metric with personality, style, inscape. "You can write a grammar of the meter," say Wimsatt and Beardsley, "but you cannot write a grammar of the meter's interaction with the sense. . . . The interactions . . . are the free and individual and unpredictable (though not irrational) parts of the poetry."[21] Thus they assume the logical and chronological priority of the meter over the sense: it is this view of meter as physical entity rather than as structure of intention that must be resisted. My point is that there is no such thing as mere identification when we are dealing with the formal-semantic entanglement that is metrical, or measured, language. As Barbara Herrnstein Smith has argued, the trouble is that traditional scansion, "since it is concerned primarily with the distribution of relative stress-values, does not discriminate other linguistic features."[22] Nor does this scansion, as a fairly inflexible matrix, discriminate any single poem's particular rules for the contravention of existing rules. Perhaps if our student were responding to a complete poem as a special kind of rule-bound communication, rather than scanning a particular detached line, the dovetailing between abstract pattern and mental enactment might be easier to specify.

Like the linguistic metrics, the New Criticism in its metrical doctrine wanted to clarify the means by which traditional metrics can produce valid analyses. Ransom, Wimsatt, and others criticize unwarranted assumptions and impressionism, on the basis that meter "is made out of linguistic objectivity, but a kind that is capable of modulation, so that a poet can use it this way or that."[23] They argue that it is misleading to resolve meaning by meter, meter by meaning; misleading to conflate the vocal with the verbal, grammar with meter, norm with rule, performance with description, prescription with description. The method is rigorous and the tone modest as they hold that "an understanding of iambic metrics is not a sufficient condition for reading certain kinds of poetry, but is a necessary condition for reading it . . . and this kind of very regularly repeated convention of form certainly affects and conditions and adds to and controls all these other things that you are talking about."[24] There is a suspicion of expressionist theory, here as elsewhere in the New Critical position; an admiration of the "narrow or technical end" of the subject, and a profound uneasiness at that "broader end, where prosody vaporizes out into cognition."[25] The distinction between meter and rhythm is a major premise. So the authority and objectivity of meter in its own sphere is protected by a willing restriction. Though, according to Wimsatt, versification is "perhaps the clearest and most firmly definable objective correlative of our response," nonetheless we must strictly forbid ourselves the impulse to "substitute the experience of the verse for the verse itself." So traditional scansion is promoted, and the discipline of prosody is a part of linguistics, "both a minutely charted and a conspicuously public study."[26] Similar assumptions permit the survey of versification in major language-types and the codification of English prosody in the various handbooks, rich in detail and often excellent in their synopses: one thinks of the works by Paul Fussell Jr., Robert Beum and Karl Shapiro, James McAuley, and Joseph Malof, all variations on the traditional wisdom but all containing flecks of originality in the presentation of the reigning theory.[27]

Doubtless there is a certain kind of critic and linguist who is drawn to metrics because of the exactness of its traditional codes, the way it seems to extinguish subjectivity. But do metrists always recognize the way literary language must continually put into question its own rule-governed behavior, its received ideas of intention, and its ontological status? More perhaps than any other thought frame in literary studies, metrics raises the issue of the relation of exegesis to formalization. Metrics as a discipline has been going through a formalizing phase since the time of Saintsbury; looking back on that era, one comes to believe the time has arrived for a leap ahead into a more powerful exegesis: for poetry and prosody to come closer to the curve of the experience. Certainly the exegetical returns of meter as it stands are very slender, partly because meter is *by definition* a code separate from the code of the meaning. Arguably a transcoding from one to the other is the next assignment for theory, if progress is to be made. The defects of unrigorous, impressionistic exegesis are by now obvious, but far more striking and pertinent for us are the defects in our techniques of formalization. (Very likely *meaning* and *voice* are themselves only partial values, less focal than rhythmic experience. Hence the need for a strong theory of rhythmic phrasing. Very likely a unified theory will come from improved formalizations, not from more or fuller exegeses. Hence the need for a historical critique of formalizations.)

In some writers the need for an authoritative, objective standard, outside the self, resistant to all expressionist theories of aesthetics, produces a kind of theology of meter. For them, meter becomes an unmoved mover, the focus of the poem and the guarantee of its merit. As example, there is Roy Fuller's terse and contemptuous sally: the chopped-up prose that almost universally serves today as poetic form "arises from unconfidence in the ability to count."[28] In such cases, traditional verse defines itself by antagonism to free verse. Usually, the correlative premise is that free verse has been trying to write iambic feet and failing. Strict meter, as a difficulty to be vanquished for the poet and a mental regulator for the reader, gains, in this ambience, an ethical force. This permeates the writings on meter by W. K. Wimsatt, John Crowe Ransom, and Allen Tate, but nowhere more openly than in the essays of Yvor Winters. "In traditional verse," writes Winters, "each variation, no matter how slight, is exactly perceptible, and as a result can be given exact meaning as an act of moral perception."[29] This moralized theory of meter, which permits slashing demotion of certain poets and the forming of a select circle of those who know how continuously to vary from an ideal norm, makes every syllable and punctuation point an ethical issue. It turns the technical code into an instrument of prescriptive judgment and allows the critic to claim his or her knowledge as objective. The abstract theoretical format of meter, as the principle of the poem's literariness and authority, separating the poem from vulgar prose or speech, tends to become the very source of poetic creativity. Wimsatt speaks of the "enabling restraints of formal bondage": a phrase similar in intent to Stefan George's maxim: "The strictest standard is also the supreme freedom." When it arrives at this position, New Critical metrical theory converges on eighteenth-century attitudes but necessarily defines innovation within a historical circumstance very much altered from that of Pope and Dr. Johnson. It must try to maintain a prescriptive and often unhistorical view of poetic composition, within a general climate of positivist description. No wonder the results are sometimes contradictory.

Others who have often worked under the wing of the New Criticism have shown more flexibility. Gay Wilson Allen's *American Prosody* (1935) discusses the variety of techniques used by American poets and takes a special interest in Whitman's rhythms. Karl Shapiro's work in prosody from the 1940s, in his *Essay on Rime* (1945), the article "English Prosody and Modern Poetry" (1948), and *Bibliography of Modern Prosody* (1948), strives to be synoptic and map theory to practice; his category divisions do not always seem to hold up, but there is a salutary reference from prosodic systems to actual recent practice. Harvey Gross's study of prosody from Thomas Hardy to Robert Lowell, *Sound and Form in Modern Poetry* (1964), comprehends work in both traditional and free verse with no bias toward either mode; his gestaltist views of "Prosody as Rhythmic Cognition" lead beyond traditional notions of meter to a theory of expectation: "meter, and prosody in general, is itself meaning. Rhythm is neither outside of a poem's meaning nor an ornament to it. Rhythmic structures are expressive forms, cognitive elements, communicating those experiences that rhythmic consciousness can alone communicate: emphatic human responses to time in its passage."[30] Barbara Herrnstein Smith's splendid study of how poems end, *Poetic Closure* (1968), is the first fully worked-out gestalt theory of reader expectation in any language. The Russian structuralist Yurii Lotman has integrated an account of meter within his general description of poetic equivalence, in a number of works that derive from Russian as well as American formalism. Walter Sutton's *American Free Verse* (1972), deficient in its historical and analytical tools, nonetheless treats its subject with serious respect; still, Sutton is absolutely displaced by a book that explicitly adopts a grammetric approach, Enikö Bollobás's *Tradition and Innovation in American Free Verse* (1986). The most historically complete of these studies in poetic form is John Hollander's *Vision and Design: Two Senses of Poetic Form* (1975), and the essays in Hollander's *Melodious Guile* (1988), about how "poems trope their own schemes" such as meters and refrains, are the most wide-ranging into devices of prosody beyond meter. Hollander is always subtly extending the premises of traditional prosody, not unfriendly to experimental poetry and yet basically more at home with strong closure, emphatic effects, the "metrical contract," in Hollander's own term.

All these studies exhibit acquaintance with the history and methods of traditional metrics, and all, in one way or another, try to dignify and extend that code, to move beyond formalization to exegesis. Taken together, they tend to suggest how prosody might develop itself into a humanistic discipline: by preserving the best elements in the recent, largely linguistic, researches toward a formal notation, but also situating our work on form in reader-response and in literary and general history.[31]

None of the writers so far taken up crosses the bridge between linguistics and criticism, at least not all the way. Nor do students of linguistic metrics cross in the other direction. Yet despite these facts the two forms of research are aware of each other and in rapport. To my mind, the differences between linguistic and literary metrics will finally seem less significant than the one commanding similarity: their shared hope for a heuristic separation between the text's meaning and its formal means. With the exception of a boldly ethical metrist like Yvor Winters, who continually if unpredictably crosses the line between his intuitive formalizations and his moral bias and thus is exemplary for the wrong reasons, both the New Criticism and the New Linguistics share a tendency to reject the notion of a speaking subject. For them, the poem is a place for the transactions of contiguous but separate systems, the least tractable of which is the semantic system.

Linguistic metrics demands analytical rigor. To attain rigor means delimiting the object for study. The choice of this object, and of the units that may be said to comprise the poem's metric for the purposes of description, will for the foreseeable future be the crucial issues in prosody. Though I am myself skeptical that linguists have isolated the proper object and units of prosodic study, nonetheless over the past three decades linguistic analysis, especially in its guise as rhythmic phrasing, has been the area of greatest progress in metrics. Actually, work by such theorists as Jakobson, Chatman, Halle and Keyser, Kiparsky, and Cureton is based on distinctions and discoveries that go back to the early years of the present century: the time of Jespersen's essay of 1900, the invention of the kymograph and oscillograph, Ferdinand de Saussure's constitutive discrimination between speech acts and the system of a language, and the Russian Formalist focus on poetic devices. Progress in metrics has usually followed progress in the knowledge of language. The recognition that "metrics is an aspect of language," that "the normal phonemic command of their language is what enables people to scan," and that "what poetry imitates is the structure of the language itself" has tended to demystify prosody and turn it from a notion into a theory.[32] The basis for a more scientific methodology was laid when these early-century theorists saw that this discipline "forces the literary student to a close intimacy with the material base of literary structure in the structure of language."[33] So, alongside the traditional scansion, from Saintsbury to Wimsatt, there has grown up another, complementary description based on the linguistic givens of English. "The metrical pattern," John Thompson has written, "is a copy, a mimicry, a counterfeit without intention to deceive, of the basic elements of our language and of their order."[34] Jonathan Culler is right to say that numerical symmetry cannot "in itself serve as a defining characteristic of the poetic function in language."[35] But power and subtlety of linguistic description have been useful as developments in formalization, which demand corresponding advances in the accuracy of exegesis.

When literary criticism can complete linguistic metrics, and when it can in turn be completed by being deepened with a cognitive psychology of the reader, and when it can be fully historicized, then we shall have a prosody adequate to the greatness and range of poetry in English. Proceeding toward that end, I intend here not an exhaustive summary of linguistic metrics; rather a judgment on its major emphases during the heady, new-paradigm years of generative grammar in the 1960s and 1970s. I shall argue that work in this area, though brilliant in its own terms, has nonetheless framed those terms so narrowly as to diminish their pertinence for the history and hermeneutics of our poetry. If this is true of prosody in general from the time of Gascoigne, it is very dramatically the case in a study that attempts to "approach an objective verification of intuitive value judgments about rhythm in poetry":[36] where the intuitive is transformed into the objective before most studies begin, *by means that are not on display.* Further, it is not yet, even now, settled whether the true contrary of *objective* is *intuitive*—especially if we define *intuitive* as our learned competence at producing and responding to strings of language. This could be settled now, if we would attend massively to work on the overarching regimes of rhythm, by Henri Meschonnic in the 1980s and Richard D. Cureton in the 1990s; what we might learn from their studies is that we must go beyond the confines of metrics and linguistics to reconcile some of the contradictions within linguistics and metrics. Cureton more than any other emphasizes rhythmic cognition in its relation to processive time, exactly the area where we may expect the breakthrough to a unifying field theory.

Meter depends on prominences, and English meter depends on the prominence of certain features of sound. Those signaling features, whether they be heard as oppositional (binary choices) or as graded (along a spectrum), are limiting conditions; in general it seems true that they cannot be countermanded by the meter. There must be a fit between the metric pattern and the pattern of speech stresses; meter is not itself a special kind of language, but an aspect or secondary function of language. That is why quantitative meter on the classical model was never possible in English, except as a mistaken theory or a consciously odd practice; it goes against the grain of this language. (The exception, unexamined so far by scholarship, is the dependence on quantity of the English dol'nik.) Twentieth-century linguists have proven this stress basis of English definitively, without, however, going on to admit by extension of this premise that neither is counting, by any measure, a usual response to English sentences. Especially recently, the possibility of making the language material amenable to counting has been the thing that attracted linguists to metrics as "clearly a subject in phonology and evidently systematic."[37] Even among scholars sympathetic to literary study, this way of framing the inquiry numerically has made some see meter as a purely linguistic problem. By contrast, Otto Jespersen in the first major study in linguistic metrics (1900) was able to find "the linguistic road to the aesthetic aim. . . . It is important for [us] to observe the effect which verse has—as a rhythmic phenomenon—on the mind of the listener, and how the reader's reactions in turn effect the construction of verse."[38] The idea of the reader's expectation of a recurring pattern, the pleasure of frustration and reaffirmation of language pattern, is somewhat conveniently and briefly announced in Jespersen, but it helps his essay make large claims. Jespersen also anticipates later work by being the first to observe the relativity of stress.[39] Other particular aspects of this early discussion are commentary on inverted stress, the effect of pause, and rising and falling pitch. The 1933 postscript responds admirably to technological metrists like Sonnenschein who say "the kymograph cannot lie": "but neither can it tell us anything of what really matters, namely stress, however good it is for length of sounds."[40] Jespersen was arguing, too, that we "would seem to require a fundamental revision of [meter's] principles, system of notation, and nomenclature," and that metrics cannot be an "exact science aiming at finding out natural laws that are valid everywhere."[41] Those statements seem more and more valid for the era of free verse and the prose poem. Jespersen's skepticism about "finding . . . natural laws" converges on the recent notion of Fred W. Householder concerning the binary opposition of phonemes: we need to make "some provision . . . for distinguishing the natural privative oppositions from the more arbitrary ones" that we invent as heuristic devices, as abstract theoretical entities.[42] That is true in metrics as it is in phonetics, and for the same reasons. When metrics is redefined as a cognitive science, it may claim its own form of exactness, but we do not yet know how the mind works; the new logics are yet to be learned.

From the time of Jespersen, Saussure, and the Russian Formalists, linguistic metrics tried to be scrupulous in distinguishing the functional from the nonfunctional in language. All this work finds its most concentrated, provocative expression in the several studies of meter by Roman Jakobson and by certain of his followers in stylistics such as Michael Riffaterre, Samuel Levin, and Pierre Guiraud.[43] The Jakobsonian formula, drastically reduced, may be expressed:

Similar sound/position/prominence → Similar meaning

Much brilliant observation is involved in the description of the similarities, and yet the connections with meaning are in nearly all instances scamped. Jonathan Culler overstates when he says Jakobson's analyses "are vitiated by the belief that linguistics provides an automatic discovery procedure for poetic patterns and by his failure to perceive that the central task is to explain how poetic structures emerge from the multiplicity of potential linguistic structures."[44] Still, in the terms of the present discussion, Jakobson's readings of Baudelaire and Shakespeare raise the dilemma of formalization against exegesis. One critique of the linguistic basis of these analyses is Michael Shapiro's *Asymmetry* (1976), which shows how the geometrizing of Jakobson's pattern recognition actually neglects crucial categories of linguistic givens.[45]

How is the poetic discourse to be segmented, weighted, built up from the smallest unit to the whole poem? For the linguist, the phonemic system of English is the base, and so from the outset research goes on by postulating abstract theoretical entities that mediate rule and behavior. The phoneme is our conceptualization of the phonetic fact, in terms of oppositions: voiced, unvoiced, and so on. At the next level are the constructive and prosodic features of the language: stress, transition, and pitch. These constructive features are, in Harold Whitehall's words, "*segmentalizers* . . . our chief scissors of linguistic perception,"[46] and one attempt of linguistic metrics in the last scholarly generation has been to cross-index those concepts against traditional meter's concept of the foot. Here as elsewhere the reason for a sharper analysis was the coming of a new formalizing schema, in this case the four degrees of relative stress, four levels of pitch, and four kinds of transition (or "juncture") proposed by George L. Trager and Henry Lee Smith Jr. in *An Outline of English Structure* (1951).[47] This schema implied a gradation mapping of stress rather than the binary opposition of stress-unstress within the iambic foot; now there were to be four degrees of relative stress (loud, secondary, tertiary, weak), and the types of division between feet were specified with a new notation.

The metrical implications of the Trager-Smith phonology were developed in a landmark issue of the *Kenyon Review* (summer 1956), where Harold Whitehall stressed "the careful working out of the integration between the three constructive features, of the manner in which they reinforce each other, of the grammatical and semantic implications that they carry."[48] Seymour Chatman, basing his phonemic analysis of a Frost poem in that issue on the Trager-Smith system, effectively raised the whole vexed issue of performance of texts. Trager-Smith, he held, may be used to juxtapose traditional meter and the suprasegmental analysis of the spoken lines, thus enabling a commentator to show the tension between abstract matrix and actual metrical instance. The attempt to show variations in intonation patterning, through a number of performances of the same poem, has the advantage of avoiding "the unfortunate assumption that performances involve 'exceptions' to some kind of norm" (Chatman), but this attempt brings in other suspect assumptions that tend to conflate the poem's meter with its oral recitation, formula with physical event. Chatman was to extend further yet his concern for performances in his *Theory of Meter* (1965), but it is the synoptic and speculative parts of that book that have come to have more importance. Trager-Smith phonology is taken to its logical limits by Edmund L. Epstein and Terence Hawkes, who proposed in *Linguistics and English Poetry* (1959) that "in English prosody there are only 6192 possibilities of iambic units," as determined by counting all stress, juncture, and pitch features for the iambic foot.[49] The insouciance of that "only," like their throwaway assumption that free verse is not patterned (12), is typical of linguistic metrics as a whole during this structuralist era of the 1950s and 1960s. Yet despite the single-minded attempt to work out the schema in all its angles and arithmetics, this argument, like Chatman's, adopts the promising position that spoken language is basic to all literary compositions (if only to be denied by devices that cannot be spoken), and that the poet and his or her audience, mutually aware, have internalized the conventions of literary communication.[50]

Another use of Trager-Smith theory is John Thompson's *Founding of English Meter* (1961), which shows how, after various sorts of bad fit in post-Chaucerian poetry, colloquial language is for the first time subtly knit in tension with metrical pattern, in the generation of Sir Philip Sidney. The book was promptly criticized by Hawkes for misunderstanding the Trager-Smith system, and by Wimsatt for treating "the shifting relation between pattern and speech" with a method that multiplies unnecessary theoretical entities, and for giving the story of English meter from Wyatt to Sidney "such clean climax."[51]

Segmental phonology proposes a continuous-scale contrast for English speech-stress, through four levels. Thompson and Chatman follow this for the pattern of the language as spoken; but then, using the concept of productive *tension,* they cannot, it seems, elegantly relate the varying four stresses of ordinary language to the simple, binary, abstract stress-unstress of metrical theory. The precise relation of the continuous scale to the binary scale is not well explained by the misleading notion of tension, or by John Thompson's idea, intriguing enough, that meter is a "mimicry" of the basic elements and relationships of English. This is the implied issue in the appendix to Chatman's *Theory of Meter*, "The Stress-Systems of Pike and Trager-Smith": by 1965 Chatman is not sure that Trager-Smith is a complete solution, indeed seems to have switched back from continuous-range fours to binary-choice twos (leading us to ask: *is* a difference there that makes a difference?). Chatman's book, full of valuable psychological and phonetic speculations, is more a presentation of varying approaches to formalizing the language material than it is a fully articulated theory. In the recent history of prosodic scholarship, this book marks the exhaustion of interest in Trager-Smith but pursues much else of interest: statistical survey of separate performances of a single poem, survey of "objective analyses of metrical properties" through research with measuring devices, presentation of relevant work in the cognitive psychology of rhythm, the history of cognitive theory, ethical and literary-critical views of the function of meter. Chatman is properly skeptical of those metrists who tend to reify the foot, which is after all a concept, "a pure metrical convention with no relation to English or to the sense of the poem" (14); in general his interest is not classificatory: "the metrist's function is not to find out how many kinds of feet there are, but rather to insure that there aren't more kinds than necessary."[52] Yet despite Chatman's scholarly tact, his proliferation of partial explanatory models, the book lacks a theory or thesis.

In a short review, "New Directions in Metrics," written later, Chatman incisively points out all the crucial problems in the definition of rhythm, prominence, scansion, and performance, without being able to devise solutions: "Meter is a simple binary abstraction derived from the linguistic relations among adjacent syllables. But there are differences about what constitutes the basis for abstraction."[53] Given the uncertain state of the discipline, we have, of course, no right to expect a solution from Seymour Chatman, and yet perhaps we come to feel, from his very tentativeness, the possibility that phonology is too limited a frame of reference. If the choice of the right formalization is itself a matter of dispute and inquiry, such dispute has the merit of denying premature syntheses; the application of an uncertainty principle to metrics should, very likely, be as sophisticated as it is in physics. Yet one cannot, here as elsewhere among the linguistic theories, help wondering whether less pressure to formalize at every step might have permitted more willingness to consider longer stretches of meter.

In the mid-1960s, the Trager-Smith phonology gave way to a generative phonology after Noam Chomsky, Morris Halle, and Samuel Jay Keyser. Halle and Keyser, in their influential article "Chaucer and the Study of Prosody" (1966), proposed a theory of meter founded on the principles of transformational generative grammar. Though the way in which the theory is generative was rarely discussed in the several studies that followed this line, J. C. Beaver's term by analogy "generative metrics" came into use in the later 1960s.[54] Halle and Keyser attempted to reestablish their description of the iambic pentameter, with corrections after the damaging debate that followed their article, in *English Stress: Its Form, Its Growth, and Its Role in Verse* (1971). Halle and Keyser take the iambic pentameter line as a sequence of ten positions, with primary stress normally in the even-numbered positions. Each even-numbered, stressed syllable, except the very last in the line, is sandwiched between unstressed syllables. Stressed positions so defined are called stress maxima. Their displacement to nonnormal positions will create unmetricality in the line. If too many exceptions are piled up in a single line, it is judged unmetrical. Stress maxima by definition cannot occur at the first metrical position. Initial trochaic inversions, using the traditional terminology, are frequent but are not displaced stress maxima; this is one of the triumphs, supposedly, of the theory. The real triumph, they would claim, is that they are able to switch from a system that allows free substitution to one that defines which substitutions are possible and which are not. The theory thus defines positions strictly by emphatic English stress. Because this metrics hopes to show metricality and position, it makes a very great deal of intersection of the intersection of stress and position; for this reason it can be arithmeticized, turned into algorithms, and programmed. Though the term *iambic* is crucial here, oddly enough the term *foot* is never used; their theory is held, by its partisans, to have demolished the old foot-stress model.[55]

The positions, stressed or unstressed, are the deep structures of generative metrics; surface structure is the actual verse-line, obtained by a string of transformations from the deep structure. That is the analogy on which this model operated, an analogy rarely described or explored for the exact linking process of the system of transformations. Scansion of verse is the reflection of a metrical competence, according to the theory, which strictly distinguishes competence from any unique performance of the text by recitation. To the degree that this schema makes features of the verse-line more explicit and amenable to better general rules, the advance over previous systems improves the code of metrics.

The initial theory was extended and applied in the late 1960s by the authors themselves, and by J. C. Beaver, Donald C. Freeman, Jacques Roubaud, and Dudley Hascall. It was attacked by Karl Magnuson and Frank G. Ryder, then by David H. Chisholm, from a linguistic point of view; and by W. K. Wimsatt from the perspective of traditional literary-critical prosody. Wimsatt is highly empirical and wary of a degree of abstraction that seems to say more about the counting of prominences than about the hearing of five full stresses, more about "complication" than about the tension between norm and utterance.[56]

The Halle and Keyser formalization is the successor in the line of Bridges, Jespersen, and Jakobson. In its extension and development in the system of Derek Attridge, where the terms *beat* and *offbeat* are substituted for Halle and Keyser's *strong* and *weak,* it once seemed able to supplant conventional literary approaches. From the mass of contentious and highly detailed argumentation within and against this new subparadigm, certain studies emerge with special promise for grammetrics. Attridge's book is a model exposition.[57] Donald C. Freeman has shown how the "basic mapping rules" of Halle and Keyser may be historicized: his essay "On the Primes of Metrical Style" (1968) demonstrates that certain periods of English literary history try to actualize all the stress maxima in the line and attain mathematical purity, by the sleights of synaloepha (one metrical position, many syllables) and diaresis (many positions, one syllable); other periods do not enforce stress regularity with anything like this strictness:

> The movement of English verse between these poles continues—from the strict regularity of Pope and Swift to the true accentuation of Coleridge's *Christabel;* from the freedom of metrical practice typical of much Romantic verse to the more formal meters of Tennyson and Arnold to the radical departures from the mainstream of English metrical tradition to be found in modern poetry. Detailed study of each of these periods in terms of this framework is needed.[58]

Jacques Roubaud's "Theses on Poetics" (1969) speculate on the curiosity of a linguistic metrics that cannot, even with the new precisions of Halle and Keyser, devise a code to describe a type of poetry whose only formal trait, at least on first view, is the fact of being segmented by lines: free verse. "The poem, here, is the sentence. . . . The essential passage from sound to sense is made in the line. The description *[codage]* of this hinge must thus be to insist in a brutal, striking way on this: there is attained a unity of another type [that is, different from traditional meter]." Roubaud is not being entirely flippant when he says that this is "perhaps a preparation for the well-considered, conceptual discovery of new laws of language: [the coming of] free verse is perhaps an anticipation of the Circle of Prague, one condition of the existence of phonology."[59] A scheme that tests metricality and its failures will not be much good for a poetry that employs a nonmetrical prosody; scanning, there, will be inappropriate, worse than useless. The Halle and Keyser theory tends to zero in at the syllable, or at most at the single line, registering four major stresses and pointedly neglecting the way the tenth position may have additional emphasis from rhyme.

Paul Kiparsky works at this limitation in his long and example-packed study "Stress, Syntax, and Meter," taking the phonological phrase as his elastic "unit." He finds that compound words, with their tendency toward level stress, and also punctuated line-ending and enjambment are things that tend to separate the line within itself and from other lines with segmentations Halle and Keyser cannot predict or even imagine.[60] In this movement beyond the syllable to larger groupings, there is the inkling of a method for relating minor form to major form, and phonology to syntax. Still, at heart Kiparsky is only interested in metricality.

Generative grammar has been surpassed. If I refer to some of its categories in my own synthesis, this is solely because generative grammar has been able to build a reference to syntax into its units. As T. V. F. Brogan and others have maintained for some time, generative grammar failed because the approach itself was fundamentally negative, not positive. It talked about what was *not* allowed in a line, not what makes a line work. Based on a linguistics that made dramatic claims about how the mind works, generative metrics ironically made no inquiries whatever into the reader's processive attention.

Plainly a method for characterizing sentencing and whole utterances, a text grammar, a grammetrics, does not yet exist. The last and best revision of Halle and Keyser is a philosophical critique of their methodology. According to Jens F. Ihwe, the real problem of generative metrics "is the question of which area it covers or should cover," and this typically involves whether we should concentrate on "literary" texts or all sorts of texts, whether the prose-poetry dichotomy is acceptable, whether the current terminology has a sufficient interpretive basis, what kinds of formalization yield the richest discovery procedures, whether metrical competence is a controllable thing, whether Halle-Keyser arithmetics can get beyond taxonomy to predictive power, whether the analogy to transformational generative grammar is based on too loose an assumption, whether the rule system of Halle-Keyser metrics can be "determined within the framework of the phonological component alone," whether rapport exists between metrics, semantics, and historical consciousness. Neither traditional nor generative metrics has up to now posed, in Ihwe's words, "the question of the interpretive basis." Not until this is faced will any new metrics find "ways to construct a genuine descriptive metalanguage": Halle-Keyser gives us a machine for scanning everything, but one that does not discriminate historical metrical styles, does not afford ways of relating line to text, text to genre. "There is not a trace of a controlled heuristics. . . . The context of the analyses and the texts is totally emaciated."[61] Nearly all of traditional and linguistic metrics have explained poetic pattern by relating sign to sign—not sign to signifier. The modesty of that delimitation of the task is a weakness: one wants to agree with Ihwe that the subject needs to be complicated by the introduction of the semantic element, hermeneutics, the psychology of the reader, and the historical basis of period styles. The conscious irony and constant wariness of Ihwe's sentences makes of them a minefield of philosophical problematics; his inverted commas may stand for the current state of the metrical discipline. In such a climate one way to make tentative progress is to be the gadfly historian of systems; my role in part 1. Another way is to propose a system, or a partial system; my part 2.

To bring this survey up to the 1990s on a far more promising note, I would cite the capacious critical syntheses of T. V. F. Brogan and Richard D. Cureton. Both have produced landmark books and powerful ancillary writings, work that should be the first recourse for anyone seeking to define the growing edge of the field.

Brogan's imagination is humanistic and historical, but he has an appetite for accurate facts about recursive structures. In his reference guide, *English Versification, 1570–1980* (1981), Brogan surveys six thousand works of metrical scholarship over four hundred years, with incisive historical and structural commentary: aiming to provide "conspectus and contour," and also "codification of the work of the past [to] focus and refine the work of the future"—and not least, in his scorching summaries of past work, "by signposting the dead ends and the unlikely avenues, [to] hasten our progress forward" (xii). In his long *New Princeton Encyclopedia of Poetry and Poetics* (1993) articles "Meter" and "Prosody," particularly the latter, Brogan confronts basic issues of bound speech, structures and effects, verse form, complexity and metricality, comparative metrics, theory of rhythm, linguistics' role in verse study. Included here are mentions of *grammetrics,* a term now added to the expanded Princeton volume at the instigation of Brogan as editor. Brogan admits that no comprehensive theory exists, and he offers nine requirements for a unified-field theory of verse (the fourth, to which my *Scissors* contributes, is: "It must make a place for syntax").[62]

Cureton's imagination is logical and linguistic, but he is able to cross his heavily notated analyses with literary-critical accounts of meaning. Cureton's early review of Attridge (1985) and his article "Traditional Scansion: Myths and Muddles" (1986) show him preparing for the work of devastation in the first two chapters in *Rhythmic Phrasing in English Verse* (1992), on current theories and myths.[63] Included in his book is a critique of grammetrics, known to Cureton through a draft version of my *Scissors.* These early chapters also discern what is productive in recent studies on syntax, phrasing, and language segmentation; the middle chapters define rhythm and rhythmic competence and offer a theory of grouping where Cureton devises well-formedness rules. What Cureton says of two other theorists, Lerdahl and Jackendoff, may be said of his own study from the point of view of logical completeness: "With its pithy constraints on hierarchy, its small number of cleanly articulated components, its short lists of psychologically 'natural' preference rules, and its revealing graphic displays, this theory offers the rhythmist an analytical tool that combines an unprecedented degree of clarity, simplicity, and descriptive power." He is brilliantly original in his accounts of grouping and prolongation. Top-down from larger to smaller structures, pragmatic, linear: those are Cureton's methodological criteria for a study of rhythmic phrasing that prefers the beat-offbeat notion to the delusions of the old metrical scansion; that can read free verse and doggerel and sprung rhythm with the same analytical tools as iambic pentameter; that can separate rhythmic levels from semantic levels when it needs to; and that, seeing the poem as having an "overarching teleology," can move all the way from the single syllable to the whole poem. By analyzing phrasal forms and not metrical ones, he turns traditional theory on its head.

Brogan and Cureton, starting from opposite sides of the literature-linguistics divide, share an extraordinary sensitivity to the cognitive process of the reader, as the reader understands a poem in sequence and in retrospect. Especially in this, also in other respects, they manage to think beyond the deficiencies of traditional metrical theory.

## Chapter 3

# Deficiencies of Traditional Metrical Theory

In a thoroughly negative chapter, I will criticize literary-critical and linguistic metrics as a single paradigm. I go on, in chapter 4, to oppose this formalizing paradigm to one I will, with some exaggeration and without espousing the term or the thesis behind it, call physiological. Each of these ways of discussing poetic technique is the essential contradiction, thus the proper supplement, of the other. Since the formalizing paradigm is the one of the two that has had prestige or centrality for metrics, I have chosen, as a hygiene, to list its fundamental difficulties, both logical and historical. The physiological versification wears its difficulties openly and has no power whatsoever, *except among poets.* The formal schemata and metalanguages of traditional versification have been developed for traditional poetries and have their successes there; the physiological versification derives from the avant-garde poetries and explains or evokes that writing's merit. The one explanation is less objective and systematic than it believes itself to be, the other less formal and rigorous than it needs to be. That is why a cognitive metrics, namely the grammetrics advanced in part 2, is likely have something new to offer.

My reason for combining literary-critical and linguistic metrics in the same paradigm, despite their acknowledged differences of emphasis, is their unhappy production of formal schemata—what George Steiner has called "fictions of isolation."[1] Here I wish to question the nature of these models. I do not question the need for any such models, to make our responses precise and publicly available. But we must ask whether the models so far advanced are adequate: whether their inventors have imagined the requirements of a full theory, in its structural-descriptive and historical dimensions. To the extent that formal schemata are revolutions against the given languages in which we conduct our lives, they achieve their control at the expense of giving up certain kinds of content. The reigning system requires ever stronger, more general rules, rules about breaking rules, and rules that protect against refutations; this reduces empirical search. That is why recent metrical scholarship exhausts model after model, in a clash of theory with, we might say, reality. (The mode of reality of grammetrics, if it has such, is yet to be defined.)

Since the materials of metrics are not as tractable as those of natural science, the normal relationship between conjecture and refutation is vexed. I will discuss briefly five reasons why traditional metrics has trouble either proving or refuting its hypotheses.

1. *Isolation*. The first assumption is that literary language is something different from ordinary language. That delimits the field. It would be more economical to assume that literariness condenses or overdetermines ordinary language by knitting it with certain conventions, but that would bring a perhaps insoluble difficulty into the heart of traditional prosody's nascent scientific system.

The second assumption is that meter inheres in the poem's language, and is not constituted by any reader's psychology, or by any oral performance.

The third assumption is that the meter comprises certain very prominent elements in the poem, primary equivalences that dominate the other devices.

Thus traditional metrics is based on the separation of one factor, metrical pattern, from the insistent possibilities presented by other factors. The restriction of prosody to metrics makes of meter the central constructive and authoritative device. For Vladimir Nabokov and Halle and Keyser, for example, rhyme is nonessential, an ornamental phenomenon.

Restriction of metrics to identification of feet as units has prevented movement beyond the level of the foot or the small group of feet that is the line.

Analyses of whole poems or period styles have been rare, because the need to document ictus has kept the study focused on units smaller than sentence or even line. This frame of reference hardly permits the investigator regularly (and correctly) to employ such terms as tone, voice, or movement to characterize a whole utterance.

The decision to assess metricality, like the earlier decision by prelinguistic metrics to identify foot structures, unintentionally makes doubtful the role of examples in traditional theory. Are quoted lines evidences, proofs, cases? The use of model lines, taken from long texts or invented as dummies, is ostensive and taxonomical, with little interpretive merit.

These techniques of fragmentation miss the relationships of literary to ordinary language, of text to reader, of measurable units to the whole poem.

2. *Reification*. The assumption is that meter is a measuring of items that can,

as building blocks neither too small nor too large to be registered, be wholly known. These units, the better to reduce empiricism, will be abstract theoretical entities: phoneme, foot, stress maximum. Their value derives from their having no audibility by the ear, no linguistic existence to muddle rational measurement by the distractions of individual performance.

Any scientific conception is a fictional construct, Roman Jakobson argues, but if we oppose, say, the phoneme to actual sound as a "mere contrivance having no necessary correlate in concrete experience," this reality check "threatens the objective value of phonemic analysis":

> This danger may, however, be avoided by the methodological demand that any distinctive feature . . . have its constant correlate at each stage of the speech event and thus be identifiable at any level accessible to observation. Our present knowledge of the physical and physiological aspects of speech sounds is sufficient to meet this demand. The sameness of a distinctive feature throughout all its variable implementations is now objectively demonstrable.[2]

But our present knowledge of the relation of stress and stress maximum to accent, ictus, and the stringing of feet in the line is not as developed as our knowledge of the basis of the phoneme. In meter we cannot make the same methodological demand with any security. Up until now, the very definition of meter has been premised precisely on not making that demand. That is why what we have just criticized as an abstraction may also be criticized as a reification.

The foot was for many generations the basis of all meter. It was found everywhere, and when it could not be observed, poetry was not present. It was reified as a physical event. (William Carlos Williams's need to invent such a concept as a variable foot, in order to defy the usual foot, shows one perverse effect of this reification.) In 1996, if anyone mentions the foot, it is used as a perfectly conventional, though sometimes convenient, concept that "does not exist independently of the line."[3]

Perhaps more than in any other area of literary study, metrics holds the acute possibility that a notional unit invented to reveal perceptions may in fact block others, which are more significant. But it was never the sole purpose of metrics to reveal perceptions!

3. *Ethical Presuppositions.* Conscious and unconscious ethical assumptions are more prevalent in literary-critical metrics than in linguistic metrics. We cannot, however, rule out the possibility that the very restriction of focus in linguistic metrics carries ideological significance.

Metrists tend to see meter as an objective principle of authority. Its presence makes poetry more amenable to descriptive schemata. The lack of interest in such other, possibly crucial, elements of poetic form as rhyme and syntax is very likely due to their being less easily formalized.

Description shades into prescription. The poet is supposed to have conquered a resistant form, won the poem, vanquished the self-assigned difficulties. The metaphors are masculine, aggressive. The idea, perhaps impossible of proof save by comparing drafts with published versions, is that formal constraint evokes unforeseen felicities from the person confronting the language material.

The use of an abstract metrical matrix and theoretical entities may also involve ethical assumptions about the relation of model to instance. Lines will either be regular and by definition unproblematic, or be irregular. If they are irregular with, say, first-foot inversion, midline caesura, a hypermetrical final foot, then they require some sort of explanation. Such lines are said to be "in tension" with the ideal matrix or norm, and a minimal gesture of relating form and sense can show how their deviation is expressive.

Such language of analysis is ethical and promotes a judgmental metrics. Seeing a disturbance in the beat, the traditional metrist goes back to find a textual reason for it. You may, said Ezra Pound in the *Treatise on Harmony,* "beat with or against the coincidence; with, to clarify; against, to complicate." Regularity affirms the rule; irregularity affords a way to avoid mechanical rhythm, individualizes the text, gives emotional drive, and enacts a special metrical style within the confines of the matrix.

Yet is there not divorce between identification and interpretation, which make irregularities but not regularities the result of "emotion"? We may wonder if this is a logically adequate procedure; especially if, in practice, it can result in such a notion as John Crowe Ransom's that the poet writes perfect meters and then roughs them up for expressive purposes.

Least convincing is the explanation of the famous "interplay" between actual line and ideal norm. As soon as the line "bucks" in this way, the metrist falls on interpretive guesses as to why the deviation is justified in the poem's emotional logic. Interpretation thus derives from watching the simple binary opposition of more/less of stress, whereas, one objects, expression is actually occurring all along the utterance.

Jan M. Meijer is right when he maintains that the deviation theory finds beauty really only in the seemingly nonnatural parts of the poem: "We will not find that the irregularities are there for their own sake as literary signals."[4] What is there in the poem had to be said in that way; any alternative construction would contain less. Covertly, in the metrical context is still the notion that poetic speech is abnormal speech, an idea that, as Meijer argues, has by now outlived its usefulness.

The belief in an untouchable norm is resurrected, it would appear, whenever metrical speculation moves into an ethical phase. The idea is a plausible one, but its results are not promising: the omission of tracts of the poem while one feature is promoted as a dominant; the relating of metrical form and poetic logic only where we have noticed a conscious oddity or wrenching point.

4. *Lack of a Historical Sense.* With very few exceptions, such as Paul Fussell's study of eighteenth-century meter, theoretical and operational studies in traditional prosody are synchronic, and use examples from several period styles as if all poets shared the same metrical assumptions. All studies that, for instance, discuss Pope, Swift, and Augustan form as if eighteenth-century premises were the same as those of Shakespeare and Tennyson, are engaged in dramatic anachronism. The syllable-stress theories that fit the poems of nineteenth-century poets and that are, in large measure, founded on their practice, are alien to the intentions of Pope and Swift and do not describe their practice. That said, I should admit that foot prosodists are by definition more historical than generative metrists.

Surely a history of poetry is a difficult, tentative task. Robert Graves has advised that we not attempt it at all, for what we have is merely a few genuine poets "and swarms of imitators." Prosodic history, like all history, is written from a standpoint, though I do not know a single case in this field where a writer has consciously analyzed and set down a perspective on the subject to alert the reader. Pallister Barkas is correct when he states, "However [one] may arrange [one's] materials for purposes of exposition, the historian must begin with the analysis of the verse of the last hundred years and work backwards."[5] But I would add that often such study is undertaken to defend or suppress tendencies in the writing of the past quarter-century, thus creating, for its own purposes, a selective tradition. All study of prosody is helplessly tied to the examples known in a given time. If the same examples are produced and reanalyzed over and over, the same theories will be reproduced with slight modification.

Prosody always wants the existence of a written, semiprescriptive poetics as a rule system; at times it has had one. The relation of prosody to poetics is a very complicated thing in a time when, as now, we lack such a written poetics. There is no implied set of rules when the "tradition of the new," and beyond that the new-new (the postmodern) is the imperative of all writing.

Looking backward, anachronism; looking forward, incomprehension. Our prosody has a horror of innovation. The present moment in writing is ruled by the coexistence of types, or the mixed genre. Traditional prosody cannot make sense of this, because it lacks redefined categories of identification, reading, and interpretation.

Traditional metrics is unable to describe the phenomena of prosodic avant-gardism and so, until recently, has avoided free verse and the prose poem. Neither of these forms employs meter in the systematic definition: thus they remain invisible to the usual discovery procedures. An account of the relation of poetry to prose, historically based, is a prior necessity, before any explanation of the prose poem. These are poetic forms that try to avoid system, but what traditional metrics has missed is a new sophistication in poetics: namely the idea that there is a system in those avoidances of system.

Metrics and poetics generally have not gauged the full extent of their modernity. Their historical sense is still rooted in traditional writing previous to the twentieth century, and their methods are still too closely tied to nineteenth-century positivism. Yet as Paul de Man reminds us: "If literature rested at ease within its own self-definition, it could be studied according to methods that are scientific rather than historical. We are obliged to confine ourselves to history when this is no longer the case, when the entity steadily puts its own ontological status into question."[6] Henceforth our work with both traditional and innovative prosodies must be based on this recognition.

5. *Inability to Pose the Question of an Interpretive Basis.* This fifth and last deficiency is the most general. All the others may be said to derive from this failure of traditional metrics to have hermeneutical first purposes. The crisis of prosodic theory, and in particular the logical gaps in traditional metrics, is only one phase of the more general crisis of commentary.

The attempt of previous prosodic theory to find a form of analysis not merely subjective found instead a false objective system that was, nonetheless, plausible. It did make gestures toward relating form to sense, but its initial formulation starved it of semantic content.

W. K. Wimsatt has said we cannot write a grammar of meter's interaction with the sense. That may not be true of meter in its traditional definition; more to the point is that, since Wordsworth and Coleridge, writers of intelligence have hoped, in the face of all linguistic fact and philosophical reason, that the formal meter could be dissolved into the poem's sense. This hope has wrenched traditional poems toward effects of spontaneity and has produced successful nontraditional poems where the lack of meter is boldly proclaimed as a signifying absence.

The poets' own demand for an informed spontaneity or nonmetrical prosody is a fact of an avant-gardist era. To match the poets' insistences, prosody itself will very likely wish to invent categories as hybrids, combining sound and grammar, meter and grammar. The notion of the *grammetrical* does begin to write a grammar of the meter's interaction with the sense. Syntax rather than phonology is the most appropriate linguistic discipline for the development of a strong interpretive basis in metrics. *Sentencing* will be an important feature of an improved descriptive language. Sentencing relates the literary and metrical signs to signifiers along the way and is part of linguistic expectation, as *counting* is not. At the intersection points of sentencing, lineation, and the smaller units of measure within the line, we will be able to mark the places where form scissors sense, sense form. When such a versification is developed for free verse and the prose poem, the units and techniques there developed will help us toward better explanations of the form of traditional poetries. It is now very late in the day to be noticing that binary-contrast, traditional metrics cannot describe the historical practice it is designed for—much less the multilinear, collage, spatial, and otherwise avant-garde prosodies that obviously explode its categories.[7]

The last decade's work by Derek Attridge, T. V. F. Brogan, Richard D. Cureton, and a few others is an exception, and most of the usual explanations do not work. The majority of explanations fail because they cannot coordinate, at an acceptable level, the operations of formalization and exegesis; they cannot articulate processive time. Both in its poetry and in its metrical theory, prosodic avant-gardism (in the actual practice, written into poems) shares with its contemporary, transformational generative grammar, a founding belief in the concept of competence. It is competence that permits the child to create personal meaning within the abstract design of grammar; competence that enables the poet to find personal meaning within the designs both of grammar and of the supergrammar that is poetic convention. (Is metrical competence distinctly different from linguistic competence? What if it is, and what if we can be competent at both at the same time, in reading? Such is my argument in part 2.)

So the issue becomes: what are the elements of a strong synthesis, and how can we include in the system a design infinite or fuzzy, such as syntax, and still be able to make the claim that we are rigorous? Poets, after all, have performed with imaginative rigor in their poems. Tens of thousands of admirable poems are in themselves the lure, if not the guarantee that an adequate theory is possible. We know how to read, so we do not need the poet or poem to teach us how to do that. What we do not sufficiently know, even after half a century of reader-response criticism, is how we do read. By watching what we do, could we teach ourselves what we do when we read? Through what frame of thought will we watch thought?

## Chapter 4

# Meter and Cognition in Open-Field Theories

That the form of verse is conditioned by economy of those
muscular movements which insure the oxygenation of the
blood is a fact which many have acted on the strength of
without knowing why they did so.
—Oliver Wendell Holmes,
"The Physiology of Versification"

In part 1 of this book, I intend a critique of modern metrics in the Kantian sense of a history-theory that examines assumptions to their root ideas. (Here, we study not the manifolds of space and time, as in Kant, but of stress and time, though visual space is also at issue; and *adding syntax* is like adding an exponential complexity, a fourth dimension. Described that way, grammetrics seems impossible, but thousands of people perform grammetrics every day, so apparently the elements coordinate with simplicity and power.) As I come to the end of the critical phase of my work, I feel the need to show that what exists in modern metrics is not a single bloc, with its own within-the-paradigm debates continuing over time. Arguably there is another paradigm, in rapport with what I have shown in the first three chapters, but recessive, nearly invisible because it comes forward not in treatises but in manifestos, interviews, and in poems themselves. The disparate genres that make up the other tradition are not usually read together, or read as theory. Most of this writing is done by poets of the avant-garde who tend to speak physiologically, metaphorically. Their commentary often takes the form of a rejection or rebuttal of official metrics, but one that does not mention or show exact knowledge of the antagonist. Describing this countercurrent by looking at what poets say about technique in their art, how they write, takes us a step closer to making statements about what readers do when they read. There is no way to get from writing to reading, in logic or in fact, but still, these operations are arguably connected, and what the poets say about form is not on the face of it any less precise than what academic metrists say. Anyone saying and not making is already by definition a reader.

Until now I have held this countercurrent in reserve, in order to map the tensions and limits of official metrics. The countermetrics is in no sense the remedy for the official one. The presence since Walt Whitman of a counter-metrics, though, shows that for a long time we have known that writers are unhappy with the analytical categories of metrists; and that the received mathematical-musical explanation has contested the field with another explana-tion, the second one phrased in cognitive-biological terms.

So, in that corner of the universe of the human studies known as metrics, there coexist without much human or logical contact two directions of research. To achieve a bold contrast, these may be parodied thus: a lay-down-the-law metrics interested in identification of snap-and-crackle premeditated forms; and this consorts with, or surrounds, an unscientific upstart prosody of breath rhythms, randomness, speed, and form-as-proceeding. The academic metrics is designed to describe the rhyme-and-meter poetry of the pre-Whitman era, and its scholarly antecedents go back to the line of treatises from Gascoigne's *Certaine Notes of Instruction* to Saintsbury; a theory distinguished and ingenious but, as I have shown, contradictory within itself; many things, not one. The other metric, which I will call *insurgent* but without any wish to summon up images of barricades, attempts to account for free verse since Whitman and all the varied techniques of a period of stylistic pluralism. The antecedents are neither scholarly nor ancient, but extending to Coleridgean theory, to Whitman's preface, to W. C. Williams's "Poem as a Field of Action" essay (1948), to Charles Olson's "Projective Verse" manifesto (1950), to the ethnopoetics movement of the last twenty years, and to the essays of Charles Bernstein's *Content's Dream* (1986) and Ron Silliman's *The New Sentence* (1987). Though I will not pursue the matter here, it can be shown, I think, that neither the academic nor the professional-poet prosodies is adequate to its preferred kind of writing; such a demonstration would be more valuable than any argument about the inadequacy of academic prosodies to assess free verse, or of insurgent prosodies to do anything but denounce metered verse. John Hollander's *Vision and Resonance* (1975) is one indication that this implicit paradigm debate is gradually being raised to a new level, where it seems possible to elude outworn arguments and enforce higher standards of explanatory adequacy. With many reservations and prudential ges-tures Hollander cautiously moves from the traditional framework, where he took his training with Auden and Wimsatt, to recognizing the poems and theories of the other tradition, at least up to Williams. In so doing he moves closer to actual contemporary practice than most prosodists and shows how flexible and undogmatic an academic criticism can be without denaturing itself or distorting its innermost structure of definitions. The other prosody will not itself become dominant while its antagonists include canny theorists like Hollander who draw the line against mystical overstatement while elsewhere they select elements of good sense in the postromantic notions of unpredictability, nonparity of formal elements, or form as instance rather than design.

For all its faults in not providing a detailed strategy for analysis, insurgent theory does not, at least obtrusively, leave itself open to the criticisms just leveled at traditional theory. This fairly large body of speculation is logically as watertight as it needs to be and is coherent within its own terms. The terms may seem metaphysical, but this theory is meant to be practical. Its intended function is as a series of ad hoc notes of instruction to enable poets of a certain character to share methods and preserve standards of judgment. (And by following such manifestos, readers can also get advice on how to read.) This is versification theory written mostly by poets themselves, with the aim of controlling that theory and preventing control by others. (That others may want control is evident from the fireworks that erupt from Marjorie Perloff's encounter with the poetics of Charles Olson.)[1]

This theory's actual intent is to call into question the kind of thinking that demands finite solution, tight definition. The same Allen Ginsberg who speaks of "the actual heart-throb or direct expression of the material," or of "language yoga," has shown himself brilliantly adept at analyzing (with provocative, nonstandard terms) the measures of Blake and Whitman, Robert Lowell, and John Ashbery; and in a recorded class (1971) speaks a Catullus poem from memory in the original and spends many minutes describing the relation between English speech-rhythms, English poetry, and classical quantitative prosody. Profoundly antagonistic to traditional poetry and prosody in this century, David Antin in his two essays on poetic technique employs the methods of advanced linguistics.[2] The poet-theorists I will be quoting now are deliberate defenders of their conception of poetry; scholars—but embattled scholars.

The historian with an interest in doing justice to the cogency of this body of writing will note its perfect complementarity with the traditional prosody; rising, in part, due to the limitations of existing theory, the insurgent prosodies have a way of filling vacuums in the received argumentation. They would be purely disruptive, and indeed do appear that way to many commentators, but for their habit of snapping new information into new patterns: patterns recognizable as such, though these are not the forms traditional writing has created or hoped to perpetuate.

Insurgent theory embroiders the view that it received from English romantic poetry and criticism: poetry discovers, constitutes, and participates in phenomenological reality. Poetry, these writers would affirm, does this by restructuring the patterns of real and imaginary experience. Its way of existing in the world is to make both reality and language more perceptible by putting them together in different ways. For the insurgents, it is in this sense that poetry is superior to reality, indeed creates reality by making new understanding possible, peeling off the dead layers. Suitably qualified, this assumption has not been anywhere convincingly demolished and remains the rationale of much of our best writing. That assumption underlies a material poetics, in which social being creates consciousness, but poetry creates new ways of formulating and responding to that social being. Through many mediations, a historical moment of forces is both masked and exposed in any period's poetry. The ideological and formal determinants can be dated as historical conditions of possibility, and thus analyzed. The only originality, here, is the intention to take the formal possibilities as seriously and as technically as the social ones, and to keep the two series in rapport.

The fragmentation of traditional prosody within itself, and its implied struggle against insurgent prosodies, is one phenomenon of a period of stylistic pluralism. Even more explicitly than the other, the insurgent prosodies hope for a more unified theory and for a poetry that brings the reader more closely into contact with the reader's own and the poem's historicity: this specifically at the level of technique. Like their ancestors Blake and Whitman, W. C. Williams, Charles Olson, Allen Ginsberg, and Robert Duncan all adopt an emphatic version of the prosody-as-rhythmic-cognition view. (I take that term from Harvey Gross, whose *Sound and Form in Modern Poetry* [1964] is a landmark text in mediating between traditional and insurgent metrics.) Williams's resistance to "complicated ritualistic forms designed to separate the work from 'reality'" is essentially the same position as Blake's in his note on the "Measure in which *Jerusalem* was written" (1804): against "the modern bondage of Rhyming," an idea of "variety in every line, both of cadences & number of syllables," and this because "Poetry Fetter'd Fetters the Human Race."[3] Clearly in the late-Augustan milieu of Ossian and Blake, the theoretical groundwork was laid for a poetry in free verse by resistance to prosody as prison: a central metaphor that has returned again, recently in Karl Shapiro's "cold manacles of rhyme."[4] The analogies for poetry change from song to speech, from enclosure to liberation. After the 1790s the typical romantic analogies for poetic pattern were music, wind harp, and moving water, but after "the revolution of the ear, 1910, the trochee's heave," in Olson's words, the analogies were most often intimate, relying on the body and its rhythms. Oliver Wendell Holmes, and more recently Seymour Chatman, have related meter to heartbeat, the literal pulse; and there is a line of theory from R. W. Emerson and Oliver Wendell Holmes ("The Physiology of Versification"), through Robert de Souza, Henry Lanz, André Spire, Stanley Burnshaw, Olson, and the phonetician David Abercrombie with his "chest pulse," where rhythm is compared to (if not based upon) human breathing.[5] This prosody is a physiology of consciousness or biology of meaning; where traditional prosody moves in a set direction, this one moves to generate a direction. The poet, as Williams so often said, thinks with his poem.

Robert Duncan, referring to Schrödinger's meditations on life, and particularly to the principle that "Living matter evades the decay to equilibrium," describes a poetry that generates complex unities easily, because the human mind is a pattern-making system, one of many in the universe:

> In the very beginnings of life, in the source of our cadences, with the first pulse of the blood in the egg then, the changes of night and day must have been there. So that in the configuration of the living, hidden in the ex-changing orders of the chromosome sequences from which we have our nature, the first nature, child of deep waters and of night and day, sleeping and waking, remains. . . . Tide-flow under the sun and moon of the sea, systole and diastole of the heart, these rhythms lie deep in our experience and when we let them take over our speech there is a monotonous rapture of persistent regular stresses and waves of lines breaking rhyme after rhyme. . . . What interests me [in Schrödinger] is that this picture of an intricately articulated structure, a form that maintains a disequilibrium or lifetime—whatever it means to the biophysicist—to the poet means that life is by its nature orderly and that the poem might follow the primary processes of thought and feeling, the immediate pulses of psychic life.[6]

Duncan says elsewhere that "poetry is not only [the] idea of making": inspiration is both the physical act of taking breath and something "that . . . comes from great spirit into a man"; however, the poet "can't just be shaken by this divine inspiration" but must "have a massive access to rhyme, to music, to everything, so when he's filled with it, it comes into form."[7] In practice the resulting poetry would not be analytical, with a meter that exists before the poem is written; rather a measure that sequences the arrival of information with the highest premium on disruption and provocation. For Williams this means a rule of *profusion* against what he took to be T. S. Eliot's *distinction;* for Allen Ginsberg this means a rule of no revision; for Olson a rule of pronunciation, each poet going "down into the workings of his own throat" and writing with a vertical and horizontal scattering of lines on the page to notate the patterning of breath breaks in speech. With these and others who come after, the poem becomes a notation or score, thus having ontological status in the middle ground between oral poem and the idea of literature.[8] If not stated as a necessity of insurgent theory, the presence of auditor or reader is implied as the other half of the poetic act. The reader is decoder of the notation, actualizer of the text; the reader too has to go down into the workings of the throat, mentally to reenact the poet's imitation of speech.

This is a prosody neither accentual nor quantitative, but, in Williams's word, "qualitative."[9] Williams meant no reference to the sentiments or ideas of the poem, but rather a minute concern for *arrangement of information*. He would begin at smallest units, though he does not specify what those are: "It is in the minutiae—in the minute organization of the words and their relationships in a composition that the seriousness and value of a work of writing exist." By 1913 Williams was writing that "Vers libre is finished—Whitman did all that was necessary with it"; after Whitman had broken the dominance of the iambic pentameter in English, it was "up to us, in the new dialect, to continue [Whitman's discoveries] by a new construction upon the syllable." To carry the speech rhythms of phrases like "I'll kick yuh eye" and "Atta boy! Atta boy!" over into imaginative literature meant a new democracy of words and rhythms, no exclusions or "sequestration (the cloistering of words)" like the ones in the fixed meters, which, Williams says, deform "all the advantageous jumps, swiftnesses, colors, movements of the day." Accordingly, not to deform language as spoken, prosody became for Williams not a finite process but a probabilistic one.[10]

In its eagerness to do battle with the fragmentary, reified nature of traditional poetry and politics, insurgent theory involves itself in contradictions of its own. Though not in the more recent figures, Antin and Silliman and Bernstein (who prefer artificiality as such), insurgent theory habitually overstates its reliance on the natural in thinking and language, suppressing for polemical reasons its awareness that naturalness is itself, most usually, but congealed convention; and that convention, if we trace it back far enough, is a congealed naturalness and began as an attempt to understand the nature of the mind. All that need be noted here, in defense of insurgent theory, is that Williams and Duncan and others among the best in this line are all aware of the need for some kind of conventions to heighten speech; and that since Whitman magnificent poems have been written on such premises, despite limitations in the theory.

In the sense that Williams employs, there is no such thing as free verse. Seeking the new in the old, as well as the old in the new, poetry by this name is structural, but in a different way. It attaches itself to "that possible thing which is disturbing the metrical table of value." This is no abstract idea of freedom, but a relative order. "Relativity gives us the clue": in both "The Poem as a Field of Action" (1948) and "On Measure" (1954), Williams applies Einstein's theory of relativity of measurements to the repeating or destroying of the rhythmic particles of the poetic line. By this reasoning he arrives at that startling scandal of form, his idea of the variable foot, something scorned by traditional prosodists, but, after all, a serious attempt to see how a "relatively stable foot, not a rigid one" might accommodate the mobility of speech. Einstein's only constant was the speed of light: for prosody, Williams sought such an anchor in "our concept of musical time," but without much confidence that that might be a solution. Profusion, accumulation, process, speed were to be gained by continuous restructuring of patterns: change itself the law behind all the patterns, the law of life, self-corrective because in motion. How modern! How American![11]

The traditional, if not feudal, images for poetic construction are making, crafting, assembling. "Field of action" poetics, with its analogies between prosody and pulse and respiration, prosody and the new physics, conceives of the poem as from its outset an area of possibility. The poem is thus not assembled but, as it were, *moved into* like a delimited meadow in which writer and reader have permission to roam.[12] The action is neither entirely determined nor entirely random. The time/space of the text has as its condensation or analogy the ideogram, the glyph, the hieroglyphic, the collage, the montage, the sequence of the musical phrase—devices where planes overlap, and the aesthetic unit is the nexus of both its position and its trajectory.[13] Every verbal unit, separately as a particle and collectively in the wave of the art-sentence, releases the action of phrase, line, and sentence. The eventfulness of all this in motion, won from sudden restructuring of information, variety in every line, creates prosodic speed. In the shifting topography of this open-field poetry, the only constant is change. Yet to believe in poetic measure, as Williams did, is to believe in the possibility of the poet's controlling change under his or her hand; and the reader's mapping it, by ear but rationally.

Williams emphasized minutiae, but it was Charles Olson who got down to the phonemic level—to a pseudophysiology of the syllable: "it is from the union of the mind and the ear that the syllable is born," he says in "Projective Verse" (1950). The ear, before the eye, was to be measurer of poetry, presumably because the ear is a better monitor of the rhythms of the breath. Olson's essay is in direct line from English romantic poetics not only in this physiological emphasis, but also in the way it knocks down partitions between prosody and meaning in the postulate (taken from Robert Creeley) that "FORM IS NEVER MORE

THAN AN EXTENSION OF CONTENT." The essay follows and develops Williams's belief in a prosody whose swiftness is maintained by continuous insight-restructuring of language: "always one perception must MOVE, IN-STANTER, ON ANOTHER!" whether the perception be of sound or meaning, syllable or image. The poet in this Williams-Olson definition had to take the risk of putting the self into the open, conceiving the job to be that of transferring "energy . . . from where [he or she] got it . . . by way of the poem itself to, all the way over to, the reader."[14] The interest of this for other, later poets is that the theory is formulated largely outside traditional models, yet it bristles with technical injunctions and the spirit of collective enterprise. "It concerns the poem as a field of action, at what pitch the battle is today and what may come of it," in Williams's manifesto-phrasing of 1948; since then what has come of it, in the work of Paul Blackburn, Denise Levertov, Charles Tomlinson, W. S. Merwin, Edward Dorn, Robert Creeley, Adrienne Rich, Allen Ginsberg, Robert Duncan, Galway Kinnell, J. H. Prynne, and others more recent is palpably a genuine discipline. Especially since 1960, anthologies have been successful in bringing the alternative poetics into poetic view.[15] Various as these writers are, I think they would share Walt Whitman's definition of their task in *An American Primer:* "A perfect writer would make words sing, dance, kiss, do the male and female act, bear children, weep, bleed, rage, stab, steal, fire cannon, steer ships, sack cities, charge with cavalry or infantry, or do any thing, that man or woman or the natural powers can do." That contains the working assumption that poetry may be assimilated to nature and to action in the world. Bravo! However, by now it will be clear that such a prosody is no more and no less fictitious than the existence of English syllable-stress meter traditionally defined.

I have said that insurgent reading is structural, but in a different way, and I have used terms like *cognitive* and *physiological* to try to define the method. Perhaps it is more an attitude than a method, and thus it will disappoint those of my readers who want examples exhaustively read. As an attitude, it is at once broader and narrower, in its address to the poem, than traditional versification.

I remember two talks on poetry given by Robert Lowell at Harvard in 1964. One, fifteen minutes long, was a commentary on the opening of "Lycidas," on the way Milton put himself and his voice into an ancient impersonal genre of elegy. The other, a whole class for undergraduate poets, had Lowell commenting line by line on eight or ten of Pound's early poems, saying things like "He's squeezed all the air out of line 5." In the class, Lowell gave no interpretations of whole poems, merely local comments on features of technique, lineation, punctuation, rhyme sounds, though by the end he had built up a vocabulary of effects and a standard of judgment—based on Pound as the most severe model. Lowell, lacking the name or coherence of theory, was performing in 1964 a conscious if idiosyncratic version of grammetrics.

It was not criticism and it was not metrics, but it had authority well suited to teaching. What do students and young writers need to know about the form of the poem? Exactly what all readers need to know: above all, kinetics, how eventfulness is achieved through energy transfer from writer to reader by means of the notation of the poem: by means of prolongation, grouping, propulsion, counterposing of line and sentence, frustration and release of cognitive energies, closure. That is structure, when the academic metrics is modified, and in the process extended and partly dismantled, by measure-not-meter metrics. Traditional and insurgent researchers have remained foreign to each other. Each has needed distance to define itself with some purity. Now is the time for massive encounter and mutual modification. Grammetrics is one place this can occur.

# Part 2

# GRAMMETRICS AND READING

Le poète doit plus de confiance à son oreille
qu'à l'Institut phonétique

★

★                                    ★

. . . . . . . . . . . . . . . . . . . . . . . . . .
. . . . . . . . . . . . . . . . . . . . . . . . . .
. . . . . . . . . . . . . . . . . . . . . . . . . .
. . . . . .Mais d'abord il faut être un poète.

—Georges Duhamel and Charles Vildrac,
*Notes sur la technique poétique* (1910)

*Chapter 5*

# The Possibility of Prosody

In an avant-garde era, poetry and poetics continually outstrip versification. Twentieth-century metrists have not gauged the full extent of their own modernity, much less their postmodernity. One way to advance understanding is simply to point out, as I have done in chapter 4, how the traditional and open-field prosodies coexist without shared assumptions; and how they attempt to describe different kinds of texts. Each prosody implicitly sees its own preferred poetry as exercising all the powers of language. Neither admits the existence of the other, or of intermediate forms between types.

Developing their schemas, metrists have been some distance behind the poets themselves in understanding the nature of this paradigm crisis. Perhaps there is no comparable era in literary history when poets themselves have said as much about technique. Since 1950, in part because of the general use of the tape-recorder, the emergence of the genre of questionnaire and craft interview has brought out an immense body of opinion.[1] If we collate these statements, we have the best survey of insurgent prosodic theory since midcentury. The tone is tentative and various, with widely different aims and directions, with free verse at exact parity with metered verse, and with universal suspicion of poetic devices while those devices are also seen to be necessary. To the question, "What books of craft would you recommend that poets keep on their shelves?" W. H. Auden replied: "Saintsbury's *A History of English Prosody.* All thirteen volumes of the Oxford English Dictionary." Yet even Auden, who looked "to see how a poem is made before I think what it says," showed himself fully alert to alternatives: "There is a reaction now against form. . . . We shall see. It may be I am getting old and can't get used to new things."[2] Roy Fuller finds that for him "free verse . . . is the constricting form," yet generously allows that free verse "obviously depends on a very acute ear, which I don't think I've got."[3] Another notably traditional craftsman, Richard Wilbur, has said that poetry "should include every resource which can be made to work."[4] That, from a defender of the enabling restraint of convention, sounds very like the kind of statement made by Duhamel and Vildrac, those witty proponents of free verse, in the headnote to part 2; and like the defense of organic form by W. S. Merwin: "Obviously it is the poem that is or is not the only possible justification for any form, however theory runs. The poem is or it is not the answer to 'why that form?' The consideration of the evolution of forms, strict or open, belongs largely to history and to method. The visitation that is going to be a poem finds the form it needs in spite of both."[5] In such a situation, any poet's decision to rhyme and meter a poem, or not, is arguably less fundamental than the general consciousness shared with all other professional poets, whether those poets are "strict" or "open." In an avant-garde era, absence of an encompassing prosody makes all prosodies provisional, suspect, pragmatic. All writing that aspires to sustained attention must use the suspect devices of equivalence both to select, and show a differential from, ordinary language. Whether strict or open in tendency, the structure of contemporary poetry, as Yurii Lotman says, "is a relation of the oral to the written text, oral on the basis of the written."[6] No escape from convention; and yet convention can be bent, attenuated, or freighted by personality. Emphatically, then, no escape from personality; the wish to escape it belonged to a classicizing current of modernism, now itself a matter to be understood historically.

It may be that a unified theory of metrics is a logical impossibility; or it may be that such a theory is inappropriate to the kind and quality of precisions necessary just now in literary study. Despite the arrival of promising new directions in the 1990s, described at the end of chapter 2, no time could be less propitious than the present to unify the field, or even to attempt yet another partial synthesis. So far the business of this book has been to map existing directions of research. My review, with its judgment on the aims and limits of the discipline, has nonetheless a few larger claims to make. The small side-chapel of metrics opens onto the larger central cathedral of poetics, with inevitable implications for critical and pedagogical practice.

Without actually developing, in the immense detail required, the whole armamentarium of a new metrical/prosodic theory, it is at least possible to foresee what a unified prosodic theory might require. The primary requirement is that theory put itself in a position where it can pose with profit the questions of history and structure that would yield an interpretive basis. Neither the traditional nor the open-field metrics is fully historical. The reason for this may be that neither is fully structural, in the sense of deriving the history of prosody and the structure of the poem *from the structure of the human mind.* If the new study of metrics gives some understanding of cognition and attention, then what we have taken to be a side chapel to literature and the humanities may turn out to have been neglected within the inmost sanctuary; may even be the whole cathedral! That is a very big if.

Analysis must itself be the extension of a total method, so that if one device of equivalence is isolated for a certain purpose, it must (sooner or later) be replaced in the context of the whole poem. Wherever possible, whole poems will be quoted, and the pressure of period styles will be acknowledged. Regularities must be reduced to rule, but in the process the analyst will at once test and resist the urge to reduce the literary device to language material: prosodic theory must follow the ethos of contemporary poetry in this, so far as possible. In the context of avoiding all unnecessary fragmentation and reification, metrists will attempt to use response entities rather than fictional ones. There will develop, instead of the one basic unit of the foot or the stress maximum or the beat, many types and sizes of units for analysis, and especially important among these will be the hybrid concepts that show the aesthetic in the cognitive, the cognitive in the aesthetic: equations of sentence measure with line measure, sentencing or syntax as a prosodic category, concepts from cognition theory like prolongation, continuation, closure. In structure and in history, we need to work out a system of partial explanations for an indescribably complex reality. It may no longer be possible, in the time of free verse and the prose poem, to locate the least parts as units and build a complex structure out of the units. What if we start, like Cureton, with higher-level cognitive processes and textual structures, and work down to lower?

In the cognitive as distinct from the historical and structural frames of reference (but always dependent upon those), it comes down to a request for the reintroduction of the reader. As participant observer in the poem's movement, the reader registers the prosodic events in human time. Prosody as rhythmic cognition will perhaps be able to deal with both traditional and open-field poetry. It will make no decisions as to value between the two and will be able to watch with greater precision than heretofore the blendings or juxtapositions of syllable-stress and other measurings. We need a phenomenology of rhythm, in which we do not separate it from meter for the purpose of analysis, except in the analysis of free verse. Regularities will be found, but such a prosody will not itself be defined by the discovery of regularities reducible to rule. Positivistic reduction will be resisted, on the ground that just such rules, though tending to reduce empiricism and the work of the analyst, are counter to the imperatives of an avant-garde era. Rules are abstract matrices with the tendency to reify into prescriptions; they rarely are sophisticated enough to involve response units. The rules that are in force before the poem is written or read are the rules that describe human cognitive abilities. To a larger extent than before, the laws of the text will be actualized by the reader's response, as an experience in human time both progressive and recursive.

Writers since Wordsworth like to pretend that no rules will be in force before the poem begins, for in that way they avoid the imputation of having antecedents. To some extent this self-disinheritance, in the realm of poetic form, is a bluffing heuristic rhetorical strategy, engaged in order to get work done and to mask the obvious fact that the style of stylelessness is itself a style.

Such poetry will contain revisions of existing poetic devices that may be responded to and, eventually, described in context. In this schema that we have deduced, the text will be seen, then, not as an object occupying space but as an experience occupying the time of human expectation. Any given point in it will be an arrested motion, the eventful moment of forces between a word's position and its trajectory in sentence, line, and poem.

My point is that in metrics, as elsewhere in the humanities, we need continually to relate our actual verbal behavior and human moral knowledge to our special codes of expertise. Before we can move out of our preprosodic moment, we need better explanations of the poem in cognition and in history. My inquiry so far has discussed the obstacles that remain in our path. Its work has been skeptical, and not a little grim. It cannot answer definitively all the structural and historical questions it poses, or entirely complete the synthesis it has imagined.

Portions of the synthesis I have imagined are already present in Richard D. Cureton on rhythmic phrasing, in Jiří Levý's work on the semantic functions of poetic devices, in Peter Wexler's and Paul Kiparsky's and Robert Dilligan's and Matthew Chen's and Eleanor Berry's studies on the relation between the verse-line and the larger units of grammar. The historical and stylistic work of Josephine Miles, Paul Fussell Jr., Barbara Herrnstein Smith, Yurii Tynjanov, Lidiiya Ginsburg, Yurii Lotman, Edwin Fussell, Harvey Gross, Marjorie Perloff, and Henri Meschonnic is exemplary, and many other names might be mentioned.

Nothing in this chapter or the chapters to follow is advanced as a discovery. These are all reminders. *Able readers of whole literary texts have always worked with such knowledge, such pleasure.* The experience of able readers gives the lie to the previous, deconstructionist generation of criticism, whose leading thesis was that the figurative nature of language frustrates reading. To make that argument Paul de Man and others compress language and literary experience into the single, static device of metaphor. The grammetrics I now put into practice returns metaphors to the temporal experience of the whole poem and enables rather than disables the reader.

## Chapter 6

# Grammetrics and Reading

These pages have more the status of a practical suggestion than the status of a coherent, integrated body of knowledge. Modesty about results is necessary, since my practical suggestion in itself involves not a little presumption. Modesty in the use of terms is also necessary: in my title, I speak of *reading* rather than *interpretation,* because I wish to remain within the skills part of the scale of competence. However, and here is one presumption, I shall be arguing that the skills ability encroaches across most of the scale and is the sine qua non for historical, ideological, judgmental work with texts. I welcome the thought that, equally in the reverse direction, the ideological reaches into a critical reader's cognitive-processing abilities, as a political unconscious of the reader; but it is not part of my brief to demonstrate that side of the equation in a book on grammetrics.

An appropriate taxonomy is one requirement of an adequate metrical theory. Identification of smaller and larger units, and the methods by which units are strung in sequence, will be indispensable. Traditionally, the whole of metrical theory for English has been made to follow from a given metrist's hypothesis about how to scan accentual-syllabic feet and how to handle exceptional cases. My experiment in *The Scissors of Meter* is to arrive at a taxonomy last, as the final articulation of a hermeneutics and psychology. Might we build up syntax as part of a notation, and thus be able to describe metrical and nonmetrical poetic texts with the same grammetrical terms? Worth a try. Is it possible that the physiological schema, whose naive premises I questioned, is related to the numerical paradigm as a higher unity: possible that breathing subsumes counting? No, except as utopian myth; of course thinking of utopia changes your reality.

Previous to any taxonomy, the attributes of an adequate metrical theory are (1) if not actually sanctioning and validating a reading, it should increase the chances of metrical study having a more direct influence on reading for meaning; and (2) having due respect for the arbitrariness of language and of meter as systems, it should show how in a poem these systems determine and are determined by a writer's will to make certain meanings. The taxonomy itself should be able to distinguish between metrical and nonmetrical poems, and between degrees of metricality in metrical poems; the more general of its criteria should be applicable equally to metrical and nonmetrical poems; the more specific of its criteria should be able to handle all the details from the smallest unit, whatever that might be, to disposition of stanzas and the whole poem with its mode of address. Like any theory, the adequate metrical theory should lead to procedures that can be either repeated or refuted by others. The way the elements are laid out should positively encourage the testing, and falsifying, of basic assumptions. Examples should be whole poems read exhaustively.

Having begun in critique, this essay looks ahead to a theory of such adequacy, but cannot pretend to solve everything. "Many extremely important problems are still beyond the scope of contemporary science," says Yurii Lotman, who rightly says that sometimes we prepare for advances by eliminating questions incorrectly posed.[1] Why have hundreds of years of metrical speculation proved so barren of interpretive hypotheses, so contentious, and so unhelpful to writers and readers of poems? Apparently theorists have failed to ask questions that would lead beyond tautology into formulations productive for thought and analysis. There has been a mistake or foreclosure in logical typing, which has in turn prevented a form of reading that bridges several levels of discourse. I suggest that we map other relevant phenomena, principally what I shall call sentencing, onto the same tautology. The conclusions to be drawn from *doing scansion* are of different logical type than those drawn from *reading a poem's semantic structures;* and yet these formalizable entities (metrical feet or, if you prefer, stress maxima) and these explicatable entities (sentences, and their segments) occupy the same space, the poem. The rules of art must not be confounded with the laws of knowledge; but the rules of poetry are only realized in and through the categories of perception, logic, and language.

To read meter and grammar as intersecting codes will tend to break down earlier explanations of meter's relation to meaning, which usually has been taken to be no relation at all. (Choice of overall metrical or stanzaic format usually has, for writer and reader, a clear emotional and ideological burden, and much valuable work has been done to inquire into such matchings; guessing meanings for local metrical effects is by contrast actively discouraged.) Perhaps this intersecting-codes method will also multiply the explanatory power of theory, for another logical product is created when we inquire as to how meter is sentenced and the sentence is metered. The name for this logical product, which I take from Peter Wexler's two studies of the classical alexandrine in Racine, is *grammetrics*—by which Wexler intends "a hybridization of grammar and metrics: the key hypothesis is that the interplay of sentence-structure and line-structure can be accounted for more economically by simultaneous than by successive analysis."[2] For Wexler, this "does not, unfortunately, mean that all we have to do is straightforwardly combine the results of a traditional grammar and a traditional metrics: in both cases the forms available are only partly relevant, though with luck better ones may emerge. Meanwhile we must rely for our analysis on categories which it is one object of the analysis to change." It may be that grammetrics as theory cannot survive, because of the atomistic preconceptions of most extant categories of meter and grammar. However, even if a more comprehensive theory comes to subsume grammetrics, perhaps there would be reciprocal benefits to both partners to this particular neologism. "Reformulation even in traditional grammatical terms can often improve the objectivity, specificity and generality of metrical categories such as *enjambement, repos,* etc."; and, continues Wexler, grammar might benefit because of the chance of exhaustively describing the rigidly restricted language of the alexandrine of French classical tragedy, whose permissible vocabulary, sequences, and syntagmatic combinations are uniquely small.

My own data differs from Wexler's alexandrines and Robert Dilligan's *In Memoriam* stanzas. Permissible grammetrical distributions in the alexandrine couplet, and in the special generic stanza of Tennyson's immense poem, present a much narrower front than the nine variously metered poems I have chosen from nine authors representing several centuries. Wexler in his sketches and Dilligan in his elaborate study employ the computer to do a grammetrics of positional distribution for sentence, clause, and group boundaries. I have used the computer to pull out certain materials from my scant 220 lines of metered text, but my aim has not been to duplicate their method. Relying on the plausibility of their mutually confirming demonstrations, I use my examples to focus from the start on the issue of how we relate inventory to commentary. Dilligan is right: "Both the Halle-Keyser and Kiparsky models deal with prosody as though it were analyzable wholly in terms of phonology and syntax," but the more powerful position "is that the basic integer of prosody is the verse period which can only be defined in terms of the meaning of the poem."[3] I think Dilligan is also correct to say that by taking meter strictly as a phonological constraint on language, Halle-Keyser has far surpassed the old foot-stress model; and yet it would be wrong, at this stage in the development of a notation, entirely to dismiss the foot stress scansion. Any trained reader's response to a metered poem is an obligatory, because ingrained and automatic, silent scansion. This somewhat artificial silent reading is the prior condition for success in oral reading or public declamation.

Most readers still scan according to the foot stress model that permits them, for example, to adjust to Shakespeare's metrically odd line, "Inioyed no sooner but dispised straight," by noticing an incomplete final foot and going back into the line to sound (but not to stress) a final syllable on "despis-ed." (Note that the first edition of the poem does not put in the diacritical mark; later editions supply it, in order to aid the reader's scansion.) This convention of the sounded "-ed" ekes out a regularity and abolishes an anomaly. It can be explained with fewer symbols in the Halle-Keyser model, but foot stress symbols retain some claim to rigor and are familiar.

Like Halle-Keyser, foot stress has no way of showing the relation of phonology to syntax, the relation of minor to major form. It is the main purpose of the present argument to show ways of describing those relations. More specifically, my task is to show the reasons why grammetrics is more powerful and versatile than meter taken alone, and to give warrants for these claims by performing more than a few grammetrical readings.

The principle of sufficient precision must also direct my handling of English grammar. Due to the variable scope of the term, grammar can mean the whole of language, or can mean something far more precise. To the modern linguist, grammar includes word structure; syntax, or the placement of words; and sentence structure. It excludes lexis and phonology, and for linguists, though not in Ronald Langacker's cognitive grammar and not here, it excludes semantics. Until recently, in a usage adhered to, for example, by Dr. Samuel Johnson's great dictionary (1755), grammar was divided into orthography, etymology, syntax, and prosody. By prosody Johnson meant the stress system of the language; not, as in this book and modern criticism, a study of the devices that constitute poetic form. Johnson, correctly I feel, takes grammar as a higher-order proposition. Language is an arbitrary system for dealing with the world; prosody, specifically poetic meter, is an arbitrary system for dealing with language. Grammar is the encompassing logical type, so we must not understand grammar as a component of meter; if we do so, we create the paradox of the class that is taken to be a member of itself. The conditions under which grammar coexists with meter in the poem will be discussed below; rather than speak of coalescence, or reinforcement, I follow Jan M. Meijer and employ the term *interference* to describe this relationship. For my purposes, it is sufficient to have a nontechnical account of English grammar's rules for employing inflectional forms, and of its other means to indicate links between words in the sentence. Wherever feasible, I draw on recent and practical formulations of these rules. For working premises and definitions, I owe much to M. A. K. Halliday's "Categories of the Theory of Grammar."[4]

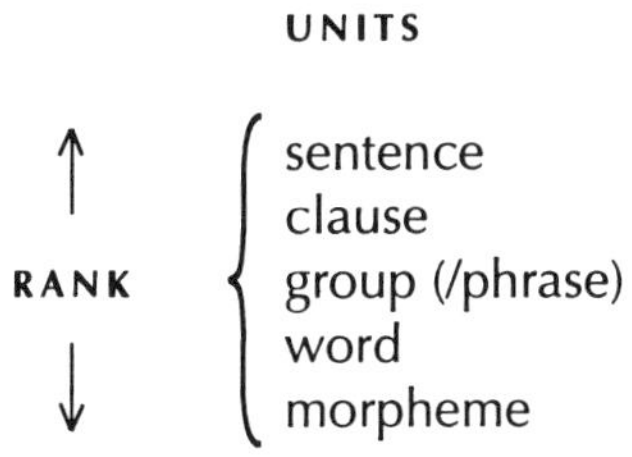

**UNITS**

$$
\text{RANK} \quad \left\{ \begin{array}{l} \text{sentence} \\ \text{clause} \\ \text{group (/phrase)} \\ \text{word} \\ \text{morpheme} \end{array} \right.
$$

*Figure 1. Halliday's ranks of grammar*

Halliday provides a framework of logically interrelated categories. Grammar he distinguishes from lexis by defining it as "that level of linguistic form at which operate closed systems" (246–47). For the description of English, Halliday specifies five units at different ranks, lower units nested inside the higher ones (253), as in figure 1. Each place is defined with relation to the unit next below; units are always wholes, and the lowest unit has no structure. The arrow that denotes rank has two directional points, signifying the ability for description to go up and down the rank scale, a procedure Halliday calls *shunting.* " 'Syntax' is then the downward relation, 'morphology' the upward one; *and both go all the way*" (262). Description "is not and can never be unidirectional," since "criteria of any given unit always involve reference to others, and therefore indirectly to all the others" (254). Shunting is constant, because language is really a kind of progressive contextual shaping. But when description reaches the lower ranks, say at the phrase and below, a new scale enters, that of "delicacy" or depth of detail. "Description depends on the theory; theoretical validity is demanded, and relative merit is judged by reference to comprehensiveness and delicacy" (246). The best description is maximally grammatical and uses more systems with fewer terms.

Very attractive to a theory of grammetrics is Halliday's rejection of the misleading analogies of language as an organism (which grows or evolves) or an edifice (which is built unit by unit, units understood as bricks). Instead, he takes language *as an activity.* Language takes place in time and relates items by "progression"; so that the relation between an item and a preceding item is one of "sequence." But Halliday sees a danger here, and that is why he places these terms describing linear progression in inverted commas. The time sequence of a text "is a variable, and must be replaced in the theory by a more abstract dimension of order" (251). Even though formal patterns are of varying extent, measurable, say, by the number of seconds taken by each part of an utterance, these formal patterns "also appear as it were one inside the other, in a sort of one-dimensional Chinese box arrangement" (250). That is to say, the text is not only a linear progression; beyond its manifestations in substance are its realizations in form, and the theory must accommodate possible disparities between substance and form. In the literary text especially, sequence does not always manifest the norms of order for English, and wrenched sequences (through unusual additions or deletions, a word order far from colloquial, and so on) must always call for extra attention. Since the verse period's recursive circuits inevitably put greater pressure on language by wrenching many or all norms, grammetrical description requires special efforts of comprehensiveness and delicacy.

A fully constituted grammetrics would show the relationship between the line and the larger units of grammar, and between the foot (or stress maximum) and the smaller units of grammar. Wexler, Halle-Keyser, Kiparsky, and Dilligan have made splendid contributions to analysis of the smaller units, and Harai Golomb's and John Hollander's essays on enjambment have much to contribute to the longer stretches. Richard D. Cureton's book is the best account of the whole range from the smallest unit to the whole poem, though, as I will have occasion to remark in my final chapter, it is possible to doubt the neat symmetry of his rhythmic contrasts for meanings at the highest levels.

In my study, I have decided to pay most attention to the middle and larger units on Halliday's rank scale, from the phrase to the clause to the sentence, and beyond the sentence to the style of sentencing. For Halliday's purposes in theory of grammar, no special status can be assigned to any one unit; but for my purposes I shall privilege in meter the line and in grammar the sentence. Between the foot or stress maximum and the whole poem, the line is the most various and volatile aesthetic constituent of the poem; between the single phrase and the text grammar of the whole poem, the sentence is another middle-level structure of variable length. Here as in my previous study (1971; 1985) of free verse, I would like to read for the coincidence and noncoincidence of line and sentence as my primary, though not exclusive, concern. As between morpheme, word, phrase, clause, sentence, and grouping of sentences on the one side, and foot or stress maximum, caesura, line, rhyme pair, stanza, and whole poem on the other, the possibilities of permutation are immense, especially when we coordinate the factors of coincidence and noncoincidence of units. It is practical to make a choice of units centering on line and sentence, but of course the hope is that this will also be the most productive level at which to train attention.

There is a whole regime of meters for certain genres and emotions, and a considerable part of poetics used to concern matching meters with shades and structures of feeling. W. K. Wimsatt and the New Critical metrists tried to get away from that practice, and to show how meter is not a style or rhetoric; they argued that it is a formula or grid. Outside the text, they showed, meter is a descriptive schema, actualized variously by numbers, notes, letters, or other markings. Without the words, for Wimsatt meter was a dummy, and that was satisfying because it drained away the feeling, the ideology. I am interested in something messier. With the embodiment or, as I shall argue, interference of the words of the poem, meter is never notional but has its positions filled by thinking, and by sentencing as the most explicit graph of thinking. Thus Gerard Manley Hopkins aptly called poetry the figure that grammar makes. In ordinary language as in poems, usually sentences are neither extremely brief nor extremely extended. The whole poem is rarely a single sentence. So usually the sentence hovers between the word and the whole poem, capable of being taken down to the one, up to the other. It is a movable, and divisible, unit within the bookends of the text. Sentences are normally quite capacious units of marked variety. Inside them devices may be realized, and outside their boundaries they may themselves be deployed in sequences according to such factors as length, complexity, shifts of active and passive voice or of tense, presence or absence of metaphor. Because sentences inhabit the same space as the lines and rhymes and metaphors, the characteristics of literariness must be equivalence, repetition, redundancy, overload of information, design upon design, interfering systems. Yurii Lotman has rightly maintained that every single artistic device is not a material element of the text but a relationship; T. V. F. Brogan has sharpened this by rephrasing: the device is the ossified or manifest form of the relationship. Grammetrics, inevitably, will be the study of the relations of relationships.

Let us study the degree of interest fourteen writers' sentences afford to us as art sentences. By *interest* I mean the complexity and density of deviance from syntactic and other norms; and multiple-function wording and sentencing. Such deviance and doubling create what I shall call *eventfulness,* which is a pleasurable frustration functional to the enjoyment of rhythm and the construal of meaning. In his essay "Literature as Sentences," Richard Ohmann takes the sentence as "the primary unit of understanding"; argues that "it is at the level of sentences . . . that the intuition of style has its formal equivalent"; and shows with examples from prose fiction how syntactic deviance (no pejorative meant) underscores meaning, how deviance tells about an author's mode of conceiving experience.[5] (Below I take up the question of the relationship of the highly deviant sentences to the others in the text; here I would hint my view that meaning making goes on everywhere in the text, not only in places dramatic because irregular.) Implicit in our processes of understanding is the ability to recognize well-formed sentences. Depending on this ability to recognize ordinary cases, deviant sentences break down categorical boundaries, focusing and doubling the meaning, forcing the reader's mind to consider the several senses that can be rammed into a single string of language. And thus, suggests Ohmann, "*syntactic density* . . . exercises an important influence on literary comprehension. (235, Chatman and Levin, 1967)." For Ohmann, as for grammetrics, our ability to see literary works as structures of sentences-as-units opens the possibility of exchanges between linguistics and critical theory. But such exchanges are possible, I think, only if we accept, as grammetric theory must, Ohmann's premise of the essential unity of poetic and nonpoetic language. There are no two languages, as Roman Jakobson and others have argued, but rather one language that becomes literary by the application of additional constraints, or by the application of a new attitude toward a stretch of language (the "intention of literature").

In postmodernity, which Jakobson did not have to contend with, literature is everywhere or nowhere, and we have an active elimination of constraints such as the formal structure of the sentence or of logic. After New Criticism, structuralism, and poststructuralism have effectively banished the reader, grammetrics with its top-down, cognitive approach puts the reader back into the text. That is why we speak of grammetrics and reading, because the time of the text is now the reader's time. In this, grammetrics participates in a general postmodern ethos of affective stylistics. Grammetrics will be ready in place when a redefined literature, logic, and sentence return. In postmodernity, whatever's writerly becomes more readerly.

This is what Roland Barthes meant in *The Pleasure of the Text* (1973), when he said that the pleasure of the sentence is very cultural. The sentence, said Barthes,

> is hierarchical: implicates constraints, subordinations, internal alignments. Whence its achievement: how can a hierarchy be able to keep itself open? The Sentence is achieved; it is that very precisely: that very language which is achieved. In this, practice differs a good deal from theory. Theory (Chomsky) says that the sentence is by rights infinite (infinitely catalyzable), but practice obliges us always to finish the sentence.[6]

The writer, like the professor, is "someone who finishes his sentences." But even more than the professor the writer is someone whose work is defined by the activity of sentencing:

> Valéry said: "one doesn't think by words, one thinks only by sentences." He said this because he was a writer. It is said by a writer, not because the writer

is the one who expresses his thought, passion, or imagination by sentences, but because *he is the one who thinks sentences:* a Sentence-Speculator *[Pense-Phrase]* (that's to say: by no means entirely a thinker and by no means entirely a sentence maker). (80)

On the horizon of possibility, also, after modernity and after Barthes, there is a reader who is by no means entirely a sentence devourer and by no means entirely a thinker; the writer who thinks sentences needs a reader who does the same.

Within the codes of meter and of grammar, there will be a hierarchy of orders of recursiveness, and the most productive reading will focus on the places where those hierarchies most evidently overlap, or scissor. Choices will be made; one seeks for prominences. By isolating the most powerful prominences, we seek to give information about the poem's way of teaching the reader how it must be read. To show the interference of the metrical and the grammatical in the text should alter the thresholds of analysis. It should thereby tell us more about how we know what we know.

Thus does grammetrics intervene as a mediating position in a wider debate. Defining the ontological status of poetry's coded language has been one primary task of interpretation theory in the twentieth century. The lines are drawn between the cognitive and the aesthetic positions, though we know already that each partakes in the other ceaselessly and fundamentally. The cognitive position, advocated by E. D. Hirsch Jr., maintains the possibility of an objective interpretation: meaning is recoverable, is validated by the shared norms of readers of goodwill, and is based on the occasion of oral speech that has been built into the written text. The aesthetic position, advocated by Paul de Man, maintains that text and author and meaning and reader are notions of deep perplexity, ultimately undecidable; meaning is most often an illusion, or an imposition; rhetoric and meter cannot be assimilated to grammar, because there is always sooner or later a moment when the cognitive element gives up.

No reconciling positions exist that are as powerful as these. More recently a definition of a critical, resistant reader has emerged: simply assuming the cognitive competence and dissolving the aesthetic as a category, thus short-circuiting the earlier debate by immersing it in a new cultural-studies paradigm.[7]

But the terms of the earlier debate are by no means exhausted. I would venture to take from the cognitive position the intent to build up reading hypotheses in good faith, and the intent to use as much as possible the whole text, not just those points (such as puns and figures) where the rhetoric seems to obtrude. Explication is not an outworn myth but remains the necessary, teachable first step, even though what seems simple sense-making is itself ideologically determined and anything but simple. From the aesthetic position I would adopt the intent to preserve the undecidable and obscured relations of a text, and to show where and why ambiguities exist. Further, I propose to show why grammetrical disambiguation is usually a mistake, because it forecloses or disperses part of the meaning.

## Chapter 7

# Sentencing as Notation: The Issue of Arbitrariness

Since the sixteenth century, the intent has always been to make metrical theory into a science, thus to define the field tightly. The field has been by definition strictly separate from interpretation. The risk of affective contamination has thus been avoided. In such logic, expression and meter contradict each other and should not be put in the same thought.

A passage from W. K. Wimsatt and Monroe Beardsley gives the central premise and the polemic style of traditional versification theory. I return to this classic essay on the concept of meter, because of their use of the term *grammar:*

> One of the good features of Mr. Chatman's *Kenyon* essay is his constant appeal to an idea of "tension" between the full spoken poem and some kind of metrical pattern. "I believe that the beauty of verse often inheres in the tensions developed between the absolute, abstract metrical pattern and the oral actualization of sequences of English sounds." (Chatman in journal, p. 436) [There follow the sentences on Wimsatt's Yale student, "stumped . . . at the blackboard," quoted in chapter 2.] This interest in tension, or interaction, is excellent. But how can there be a tension without two things to be in tension? . . .
>
> You can write a grammar of the meter. And if you cannot, there is no meter. But you cannot write a grammar of the meter's interaction with the sense, any more than you can write a grammar of the arrangement of metaphors. The interactions and the metaphors are the free and individual and unpredictable (though not irrational) parts of the poetry. You can perceive them, and study them, and talk about them, but not write rules for them. The meter, like the grammar and vocabulary, is subject to rules. It is just as important to observe what meter a poem is written in . . . as it is to

observe what language the poem is written in. Before you recognize the
meter, you have only a vague apprehension of the much-prized tension.[1]

The student here described "stumped . . . at the blackboard" was attempting to
do rudimentary research in grammetrics. But he lacked a justifying theory and a
set of procedures. Wimsatt and Beardsley are of course right: scanning cannot *by
itself* show the interaction between the meter and the sense; but they are also
wrong to use "grammar" in the metaphorical sense ("You cannot write a gram-
mar of the meter") and in the literal sense ("like the grammar and the vocabu-
lary") in the same argument, because this serves to rule out in advance any strong
theory of interference between meter and the sentence.

As metrist, Wimsatt wishes to speak of versification, not of that "prosody"
which applies equally to ordinary as to literary language; as metrist, he draws a
broad line between rhythm ("not a physically measurable linguistic fact") and
meter, placing outside of the discipline the broader end of the study—"where
prosody vaporizes out into cognition or into just whatever shape or form or
knowledge of feeling you get from any rhythm or movement of words."[2] "Va-
porizes" is polemic, and "you cannot write a grammar of the meter's interaction
with the sense" is preemptive, premature. By showing the mutual scissoring of
syntax and metrical pattern in the verse period, grammetrics revises this conven-
tional wisdom: precisely by showing stronger relationships between the broader,
cognitive end of the study and the narrower front of scansion. Since the grammar
(in the guise of sentencing) *is in fact the sense,* a perception-oriented theory of
meter should at best not vaporize into cognition. It should be delicate enough to
show how the interference of grammar and metrics is not "free and individual
and unpredictable," as traditional versification would hold, but displays describ-
able regularities. Those regularities are discursively describable in chapters 9 to
11.

In justifying the term *interference,* used here in preference to *reconciliation* or
*interaction,* we explode the single most impressive argument in the path of estab-
lishing a grammetrical theory. This is the argument against Cratylism, a modern
literary myth that takes its name from Socrates' antagonist in Plato's dialogue.
According to Gérard Genette, a recent denouncer of this outworn, but still
seductive, thought, those who adhere to Cratylism see the poetic function "as a
compensation for and a defiance of the arbitrariness of the sign. . . . [Cratylism
is] that great secular myth which wants language to imitate ideas and, contrary to
the precisions of linguistic science, wants signs to be motivated."[3] Since the work
of Ferdinand de Saussure, unmotivatedness has been the first principle of the
linguistic sign, and it is a similar admitted arbitrariness (clearing the decks of all

but "physically measurable linguistic fact") that Wimsatt and Beardsley demand in a responsible metrical theory. Defending the fundamental principle of the arbitrariness of the sign, they require a metrical theory not assimilable to grammar or to cognition. They show existing and conceivable opposing theories as dominated by a naive hope to "motivate" meter everywhere with presence, intention, consciousness.

There are, however, other logics than the one traditional metrical theory has employed. Grammetrics assumes that meter and grammar can be scissored by each other, that the cutting places can be graphed with some precision—and this without abandoning the principle of the unmotivatedness of the linguistic sign or the metrical unit. Pope's "fatal engine" is the symbolic implement of this action, because of its steely refusal to participate in the materials it works on:

> The Peer now spreads the glitt'ring *Forfex* wide,
> T'inclose the Lock; now joins it, to divide.
> (*The Rape of the Lock,* canto 3, ll. 147–48)

One blade of the shears is meter, the other grammar. When they work against each other, they divide the poem. It is their purpose and necessity to work against each other. Meter is not a set of physical objects; rather a system intersected by, and thus in rapport with, the other major system of grammar. It marks a shift in theoretical assumptions to break literary structures down into relations rather than into substances.

The plural noun of the scissors in my title intends primarily a relationship: not one without the other, no results without continuous interference. One blade of the shears is an aesthetic structure, the other a cognitive structure. (Let us treat them as separable for now; *an open scissors.* When they have closed on each other they are one, and the same piece of text contains both, and the oddity of the term *aesthetic* for just one of the blades disappears.) *The Scissors of Meter* thus provides a particular instance of Jan M. Meijer's thesis in his constitutive article "Verbal Art as Interference between a Cognitive and an Aesthetic Structure" (1973).[4] It is the purpose and necessity of meter and grammar to work against each other: on every level of the poem, and fundamentally, Meijer holds, "the notion of conflicting structural principles [is] a specific property of literary art" (223). The components of Meijer's work are Russian Formalism of the 1920s and of the present day in Yurii Lotman and the Tartu school, and also information theory. He studies the relationship in the text of sequence and order, trajectory and position. Reading and writing seem to be linear activities, but are in fact the results of to-and-fro processes in the brain. How is it that energy, in the form of reader interest, is intensified in and through the text, rather than dissipated? Meijer answers: *through the mutual interference of systems.* Meijer argues that the intersection of systems is the identifying property, indeed the very definition, of verbal art:

> Every system has its inertia, every information its entropy, and every chan-nel has its noise. This law is not undone by art, but its action is counteracted by the intersection of systems. The intersecting system adds new energy to the intersected one, and vice versa: a rhyme never only rhymes, it also means; a meaning, in a poem, never only means, but it "rhymes," or it "meters." . . . It is our view that each level represents a structural principle, for which other levels are "material"; at least it tries to reduce its milieu to matter. . . . In that sense the operation of a structural principle creates a negative quality: for the operation of rhyme one meaning is as good as another, from the point of view of meaning one kind of rhyme is not preferable to any other. (217)

Let's assume that we are discussing meter and syntax *within the poem,* not as separate entities but in rapport with each other. Meter relies on the grammatical-cognitive code, on the poem's very words, in order to actualize itself. Equally, sentencing relies on meter or some other formal convention to achieve a certain sound-shape. If we isolate either structure, we abstract from the work itself and prevent the scissors from cutting: granted, when the scissors is taken apart at its hinge, meter at least retains meaning as a physical response, and phonetics and linguistic prosody retains a minimal sound-shape.

Developing further Meijer's basic formula of an opposition in rapport, for convenience the interferences may be shown in two columns:

| | |
|---|---|
| cognitive | aesthetic |
| grammar | meter |
| optional | arbitrary |
| quantity | number |
|   (product of measurement) |   (product of counting) |
| analogue system | digital system |
| prediction | description or taxonomy |
| approximation | accuracy |
|   (no jumps between items) |   (discontinuity between one integer and the next, so numbers can be exact) |

grammetrical analysis                    phonological analysis
(probabilistic)                          (numerical)


Cognitive systems like grammar vary continuously and in step with magnitudes in the originating event, here the intention of a sentence. Aesthetic systems like meter have the on-off characteristic, and that is why the Halle-Keyser stress-maximum theory has been so adaptable to computer research. Not the least persuasive thing about Meijer's formulation is its strong account of the combined (rather, interfering) freedom and necessity of lyric form. Precisely because the cognitive and the aesthetic are differing logical types, they can and do scissor each other in the text. There would be no interest, no eventful energy, if the aesthetic pattern could not scissor and be scissored by grammar, logic, or rhetoric, those open options of thought.

When Meijer says that "the intersecting system adds new energy to the intersected one, and vice versa," the energy he refers to is mental. The reader pays out more attention to cognitive structures when they are in interference with aesthetic structures. Two or more types of information must be called back from the same stretch of language. I suppose this is why Craig La Drière, in an article earlier than Meijer's, wrote that "the power of the aesthetic structure to absorb, if not to consume, is very great."[5] Meter and grammar try to reduce each other to matter, try to consume each other, but succeed in the mutual modifying I call scissoring. In the context of the poem, neither is what it might be if taken separately, neither has priority. La Drière: "It is hard to say whether meanings or sounds more often initiate the poetic process, but there is no theoretical reason to suppose any primacy of either. The great fact is that, once the process is begun, all the elements have *a priori* equality." *Once the process is begun,* and actually, I think, before, meter has a dynamic trajectory and a cognitive dimension; and phrasing has an aesthetic dimension. They are in rapport with each other because of their antagonism, but also because of their degree of overlap and mutual influence.

That they achieve their equality by literally fighting for it can be shown by twice rewriting an unassuming poem. Edward Thomas's "Tall Nettles" comes in two conventional iambic pentameter quatrains:


Tall nettles cover up, as they have done
These many springs, the rusty harrow, the plough
Long worn out, and the roller made of stone:
Only the elm butt tops the nettles now.

This corner of the farmyard I like most:
As well as any bloom upon a flower
I like the dust on the nettles, never lost
Except to prove the sweetness of a shower.[6]

The first travesty, which need not be given space, would omit all punctuation, and would put the rhymes in boldface. These alterations, taken with the poetic convention of capitalized first letters in each line, would step up the proportion of the aesthetic. Grammatical relationships would tend to blur, resulting in a loss of coherence. To a degree, meaning would be lost, as the words were rendered more as matter. The second travesty subordinates the metrical structure to the sentencing. Line-opening capitals are omitted, and lines are marked by slashes alone. Sentence nuclei of subject and main verb are grouped at midpage, and to the left and right are qualifying elements of various sorts (e.g., appositions to the left, tag clauses to the right):

> Tall nettles cover up
> as they have done/these many springs,
> the rusty harrow,
> the plow/long worn out,
> and the roller made of stone:/

only

> the elm butt tops the nettles
> now./

This corner
of the farmyard
> I like most:/
As well as any bloom
upon a flower/
> I like the dust
on the nettles,
> never lost/
> except to prove
> the sweetness of a shower.

Now sentencing triumphs: meter and rhyme lose much of their scissoring powers. The first version is overinsistent, the second slack. Between these two polemical distortions is situated Thomas's actual poem. Experimentally, the distortions relax one side of the interference to see what might happen.

Thomas's poem is minor and modest and yet serves to suggest how forbiddingly difficult it will be to coordinate grammatical signals with phonological description of stress. The pregrammetrical and partial reading of one word, "now" at the end of line 4, for instance, involves a series of hypotheses about the relationships of metrical lines, stanzas, rhymes, and sentences and their words. "Now" is the least convincing of all rhymes at line end in the poem and yet is not palpably bad—partly I suspect because it combines with "Only" in the first part of the line to sandwich the ready-made subject-verb-object segment neatly within two optional and movable items. (Though an uninflected language, English yet has to quite a high degree the capability to shift words around within the sentence and still be clear, correct, and unremarkable.) "Now" could have been put before "Only" or after "butt": the sentence would permit that, but the meter and rhyme would of course suffer major reallocation. Analysis of longer groupings such as modifiers "Long worn out" placed after their controlling noun, or the placing of direct object before the subject and verb in "This corner . . . I like" (l. 5), would plainly bring out the author's extensive supply of choices in this language continuum of the short poem. Few lines, hundreds of choices. The printed poem omits all but the last prosody-constrained grammatical choice. This, and not the rejected options, must be the basis of the reader's response and the analyst's interpretation. Nonetheless, the constraining of lexical choice and syntactic placement by the meter, and by the rhyme scheme, is a legitimate object of study. If it has been neglected, that is because we have lacked the speculative and practical instruments of investigation.

The instrument to be tested here is grammetrical prediction. Inevitably one adopts a perception-oriented theory of meter and of grammar, in order to use *prediction* in this special sense. As the text carves its shape in time, it continuously raises and fulfills expectations, rouses and settles the energies of thought in the reader. And as it progresses further, it tends to close off more and more avenues to expectation. The text, like a global expansion of a sentence, moves from indeterminacy to determinacy, from the pleasurable suspense of the first word or line to the pleasurable "expectation of nothing" of the last.

The fourteen examples arrayed in the following chapters are detached from their historical moments and from the rest of their writers' work; and yet we can, without too much trouble or space, establish for each poem the norms of a contract between the reader and the meter and grammar. The contract is based on the qualified reader's learned abilities to recognize what is well formed and normal in grammar and meter. For the reader of English, the normal case in grammar is subject, verb, and object in that order; and in English meter is a patterned alternation of unstressed and stressed syllables. Indispensable too is the ability to recognize, and to process, exceptions to these normal cases. It will be one of the hypotheses of this study that exceptions frame, underscore, focus, point, and turn meaning. Here are the possibilities.

> Normal sentence, normal meter
> Normal sentence, exceptional meter
> Exceptional sentence, normal meter
> Exceptional sentence, exceptional meter

The last of these will produce the greatest ambiguity of relationships in the text, the greatest energy of cognitive search. A high degree of unpredictability in exceptional sentences and lines makes for intensity, that exponent of attention.

There is a larger historical exception. Certain late-twentieth-century experiences in poetry will fail to be addressed by my kind of grammmetrics. Concrete poetry, talk poetry of the sort David Antin practices, and Ashbery-like postmodern writing that discourages closure and integration will elude my definitions of eventfulness—these declare the event in an eye blink or defer all events forever! Eventfulness is notably a value in poetry between Shakespeare and, say, Adrienne Rich, with notably strong preferences for surprise-effects in modernism. If we can develop an account of eventfulness in the majority poetry of the past few centuries, then we can mount a grammeasures of its postmodern dissolution in the next phase of the theory.

*Chapter 8*

# The Elements of Grammetrical Theory

The exposition in this chapter will contain some diagrams and numbered lists, whose purpose will be to compress information. I mention this sole purpose, so that no one is misled, even after my part 1, into thinking grammetrical theory is deductive in form. An explanation may be adequate, if not strong, even though it is not clothed in the conceptual garb of the deductive paradigm.

Traditional metrics massacres reality and reconstitutes it in a drastically simplified model; it purchases universal rules at a cost of excessive narrowness. Grammetrics in my version seeks relational propositions that show the interaction of metrical and grammatical segments of several sizes, and that lead in turn to interpretive hypotheses; it snatches descriptive wealth from the jaws of indefeasibility.

Reference to purpose can provide criteria for evaluating explanations. The audience of traditional metrics is metrists—and also beginning poets and students who read handbooks. The audience of grammetrics is the ordinary competent reader, the broad mass of persons in the middle. Traditional metrics is taxonomic, though not exclusively; hence the limitations and achievements I discussed in part 1. Sometimes, as in Paul Fussell Jr.'s *Poetic Meter and Poetic Form* (1979), traditional metrics does aim to be interpretive, but through and by means of the taxonomy. Now taxonomy is not as such an error, and more interpretation is not better interpretation; what matters is the questions asked by taxonomist or interpreter, and the way the taxonomy serves the interpretation. Grammetrics aims to aid interpretation by showing more narrowly and fully than before the meaning of form and the forms of meaning in the text. Traditional metrics up to Halle-Keyser delivers its research as a set of rules and exceptions. Grammetrics, however, gives a set of steps that might lead to a reading of the whole poem: a sequence of operations that should be fruitful for hypotheses about the relationship of the poem's aesthetic-cognitive subsystems.

Grammetrics studies the mutual interference in the poetic text of cognitive and aesthetic impulses, as these are represented respectively in the grammar and meter. When the scissors is shut and folded, in the experience of reading, the cognitive and the aesthetic are one, with invisible interface. Grammetrics opens the scissors, to produce an explanation of the normal, but in the process entirely aware that the prising apart is nonnormal.

Grammetrics is a perception-oriented theory of poetic form that shows how the determinate text directs a competent reader's investment of attention— how cognitive energies are fulfilled or frustrated, or otherwise exercised, by the phonetic-semantic sequence of the poem. The why, where, and how of mutual scissoring of grammar and meter is the focal concern.

Different historical periods, different writers and different texts will manifest different scissoring points. Accordingly, the implications for exegesis will differ too. For all periods, writers, and texts, the variable defined below as the *style of sentencing* will be the most pertinent for exegesis. An eventual grammetrics will have to be fully historical; here it is possible to suggest some historical differences by the choice of examples and the way they are described, but this is not the place to develop a historical grammetrics.[1]

Earlier I quoted the prediction of W. K. Wimsatt and Monroe Beardsley, which this book aims to disprove: "You cannot write a grammar of the meter's interaction with the sense. . . . The interactions . . . are the free and individual and unpredictable (though not irrational) parts of the poetry. You can perceive them, and study them, and talk about them, but not write rules for them." The position of grammetrics is that the grammar (syntax + lexis) portions out, and for most purposes is, the sense; and in the poem the grammar is at all points inseparable from the stress system of English: inseparable from the meter, in the rapport that I have called mutual scissoring. For the writer engaged in adjusting sentences to lines and rhymes, for the reader performing the text in the lapses of time, everything counts and is counted. The same must hold for grammetrical explanation too, as it borders on the edge of circularity, trying to create a theoretical isomorph for the empirical situation. Once a grammatical item, any item, is within a poem, there are constraints on its action; it is only free, individual, and unpredictable relative to a hierarchy of orders of recursiveness, structured by the reader's responses to the writer's choices. In a successful poem every item of grammar has its use as interfering with a metrical or otherwise formal unit in that locale; no locale is any more poetic than any other unless the poem is somewhere slipping away from success.[2]

A step on the path toward grammetrics is the position of Roman Jakobson and Mac Hammond, both of whom consider the "figure of grammar" in studies of such devices as the additive conjoining of a series of nouns, adjectives, or verbs;

the syntactic devices of apposition and anaphora; and successive sentences or clauses such as a series of questions or imperative commands.[3] Study of these items is certainly part of any fully fledged grammetrics, but the theory ought to go further than the juxtaposition of boldly obvious syntactic structures with metrical units. The whole metrical poem, with the full complement of structures at every rank-level of the grammar including the types of pauses that punctuate those structures, is the likely field for grammetrics. Of course, though it might be possible to demonstrate interferences of meter and grammar at every point, the results would be unparsimonious and boring. We require analytical principles that will reveal where the reader's energies of attention are liable to be most focused to intensity.

## The Grid of Scissoring Points, with Definitions

Using the diagram of grammetrical coordinates (fig. 2), let us begin to isolate these points of focused intensity. Since our explanation is not deductive, we can begin to describe the most complex case and work our way down to the smaller units. Such a method will be used again below, and wherever it appears it may be understood as a rhetorical gesture designed to place primary emphasis on the interpretive capabilities of the larger units of grammar. The larger units of the sentence are of course built up by means of the smaller ones, but normally the smaller ones do not comprise enough meaning to be worth discussing by them-selves. In meter, the situation is reversed: the lesser ranks in metering are more productive than the greater ones, because these determine the fundamental structure along the line of the aesthetic coordinate. We may speculate, in passing, that this difference of value between lesser and greater units is what makes grammar and meter so apt to interfere with each other, so suitable as scissoring antagonists. The middle ranks of the scale, particularly those of sentence and line, are busier than the ranks on either end, because they are more able to be taken either to ranks above or below them in size. Having more intersections offers more points where line and sentence might scissor each other.

Information in the grid of scissoring points may be displayed by working from top right, where the sixes intersect, to zero degree at bottom left.

1. The vertical axis is that of grammatical rank; the horizontal axis is that of metrical rank.
2. Intersection points of the two axes are shown by circles where the axes meet; small circles for minor coordinate points, large circles for major ones.

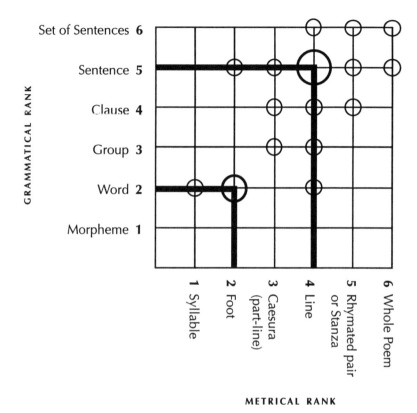

*Figure 2. Grammetrical coordinates*

3. Of all the possible intersection points that exist on the grid, only sixteen points are circled because only those sixteen points are normally filled in a poem.

4. The sixteen scissoring points may be shown in two clusters, defined by their centers at the major coordinate points of word-foot and sentence-line (large circles). Actually, these are not just scissoring points—also techniques (caesura, enjambment) that divide and suture the points.

5. Usually a whole poem is more than one sentence, more than one line. At the upper-right-hand corner this coordinate system goes as far as it can into context by marking the intersection of the group of sentences with the whole poem.

6. It is a rare case and a special effect when a sentence intersects with the rank of whole poem (5 up, 6 across).

7. More frequently, a group of sentences (two or more) may constitute a rhyme-mated pair of lines or a whole stanza (6 up, 5 across).

8. Sentence and clause frequently overlap with the rhyme-mated pair or stanza (5 and 4 up, 5 across).

9. Very rarely does a group of sentences overlap with a line; when this happens the effect is produced of brokenness and laconicism (6 up, 4 across). These atypical intersections are also eventful. (At this stage we have no systematic way to distinguish metrical from graphic lines, which are not necessarily coextensive.)

10. The sentence and line axes are specially marked because 5 up and 5 across encounter the greatest number of intersection points and thus, in this explanation, produce in their interaction the greatest number of effects of eventfulness. Sentence and line in their joined track in the poem have as many as six intersection points on aggregate. It is not only a matter of number of intersections, though, because the greater the number of intersections along a line, the greater the range of types of segments included; more types, more eventfulness.

11. Up to sentence rank on the grammatical scale and up to line rank on the metrical scale there are *successive increments* in quantity of text. After sentence and line there are *sudden jumps* in quantity of text. Usually poems are longer than sentence and line, and usually above the rank of sentence and line the text has already set in place a sort of grammetrical contract with the reader: implicit promise to build the whole according to principles in the first sentence and line.

12. From word to group to clause, there is an increasing chance that the item will be equal to a line; the likelihood declines again after clause: line-sentence less probable than line-clause. Obviously, though, the shorter the line (as in trimeter rather than pentameter) the more likely it will be equal to the subsentence ranks.

13. Group and clause are very likely to be equal to the half-line in a caesura-divided line, especially if the line is as long as a pentameter. Usually, it seems, group and clause will be part-line entities; only rarely will they be taken up to full line.

14. Only rarely will sentence be equivalent to part of a line or to anything smaller.

15. Word is possibly line, but only very rarely. Usually the word operates by cutting either syllable or two or three syllables, in order to build up a metrical unit. The infinite variety of part-word equal to part-foot, combined with word-foot, makes for a great deal of unpredictability at these lower ranks of the grid.

16. There are no positions filled on either the vertical or the horizontal
    baselines; neither the cognitive nor the aesthetic axis can exist without
    interference, within the poem.

17. Fully eight of the total of sixteen scissoring points are tightly grouped at
    the rank of sentence and above on the grammatical scale; and ten of the
    sixteen are at the rank of line and above on the metrical scale. That it is
    semantic force that powers the poem, and ends the poem, may perhaps
    be inferred by the grouping of scissoring points in this high-right end
    of the grid.

18. Several assumptions must remain undefended: the uncircled blank in-
    tersection points represent impossible or unproductive convergences;
    word-foot and sentence-line are the most prominent convergences,
    and thus get most critical attention; above-the-sentence and above-
    the-line ranks contain the most information for the construction about
    reading hypotheses on overall meaning; terms like "rare," "likely,"
    "more/less probable" are educated guesses, based on knowledge of
    metrical poems in English. Concrete, short-line, oral, and certain kinds
    of prose and free-verse poems are less well matched by the grid than the
    fourteen items in my array in chapters 9 and 10.

The largest assumption is that the diagram of coordinates is a useful repre-
sentation of the reality of reading. There is cause for doubt, first because meter
and grammar are partial sciences (actually we know more about syntax than we
do about meter); in addition, individual rank items are suspect on both axes. The
grid is a tool for thinking and will soon be criticized and surpassed.

Some borrowed or invented definitions will further extend the explanatory
capability of the diagram.

The *verse period* is the sentence within the poem, whether it equals the line
or is shorter or longer than the line. Length of verse periods, precise positions
where they begin and end, are data of some importance. The term is already in
common use: is, for instance, the basic unit in Robert Dilligan's thoughtful
computational study of Tennyson's *In Memoriam*.

The *style of sentencing* applies to all poems longer than a single sentence and
describes how sentences in the poem consort with each other: how varied as to
length, continuity, metaphorical content, and so on. The style of sentencing,
often based on studies of the behavior of the verse period, will in what follows be
taken as a major link between grammetrical observation and reading hypotheses
about the meaning of texts.

The two terms already presented, like *grammetrics* itself, are both in the form
of resolved antinomies. The same combinatory quality is evident in *grammeasures,*

a term invented to cover free verse and the prose poem, those nonmetrical prosodies. In poems in free verse and in prose poems, the interaction between grammar and structuring elements other than meter will be studied. In free verse, for example, the relation of sentence to line will be a measure more crucial than in metered verse, which has in the foot or stress maximum a determining unit smaller than the line. My fourteen-poem sample begins with a prose poem and four free-verse poems; these five poems, to be analyzed for grammeasures, will act as a control on the nine metered poems.

One of the oddities of traditional metrics is the caesura, the syntactic break within the verse line. Apparently this concept was brought in to label something traditional metrics could not describe, the midline end of a sentence or segment. The caesura is a telling absence, a no-thing and a no-place, a rip in the fabric of the syntax and the meter that neither syntax nor meter taken singly can account for. Though its function has been politely cloaked in Latin, the caesura of course *scissors* both syntax and meter: it is that type of pause which divides the line into metrical clumps. The caesura thus represents the anticipation of grammetrics within the very citadel of the old metrics. Its anomaly as a hybrid concept entirely disappears within the new explanation.

## The Semantics of Form: Categories from Jiří Levý

Most scholars of metrics have insisted on the arbitrariness of the aesthetic-executive part of the poem, on the grounds that meter's total separation from expressivity makes it suitable for the control required in exact structural study. They have been correct to argue that meter, considered as an abstract normative pattern, has no "meaning," has to be informed by (I should say interfered by) the content of the text's very words. Separation of meter from meaning has been a way to free readers from one kind of inquiry, so to find ingenious symmetries, so to find facts that have aided interpretations. This position, I have been arguing, has had a useful term of life and may now be subsumed. Once we replace meter as abstract pattern within the actual row of words in any poem, both the norms and the words are seen to influence each other as they strive unsuccessfully for dominance. We need to explain that mutual influencing, without returning to the expressivist position that provoked the abstract-pattern metrists into premature rejection of any and all perception-oriented theories.

Traditional metrics has correctly argued against the folly of searching for any one-to-one relation between segments on both levels, acoustic and semantic. But, except for Jiří Levý's brilliant essay "The Meanings of Form and the Forms of Meaning," a more productive relation seems not to have been explored.[4] This is the relation of systematic homomorphism, what Levý calls "a parallel mor-

## Forms of Linear Arrangement

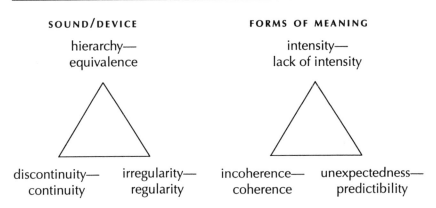

*Figure 3. Analogies between structural-acoustic and semantic levels*

phology of the two systems as wholes." Levý's classifications are basic to any
study of the semantics of poetic form, and indispensable to a future grammetrics.

We have been, Levý says, backward in the description of the semantic
effects of verse: "we are probably not going to have any reliable terms and
methods unless we succeed in formalizing, to a certain extent at least, our theory
of the semantics of verse . . . unless we find by structural analysis a limited set of
incontestable semantic functions performed by verse" (45). Levý's first and con-
stitutive hypothesis shows him centrally within a gestalt- or perception-oriented
tradition of analysis: "The basic structural feature of an [artistic] utterance is its
linear character: it consists in a sequence of consecutive segments," as for instance
in effects of meter, lineation, rhyme. Now the remarkable thing about "mean-
ing" is that it, too, "is linear in character, if we regard it as a process, i.e., as a
gradual apprehension of semantic segments." Levý specifies three elementary
formative principles of arrangement within a series on the physical, or acoustic,
level; and correlates these with three corresponding arrangements on the seman-
tic level. The morphological analogies may be diagrammed as two matching
triangles, with basic principles and their opposites at each of the points (fig. 3).
The three points on the structure triangle correspond to the three points on the
meaning triangle. Paraphrasing or quoting Levý:

1. The continuous or discontinuous arrangement of physical segments has
   its analogue in semantic coherence or incoherence, in a more compact
   or dissolute organization of context.

| PROSODIC DEVICES | ACOUSTIC PRINCIPLES OF ARRANGEMENT | PRIMARY SEMANTIC FUNCTIONS |
|---|---|---|
| Pauses | Discontinuity | Incoherence |
| Rhyme Repetition | Hierarchy | Intensity |
| Rhythm | Irregularity | Unexpectedness |

*Figure 4. Prosodic devices in relation to acoustic and semantic levels*

2. The prominence of one physical segment over another, on the sound/ device side, has its analogue in intensification (or minimization), the most common case of which is emphasis.

3. Regularity or irregularity in the arrangements of unequal units, that is, a higher or lower entropy of the series, "has its analogue in unexpectedness of semantic arrangement (lower or higher degree of predictability)" (46).

Both congruent systems are further congruent to prosodic features (fig. 4).

In this "preliminary draft of a system," Levý has speculated about fundamental relationships between the aesthetic and the cognitive in a poetic text. Working with his small number of basic relationships, we may construct a far larger number of permutations. "The three sets enter into manysided relations, some of which are stronger than others" (53). The hypothesis thus satisfies metrical theory's hope for parsimonious statement of a combinatory model.

Levý notes in passing a major qualification that is pertinent to the claims of a study on grammetrics and reading. Semantic values, he says, "are results of a quantitative arrangement of acoustic segments and are not meanings sensu stricto, but forms of meaning. It is in most cases through these forms of meaning that the meaning of the line is affected by the acoustics of verse" (54). Grammetrical study cannot pretend to give over the poem's meaning or meanings, compressed or dispersed as the full sense might be; but it can at least insist, with empirical evidences, that the full sense is locked in a system of interferences with certain determinate structures. Grammetrics is thus a tool for reminding the reader that literary meaning is inseparable from the sound and form of the text's words. Grammetrics loads stylistic concepts with semantic possibilities.

Two or even all three of the primary semantic functions may work at one time, forming composite semantic values: for example, repetition + emphasis =

gradation. Or, according to Levý, they may "stand in relations of direct ratios to each other, constituting a simple system of proportions." The compressed statement of these ratios will help to direct our grammetrical inspection of the chosen sample texts:

A. *Incoherence—Intensity*
   1. The detachment of a segment of speech (word or phrase) generally results in emphasizing that segment; and vice versa (a close attachment of the segment results in lessening its semantic prominence.)
   2. Emphasis usually takes the word out of the context, and vice versa.
B. *Incoherence—Unexpectedness*
   1. The separation of a segment from the remaining context as a rule makes this segment (as well as the following one) less predictable, and vice versa.
   2. A decrease in predictability (unexpected metrical, stylistic, or contextual situations) as a rule lessens the coherence of context, and vice versa.
C. *Intensity—Unexpectedness*
   1. A decrease in predictability (based on deviations from a regular sequence) has, as a rule, intensifying effects, and vice versa.
   2. Emphasis, usually, breaks down regularity, and therefore lessens predictability, and vice versa. Emphasis can also signal *arrival,* a disentanglement from a previous unpredictability; Levý does not mention this.

Levý guesses that, among the three functions, intensity is the dominant one. This implies that the reader will rouse search behavior and be able to process a great deal of incoherence and unexpectedness, so long as the lure of semantic intensification can be maintained. Such seems to be true in the fourteen sample texts, where intensity comes as an unplanned side-effect of their choice of inclusion on the grounds of excellence, brevity, and a high degree of difficulty.

## Steps in Grammetrical Analysis

The acts of writing and or reading oblige us to record, and retain, many simultaneous observations. As grammetrists and critics, and thus as observers of these primary observations, our capacities are limited. We must model only that which can sensibly fall within the ranges of observation and comprehension. Although as readers we understand meter and syntax together, as observers of ourselves reading we must separate the two systems for inspection. Then at a later stage we can try to explain how they coexist. The hypothesis of grammetrics is that coexistence is really a mutual interference, here called scissoring; and further, that, in Levý's words, there is not "a one-to-one relation between segments of both levels, but . . . a parallel morphology of the two systems as wholes" (58). That is, both systems are subject to three principles of linear arrangement: continuity (coherence) versus discontinuity; equivalence (lack of intensity) versus hierarchy; and regularity (predictability) versus irregularity. The task will be to read these principles back into the linear arrangement of whole poems. This may be approached by a method that shuttles between hunches, postulates, and evidences, testing each in the process. This might be a logical reconstruction, which slows down the process of reading, separates for inspection what the process effortlessly integrates, and finally attempts reintegration along an order of steps within three major stages. Here these stages will be called preliminary recognition, grammetrical inspection, and interpretive grammetrics. In the sample analyses in the next three chapters, the stages will have been performed and reperformed beforehand, so the reader will receive a rather specialized rhetoric: one mind reading grammetrically, trying to repossess the high points of an integrated parallel processing, forcing attention to the eventful moments, but neither reading for simple comprehension nor for ideological judgment.

Since our intent is teacherly and practical-critical, the steps will be phrased as imperatives.

### Step 1: Preliminary Recognition

1. Mark the meter according to Derek Attridge's pattern of strong pulses (beats) and weaker pulses (offbeats), representing a beat with a capital *B* and an offbeat with a small *o*. Attridge shows deviations with diacritical marks on these basic symbols:

double offbeat = ŏ     triple offbeat: ŏ̵
demotion = ó̦    promotion = B̄    implied offbeat = ô

Axioms to be tested on the metrical system are

a. Infringement of the metrical contract set up in the first line or stanza breaks the acoustic pattern, changes the reader's process of cognition, and always in some way serves to reinforce or otherwise change the meaning of the words affected.

b. Deletion of expected stresses, what Reuven Tsur calls "stress valleys," has a pouncing effect that emphasizes the stress when stress returns; superaddition of stresses where not expected concentrates and redoubles emphasis.

c. Beginning and end of line have permissible optional distortions; since these may to a degree be expected, they have less force than infringements elsewhere in the line.

d. If the reader feels more comfortable with Saintsburyian-traditional scansion, employ that to start off, and modify if possible with strategic mixture of methods from Attridge and Halle-Keyser.

e. Neither Attridge nor Halle-Keyser nor Saintsbury are adequate or appropriate to the measures of prose poems or free verse. These require ad hoc recognitions of form, often with particular reference to the single poem or part poem: verset or stanza grouping, line structure both internal and in conjunction with lines before and after, white spacing and visual form as instance and not design. Fortunately the range of possibility though huge is not infinite, and there are broad regular types. (We can, with Annie Finch, find "the ghost of meter" in American and other traditions of free verse, but this is to assimilate free verse to the very prosody it is abandoning, and to avoid the work of finding a prosody that will describe measure as well as meter.)[5]

2. Mark the grammar. Every word will need to be tagged for its place in the sentence, and the rank-scale of the sentence will have to be determined at least down to the constituent levels defined by Halliday. Here too, as with meter, norms and their infringements will have to be classified. Also to be marked: sentence length, sentence complexity, and the way the poem's sentences consort together as a group; the beginnings and endings of verse periods (attention to punctuation, and where punctuation is absent by virtue of naked stretches of syntax); the way the poem employs phrasal breaks and pauses of various lengths within the sentences.

Axioms to be tested on the syntactic system are

a. Infringement of the ordinary well-formed sentence breaks the syntactic pattern: changes the reader's process of cognition, forcing the reader to consider new (or several) possibilities of construing.

b. Deletion of syntactic elements (verbs, connectives, pronouns) forces in the reader the energies of search behavior: to find and supply what has been elided.

c. The further the distance in the sentence of referents from their connections, the greater the sense of skewing, of unusual energy, of mystery in causality.

d. Active constructions foreground the subject or actor; passive constructions foreground the object of the action.

    e. When a verb demanding an animate object is given an inanimate object, or when certain verbs demanding human subjects are given abstract ones, categorial restrictions are abolished: thus converting (as the case may be) juxtaposition into action, inanimate to human, abstract to physical, static to active.

    f. Multiple-function wording and sentencing, and nonnormal syntax, achieve density of texture, conversion of one category into another, and unexpectedness of movement. These focusing and distorting powers produce cognitive eventfulness from the linear arrangement of meaning.

### Step 2: Grammetrical Inspection

Here or nowhere grammetrics justifies itself by reproducing, in theory and observation, the relationships that exist in the ordinary competent reading. Levý's three functions of incoherence, unexpectedness, and intensity (and their opposites) must be studied at every rank-level of the syntax and style of sentencing; and must be studied simultaneously, or alternately, in the structural-metrical segments.

1. Study the working of the three functions in syntax-lengths below the length of the sentence. Plot word, compound-word, and part-line caesural groups against the beat-offbeat structure; note frequency and placement of scissoring, and translate this data into hypotheses about degrees of incoherence, unexpectedness, and intensity in the poem as a whole. Are there nodes where the functions are found to be especially strong?

2. Study the working of the three functions in the verse period proper. The fact of greatest interest is the coincidence or noncoincidence of sentence and line. Coincidence tends toward maximum stability, in the gestalt formed by the line in the reader's attention; optimum stability would come when the line equals the sentence. Optimum instability would come when the line is enjambed, by a noncoincident sentence running longer than itself, "and all the stanza is one long strain" (in G. M. Hopkins's phrase). The verse period is the most volatile of the classifications, thus the most productive for grammetrics: there are more possibilities for the three functions to be taken toward their limits, thus for greater metrical and syntactic density. Hypothesis: the greater the variety of the verse period, the smaller the chance of a stable, predictable relation of sentence and line; and accordingly the stronger the intensity of the reader's local response.

3. Study the working of the three functions in the style of sentencing. The linear arrangement of sentences is one variable: modes of attachment to the previ-

ous sentence; changes from one sentence to next in number of elements, in overall structure and length, in particular rhetorical frame. (Listing syntax, poly-syndeton, asyndeton, hyperbaton, for example, all change the number and length of metrical groupings and thereby produce differentials in the functions.) Through precision rule-keeping, in the array of examples below, Swift as poet unleashes joke rhymes at every sixteenth syllable and every eighth stress, whereas Wordsworth's blank verse permits sentence after sentence of exploratory, enthusiastic self-display: to say even this much is to begin a reading on the basis of determinate styles of sentencing.

### Step 3: Interpretive Grammetrics

1. In the text under study, identify specially prominent effects of meter and of syntax. The most productive points will very likely be where such prominences coexist: wrenching points where pausing or grouping or stanza-breaking reveals grammetrical densities, ambiguities on several levels.

2. Can these prominences be related to an authorial or period style, a larger context of preferences? If so, we already have an opening to interpretation.

3. As in the brief characterization of Swift and Wordsworth just above, identify a *grammetrical dominant*. This involves a hypothesis about overall meaning and should as far as possible make statements that integrate metrical and semantic observations.

4. What are the recessive traits in the text, and how are they related to the grammetrical dominant?

5. Interpretive grammetrics begins at the upper end of all scales, with events rather than units, and with style of sentencing as this leads to hypotheses about point of view and tone of voice.

Probably all acts of ordinary reading, and also many published interpretations, will give evidence of a simultaneous processing of a poem's meter and syntax. As it tries to make this implicit grammetrics more explicit, my study of fourteen poems will blot out some empirical perceptions and allow others to show through. This happens as a matter of course with every set of concepts that is used to load a conceptual system, and thus to act as a focusing device. The gain in explicitness of articulation is what justifies the theory, keeps it out of mere tautology, and makes it suitable for conscious use by other readers.

## Chapter 9

# Shakespeare's Sonnet 129: A Grammetrical Reading

The poem has a few metrical irregularities in addition to the very vexed line 4, but these are minor and forgettable deviations from an extremely high degree of regularity or, to use Yurii Lotman's term, of structural inertia. The variable of meter is held steady, so that the very lines (but for 1–2, 6) are self-contained by end punctuation. Against this steady metering, the sentencing is varied from the norms of English syntax, distorted and driven to the verges of intelligibility. Shakespeare apparently decided to use this sonnet as an experiment, in a venture to see how heavy manipulation of the syntax and logic might have consequences in the rules of formal sonnet structure. In any event, he performed a casebook example of cognitive-aesthetic interference. The sonnet is great by virtue of its greatly deviant sentencing—the way the discourse is driven across the divisions of the meter.

This grammetrical reading bases itself on the Quarto version of 1609. Despite the presence of a seventeenth-century printer's error (line 11, "and proud *and* very wo"), this text is closest to what must have been Shakespeare's own punctuation, closest to Shakespeare's own scissoring of phrase and line.

1 Th'Expence of Spirit in a waste of shame
2 Is lust in action, and till action, lust
3 Is periurd, murdrous, blouddy full of blame,
4 Sauage, extreame, rude, cruell, not to trust,
5 Inioyd no sooner but dispised straight,
6 Past reason hunted, and no sooner had
7 Past reason hated as a swollowed bayt,
8 On purpose layd to make the taker mad.
9 Made In pursut and in possession so,
10 Had, hauing, and in quest, to haue extreame,

11 A blisse in proofe and proud and very wo,
12 Before a ioy proposd behind a dreame,
13   All this the world well knowes yet none knowes well,
14   To shun the heauen that leads men to this hell.[1]

Sonnet 129 is an expanded definition of male human lust, and perhaps more generally of the lust for power. It costs ("Expence") spirit and consciousness and human time to lust, and yet we pay and keep on paying. Having said this, I am already aware that it is not so simple at all, for lust (or lust for power) divides us against ourselves, prevents us from living the ordinary experience of present time. Lust "in action" (l. 2) may be "heauen," but it leads to an inevitable "hell" (l. 14), to a "waste of shame" (l. 1), and to madness (ll. 8–9, "mad./Mad(e)"). But the before and after of lust are related states that last far longer, states where we are both hunter and hunted, hunter and bait (ll. 6–8), dreamer and dream (l. 12). Already the syntax of the paraphrase is beginning to mime the syntax of the poem, as we describe the speed of the action, the way it is leaped over in this text ("in action, and till action"; "Before . . . behind"): an ecstatic but fugitive instant amid the tracts of before and after. Lust through the cycle of its time phases is thus essentially contradictory. Shakespeare's pun on "Spirit" as both semen and con-sciousness is the epitome of the whole poem's effort to define the undefinable.

Trying to define the undefinable, the speaker, Shakespeare for short, essays phrases, showers examples, turns up contradictions, condenses his multiple meanings in metaphors. The best way to read the poem is as a single sentence, many times divided, whose subject is "lust," the to-be-defined that is the second word of the second line. We get a definition (1) and then the word defined "Is lust" (2); and then the before, during, and after of lust are listed in rather bewildering sequence in 3–12, and 13–14 are a summary plus comment. The poem has quite stupendous propulsion, as all the commentators have remarked.

But also, and more to the point, the extraordinarily high degree of in-coherence, unexpectedness, and intensity of the sentencing, as these semantic functions play against the metering, has some bearing on the sense of the poem. Indeed, it may even be said that metrically portioned-out sentencing is in large measure the sense of the poem. Lust, as we have claimed, is here taken as an inescapable condition, and what we (we males!) cannot escape is ourselves, or part of ourselves. Shakespeare shows himself caught in the toils of his angry sentencing, yet his impetuousness, his gigantism, are occupying the same space as the decorum of meter. When the reader enters the utterance with a mental or oral performance, the long sentence is known to be portioned out with and against a coolly regular system of iambic pentameter.

The structural method of Sonnet 129 is that of expansive, propulsive sentencing, developed with and against regular metering. (Helen Vendler's idea, that these are really four-stress lines pretending to be pentameters, seems to me a mistake.)[2] The tone of voice is that of hatred or self-hatred. Since the poem lacks direct address, lacks even a single pronoun, the reader (with no surrogate self indicated in the words) rather overhears than hears the tones of anger. The definition of lust is prosecuted with such energy, and at such length, across so many grammetrical divisions, precisely because it cannot be brought to satisfactory rest. So the rhetorical genre and grammetrical dominant of Sonnet 129 may be called that of the *frustrated definition*. In a poem so forward leaping, brief yet comprehensive, such a dominant will be strong enough to control even the seemingly casual metaphors that might in another poem be considered recessive features. Here, for example, the figures of "Expence," "Spirit," "bayt," "dreame," "heauen-hell" actually compress the contradictions of active-passive, spiritual-physical that initiate, while they also frustrate, Shakespeare's rhetoric.

Before suggesting a notation that justifies the reading given here, let me explain my claim that the poem is a single sentence. The 1609 printer has put a period at the end of line 8, thus dividing the octave from the sestet and counterposing the first eight against the last six lines. But in this case the division is as slight as may be, not only because the octave break is weaker in Shakespeare's three-quatrain + couplet rhyme scheme than in a Petrarchan sonnet schema, but for three even more important reasons: the punning repetition of "mad" (end of l. 8) in the next word, "Made," produces a continuity of sense and of sound that overrides the period and the line break; "Made" does not begin a new freestanding sentence but is a past participle controlled by the copula verb "is" in 3 and by the subject of that verb, namely the twice-repeated "lust" of 2; the argument of the poem carries past the notional break at the end of 8, and 9 is part of the same listing procedure as the lines previous to it (3–12 forming a unit). I doubt that there is another sonnet by Shakespeare that so insistently overleaps all of its quatrain divisions by the effects of syntax and argument. Here, there are three notional "sentences," or at least three independent propositions: (1) the definition down to "action" and the first comma in 2; (2) the description of lust in a series of words, phrases, and line-long clauses to the end of 12; (3) lines 13–14, a summarizing statement set off by indentation but not treated as a new free sentence by the 1609 printer. The subject is "lust," and the copula verb "is" controls in lines 3–12 a dazzling series of past-participle free modifiers (not absolute phrases, as one might at first suspect). After the series of predicate adjectives in lines 3–4, the past participles give the propulsion: "inioyed," "dispised," "hunted," "had," "hated," "made." Then in line 10 comes the clever conjugation, "Had, hauing, and in quest, to haue," the first break with the strict past-participle progression—and each verb summarizing in reverse order of time.

It is certainly possible, I think preferable, to see the poem as a many-times-divided hierarchical sentence. This preserves the grammetrical ambiguities that constitute the sense of the poem. To take the poem as one sentence that complicates the order of its clauses, and refuses to supply elided elements, raises the basic question of *What is an English sentence?* Shakespeare has obscured the relations of his sentence, apparently to defer an easy or early understanding, and to challenge the normative frames of mental processing. This was the appropriate method of sentencing for a poem that proposes to itself the task of defining the indefinable. Here he wished never to permit a line and a sentence to be firmly coincident—so he rested on a full period only after the last word: sentence coincident with whole poem.

The sentence does, in the end, sort itself out. It is exceptional, but grammatical. What is exceptional is the compression of the opening definition (ll. 1–2), as this is followed by the expansion and development of that definition of human lust (ll. 3–14). The poem opens by giving the definition before the word to be defined, placing the object before the verb, the verb before the subject. Then the poem develops a listing-subordination, regularly right-branching (lust is A, B, C . . .), but extended over enormously more items than usual. "It is a dominant tendency of syntactic structure," according to Randolph Quirk, "that the greatest depth of subordination or embedding is reached in the final part of the sentence."[3] Sonnet 129 is an emphatic exception to this tendency of English. Shakespeare's poetic sentence opens with an initial subordination of some complexity (two *ofs* and two *ins* within thirteen words, including "of Spirit in a waste of"). The middle part of the sentence makes a syntactical about-face, from line 3 down, moving into a more conventional right-branching subordination of great depth. "We have a clause with multiple predicates, each of which takes focus at this [subject-predicate] level . . . a clause with a monosyllabic subject followed by [a great many] predicates linked only by asyndeton" (Richard D. Cureton in a note to me). So, overall, subordination, skewing the relations, is used to develop intensity through incoherence and unexpectedness.

The result is that words and segments are detached from their contexts. This makes for emphasis. The kind and degree of isolation of items on the rank scale of syntax is thus what grammetrics studies. It means looking not only at the items themselves in their different lengths, but also at the nature of the spaces between items. Period, dash, comma, unpunctuated space, indenting have all a different specific gravity, which must itself vary according to situation before, within, or after the line.

**Th'Expence  of  Spirit  in  a  waste  of  shame**    1 2 3 4 5 6 7 8 9 10

o    B    o    B    o    B̄    o    B    o    B            10

def. art.    N    prep.    N    prep. indef. art.    N    prep.    N            1 group

 

**Is  lust  in  action,  and  till  action,  lust**    1 2 3 4 5  6 7 8 9  10

o    B    o    B o    B̄    o    B o    B            5      4      1

V    N    prep.    N    coord. conj.    prep.    N    N            3 groups

 

**Is  periurd,  murdrous,  blouddy  full  of  blame,**    1 2 3  4 5  6 7 8 9 10

o    B o    B    o    B    o    B    o    B            3    2    5

V (present)    Pred. adj.    Pred. adj.    adj.    adj. prep.    N            3 groups

 

**Sauage,  extreame,  rude,  cruell,  not  to  trust,**    1 2  3 4  5  6 7  8 9 10

B    ŏ    B    ò    B o    B    o    B            2    2    1    2    3

adj.    adj.    adj.    adj.    adj.    V.    inf. (particle)            5 groups

*Figure 5. Lines 1–4 of Sonnet 129, with grammetrical notation*

The place in line inevitably implicates pause. For example, and to begin a closer inspection, Sonnet 129 opens (the first line and a half) with fifteen "places" unbroken by punctuation, ten of these in line 1 fully unbroken by line end or caesura. Then in lines 3–4 small-scale grouping goes wild. The movement from an unbroken to a heavily broken stretch of language is very marked (fig. 5). As we come closer to the grammetrical matrix of the sonnet, it is well to remind ourselves that, after all as the last word of the poem says, this is an account of *hell,* and hell is very busy and confused. Hell-as-lust confounds the relation of time, of before and during and after; blurs the relation of thought to action, and the relation of self to self and to others. Lines 1–4, quoted here, initiate the difficulties. In the first one and one-half lines, we have six nouns woven into relationship in the space of thirteen words: "The blank of blank in a blank of blank / Is blank in blank." "Th'Expence of Spirit" is itself a compressed and knotty phrase, but when it is shown spatially in "a waste of shame," and then shown to be the definition not only of lust but of "lust in action," the degree of syntactic depth and cognitive tension is already marked, already enough for a very dense sentence—but the sentence goes further, turns on the pivot of line 2 to introduce new complications.[4]

The complications are, or quickly become, cognitive. At the beginning of the poem, two successive lines enjamb onto the verb "Is" beginning the next line; but from line 1 to line 2 the definition comes before the thing to be defined (B before A), a feature that is reversed from line 2 to line 3 (A before B). The first definition is reversed from normal order and highly compressed; then the second is put into normal order and expanded to consume the rest of the poem. The one definition is unbroken, the other divided into as many as fifteen grammetrical clause-groups between lines 3 and 12.

Cognitive depth in the first definition gives way to cognitive expanse in the many-times-divided second definition. Both procedures hamper comprehension. Line 1 judges while it displays the mode of "lust in action," showing how action is consumed, over before one realizes what has happened. What leads up to "action" and away from it is then shown, by listing and denunciation, in the rest of the poem:

> till action, lust
> Is periurd, murdrous, blouddy full of blame,
> Sauage, extreame, rude, cruell, not to trust.

After these lines the metrical groupings are a line long, but here in 2–4 we have eleven groupings, marked by commas, and eight caesuras in three lines. I should say this is the moment of highest cognitive intensity in the poem, defined as search for coherence. These lines come after the deep subordination-structures of the first one and one-half lines, and, reversing ground with another structure, these lines proliferate the most detached segments in the smallest space. Starting with 5, the reader begins to see the direction of the long sentence, but the list of lust's human attributes in 3–4 is especially incoherent and unexpected. Despite the incoherence, about here in the poem the reader begins to understand that Lust is being used as a figure of personification.

A poem about impossible self-definition here engages in almost frantic intellection, throwing out guesses that are also curses. To say this possibly accounts for the absence of a comma after "blouddy," a term that is at once literal and figurative, at once a detached adjective and a swearword modifying "full of blame." I think it also accounts for the special pertinence of metrical irregularity at just this point. Shakespeare deletes a syllable from *murderous* to make line 3 regular, but line 4 suffers a peculiar breakdown hard to interpret by means of the stress maximum or traditional foot-meter theories taken by themselves. Before line 4 regularizes itself and arrives at its rhyme word, it has followed two adjacent unstressed syllables by three adjacent stressed syllables. The "reversed" first foot effect is a permissible variation in both the stress-maximum theory and in traditional versification, but what occurs here is far more exceptional. One would expect the line to get back on the metrical track with the word "rude." But because this is scissored on either side by a syntactic break and a caesura, and perhaps too because it rhymes with the next syllable, "rude" takes a strong stress. It disrupts a line already disruptive, and to return the line to regularity Shakespeare must cut *not to be trusted* back to three syllables by ellipsis. I shall not argue that line 4 is "Sauage, extreame, rude, cruell, not to trust" because that is what it is about, but rather that the very exceptional discontinuity and irregularity of the line's meter is homomorphic with the incoherence and unexpectedness of the syntax, and that this kind of grammetrical scissoring creates cognitive intensity and a tone of suppressed fury. Alliteration and internal rhyme also contribute to this tone, but the end rhymes seem to have unusually strong semantic relationships in this quatrain: "shame" the result of "blame," "lust" the neglect of "trust."

Now the poem moves into a new quatrain and a new phase of sentencing: whole-line segments or (as in ll. 6–7, 7–8) two-line segments, larger clumpings usually structured as contrasts in logic such as the *Inioyd-dispised* of line 5 (fig. 6). The second "and" in line 11 is an obvious printer's error; rather than a conjunction, this should have been an indefinite article. But why was that reader, the printer, led to this and-stringing error? Perhaps he was caught up, like any reader, in the hurtling syntax and made it go faster yet; and perhaps in this and the next line he dropped a comma for the same reason.

At this point, we may comment on a feature of the poem we would not notice without Attridge's beat-offbeat notation: the curious break at midline, caused by either promotion (B) or demotion (o), in all the first seven lines except line 3. The poem at its opening seems to break on little function-words (*in, and, as*) into half-line segments, even as the syntax and logic plunge forward. Line 5 is typical of every one of these lines in the way *action* is elided by syntax, making what is *inioyed dispised,* showing that sexual ecstasy and sexual anguish are really the same thing temporally ("no sooner but . . . straight") as well as morally. To make *action* disappear, or at least make it brief, to overleap action in cognition is the method and meaning of the poem's long sentence.[5] Lingering for a moment on the incoherence-unexpectedness relation of these lines, I should say that lines 5–12, because they are coincident with internally contradictory groupings of clauses, are far more predictable in overall structure than lines 1–4. The long

| *Inioyd* | *no* | *sooner* | *but* | *dispised* | *straight,* | 1 2 3 4 5   6 7 8 9 10 |
|---|---|---|---|---|---|---|
| o   B | o | B   o | B̄ | o B o | B | 5        5 |
| V (past) | adv. | adv. | conj. | V (past) | adj. | unbroken |

| *Past* | *reason* | *hunted* | *and* | *no* | *sooner* | *had* | 1 2 3 4 5   6 7 8 9 10 |
|---|---|---|---|---|---|---|---|
| o | B   o | B   o | B̄ | o | B   o | B | 5       5 |
| prep. | N | V (past) | conj. | adv. | adv. | V | unbroken |

| *Past* | *reason* | *hated* | *as* | *a* | *swollowed* | *bayt,* | 1 2 3 4 5   6 7 8 9 10 |
|---|---|---|---|---|---|---|---|
| o | B   o | B o | B̄ | o | B   o | B | 5       5 |
| prep. | N | V (past) | conj. | art. | Pred. adj. | N | unbroken |

| *On* | *purpose* | *layd* | *to make* | *the* | *taker* | *mad.* | 1 2 3 4   5 6 7 8 9 10 |
|---|---|---|---|---|---|---|---|
| o | B   o | B | o B | o | B   o | B | 4       6 |
| prep. | N | V (past) | V (inf.) | def. art. | N | adj. | unbroken |

| *Made* | *In* | *pursut* | *and* | *in* | *possession* | *so,* | 1 2 3 4   5 6 7 8 9 10 |
|---|---|---|---|---|---|---|---|
| B | ŏ | B | o | B | o B o | B | 4       6 |
| V | prep. | N | conj. | prep. | N | adv. | unbroken |

| *Had,* | *hauing,* | *and* | *in* | *quest,* | *to haue* | *extreame,* | 1   2 3   4 5 6   7 8 9 10 |
|---|---|---|---|---|---|---|---|
| ȯ | B   o | B̄   o | B | o B | o | B | 1    3    2 |
| V (past) | V (pres.) | conj. | prep. | N | V (inf.) | adj. | three caesuras |

continued

*A  blisse  in  proofe  and  proud  and  very  wo,*

| o | B | o | B | o | B | o | B | o | B |
|---|---|---|---|---|---|---|---|---|---|
| ind. art. | N | prep. | N | conj. | V (past) | conj. | adj. | | N |

*Before  a  ioy  proposd  behind  a  dreame,*

| o | B | o | B | o | B | o | B | o | B |
|---|---|---|---|---|---|---|---|---|---|
| prep. | ind. art. | N | V (past) | prep. | ind. art. | N | | | |

*Figure 6. Lines 5–12 of Sonnet 129, with grammetrical notation*

sentence is beginning to sort itself out after the cognitive onslaught of the first quatrain.

The first quatrain isolates for emphasis; the second quatrain repeats. Line 6 picks up "no sooner" from line 5, but moves it nearer the line end; and line 7 picks up "Past reason" from line 6 and exactly repeats the phrase's position at beginning of line. The change comes in sound and sense, not position:

> Past reason hunted and no sooner had
> Past reason hated . . .

Shakespeare substitutes one letter for two others and so permutes desire into undesire: requiring one of the poem's scant three enjambments to perform this slight expansion of the rhetoric of contradiction we have seen in line 5. Repetition of "Past reason," in the sense of "beyond good sense or balance," reinforces the special emphasis on the twice-repeated (4, 10) term, "extreame."

This meaning is extended further by example in the line-and-a-half-long analogy of the purpose-laid bait that makes the taker mad. The lines do not specify who laid the bait, the victim of lust or the luster. The relation is left unresolved, a blurring of active and passive that permits the reader to understand the hunter of lust as the actual victim, deceived by his human bait but also, and primarily, self-deceived. The one who "has" is "had"—a Renaissance joke about love underlined by the *had-mad* rhyme, which forces a semantic connection between lust and derangement.

Lust is the animal in the human being; hence the metaphor of the frustrated hunt: "Past reason hunted" because civilized understanding cannot capture or

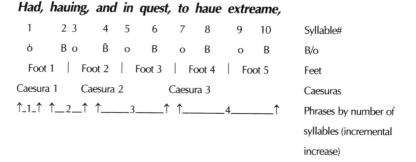

*Figure 7. Caesuras and syntax in line 10*

control this force. Physical love may seem glorious, but thinking about it consumes and distorts so much of life. Quatrains 2 and 3 show this through their images of hunting, being mad, and dreaming, but also by rhythmic and logical parallelism of the lines. Semantic intensification may operate by rhythmic breaks, as in the first quatrain, or by means of the repetition and parallels of the next two quatrains that argue the moral complexity and temporal extension of lust. To *inioyed-dispised* and *hunted-hated,* we may now add *pursut-possession, a blisse-and very wo, a ioy-a dreame:* doublets and contrasts used by Shakespeare to elide present time while showing how extremes meet.

The effect already noticed, where the poet leaps in thought beyond the end of line and sentence at lines 8–9, making a highly unusual link between quatrains, may now be seen as contributing to this same structure of contradictory thinking. "Made" beginning line 9 picks up warrant from both "to make" and "mad" in line 8, extending both in the same word, a connection both of sound and sense between the second and the third quatrain. Similarly, the beginning of line 10 picks up the rhyme end of line 6 and develops it into a whole verb-conjugation, a reversed summary of the poem's complete time scheme of lust in action. Grammetrically speaking, along with line 4 (which also has "extreame"), this is the most fascinating line in the poem (fig. 7). Here are three scissoring caesuras making four segments, which increase in size by syllable increments from one to four syllables. It is a tidy progression made possible by the original printer's commas. The other, more obvious progression is that of the verb conjugation that in one line runs through the whole of the poem's beginning-middle-after time frames, making up a rudimentary alliterative form of rhyme on the paradigm changes.

Scansion of the line by traditional feet shows the first and second feet broken by caesuras; nothing very remarkable, except that this plays stress against syntax to give extra emphasis to the times of the verb of lust that will, with the word "extreame," soon be seen to be morally equivalent. Scansion by Attridge's beat-offbeat shows that this line has a demotion, or stressed syllable pulled down to an offbeat by position, and also a promotion, or unstressed syllable between two other unstressed syllables, in the same complex line: the only time this happens in Sonnet 129. The past, present, and future of human lust are all extreme, for no time is exempt from this passion.

With its requirement that the stress maximum occur between two un-stressed syllables *in the same syntactic constituent,* the Halle-Keyser scansion will have more trouble with this line. Scissored as they are into isolation, are positions 2, 4, and 6 proper stress-maxima, and if they are not, what are they? This line works systematically to divide the weak from the strong stress, so that (counting syllables from start of line) the only true stress-maximum by definition is at position 8. Heavy, detaching, unpredictability-producing caesuras fall between positions 1 and 2 and between 3 and 4, prior to strong-stress positions, but a lighter caesura falls between 6 and 7, after a strong stress deemphasizing the comma after "quest," pulling "to haue" and "extreame" back into the attraction of the earlier half of the line. Shakespeare integrates the rhyme word more successfully within the whole line's syntax and thereby helps "extreame" apply more adhesively to all three stages of lust, and not just the stage of unfulfilled desire.

Where the earlier attribute "extreame" was lost in midline (4), it is here repeated and given special emphasis by being applied to its line's three verbal stages, and by being placed in rhyme position at line end. For further emphasis the mating rhyme, "dreame," is another attribute of lust, and the other rhyme pair in the third quatrain doubles the judgment because "so" is a substitute for *mad* in the syntax of line 9: *mad-woe-extreame-dreame* form their own semi-autonomous line-end paradigm of condemnation.

In the lines that end quatrain 3,

A blisse in proofe and proud and very wo,
Before a ioy proposd behind a dreame,

the speaker takes to the furthest point in the poem our sense of the contradictory nature of lust, and our sense of the way it consumes human time in the paradigms of desire. (If you slice close enough, there is no present moment, only memory and anticipation; *that* is what the poem is about.) Both lines, with *in proofe and proud* [proved] and *before-behind,* elide time and overleap the present moment, and they do so as whole-line groups that are self-divided into the speaker's reigning contrasts. The first of these lines uses *and;* the second juxtaposes "Before" and "behind" without conjunction or comma. The very compression of syntax here is probably what has outfoxed the original printer, who becomes the first reader in the history of the poem to act to simplify and routinize, and to make a pattern that was not found.

At line 12 ends a series begun with the first pivotal predicates. "Is," twice stated in the openings of lines 2–3, will be many times omitted but implied in what follows: is perjured, is murderous, is enjoyed, is past reason hunted, and so on. As I have argued, the definitional structure that sets out to say "lust is A and B and C" is frustrated because the defining terms are themselves paradoxes, giving an increasing sense that lust is antithetical in its nature, not subject to definition. In the 1609 Quarto the body of the poem ends, however, not with the conclusion of a heavily subordinated periodic sentence at the end of 12, but with a comma. The sentence ends in thought but not in fact, and the reader moves by comma splice into the concluding summary couplet, confirming once again (as with the end of the second quatrain) that grand elementary principle of concatenation that Helen Vendler sees "riding over all . . . antitheses in the rhythm and the logic and the rhetoric, [and] which appears semantically, rhetorically, grammatically, phonologically, and thematically."[6] The couplet is set off visually by indentation, and otherwise by being entirely monosyllabic ("heauen" is elided to make the meter fit), by having contiguous lines that rhyme with each other, and by using figurative language to give a little résumé of all that has gone before (fig. 8). The last two lines are without marked internal breaks or pauses, each word equal to a numbered slot in the line, if we go by the Halle-Keyser kind of tally. This in itself marks a change from the previous twelve lines and perhaps signals a gesture of closure—as does the change from alternate to successive rhyme, the completion of a new pattern on the poem's last word. The grammar of these lines is also very regular, two halves halved again: "well knowes"/ "knowes well"; "heauen"/"hell." The couplet extends thereby the paradoxical parallelisms of the earlier six-sevenths of the poem. Line 13 contrasts *knowledge about* and *know how,* two distinct meanings of *know* (I. A. Richards's point); and line 14 makes explicit what we have been inferring from the start, namely that lust is by definition both ecstatic and shameful—attributes inseparably twisted together. This last sentence, which is itself a final clause in the larger sentence that is the poem, manages to prolong the speaker's state of impurity and self-contradiction. It does so by working very hard the contrast of "well knowes" and "knowes well," a weighty distinction posed in a trope heartbreakingly flashy: moral values known but not acted upon. Irresolution is preserved to the end,

| *All* | *this* | *the* | *world* | *well* | *knowes* | *yet* | *none* | *knowes* | *well,* |
|------|------|------|------|------|------|------|------|------|------|
| o | B | o | B | ó | B | o | B | ó | B |
| adj. | N | def. art. | N | adv. | V (pres.) | conj. | pro. | V (pres.) | adv. |

| *To* | *shun* | *the* | *heauen* | *that* | *leads* | *men* | *to* | *this* | *hell.* |
|------|------|------|------|------|------|------|------|------|------|
| o | B | o | B | o | B (ô) | B | ŏ | | B |
| | V (inf.) | def. art. | N | rel. pro. | V (pres.) | N | prep. | adj. | N |

*Figure 8. Stress and syntax in lines 13–14*

when the last line, with its Calvinist urge to shun the false heaven that is lust in action, is presented in the context of being absolutely denied by the second-to-the-last line. What is *known well* and what is *hell* undermine each other, so that even the rhyme is ironic. The beat-offbeat notation yields two further forms of irresolution in the concluding couplet: in 13, "knowes" is repeated, once as a beat and once as an offbeat; and in 14, there is an unusual double offbeat (*to this,* ŏ) in the position just before the last word, producing a closural, stumble-then-hard-step onto *hell.*

Thus has Shakespeare concluded the poem without dissolving its perplexities. The couplet lives up to the rest of the poem as it looks back to it through anaphor ("All this"), through symmetrical repetition of the figure of epanalepsis ("or the Eccho sound, otherwise the Slowe Returne": Puttenham) from line 2 ("lust in action, and till action, lust"; "the world well knowes yet none knowes well")—and through the antithetical parallelism of lines 1 and 14 (spirit/shame; heaven/hell).[7] The ending also returns to the punning and metaphors of line 1 and to that line's definitional urges, adding a new trope to the system of definitions: lust = action = heaven = hell, so we end with *hell,* a religious image for desperate sexual guilt (by Renaissance convention, "hell" also referred to a woman's genitals). Grammetrics cannot by itself explain the full meaning of that image, which is beyond its scope, but it most certainly can explain the position of *hell.* Its position, as prolonging and intensifying irresolution up to and beyond the last word of the poem, is a part of its meaning that is all too easily missed. But more than elsewhere in the poem, position in Shakespeare's verse period would be a void without the converging, figural force of the term saved for this place. In these lines, both meter and grammar take a turn toward greater coherence and predictability, as the poem hints its closure, but the figure in the final line's final word cuts across grammetrical regularity to maintain the impossibility of self-definition—thus to disrupt stability of meaning by another method.

Since I am not claiming to offer an innovative reading, but rather trying to show some of the literary processes that make any acceptable reading possible at all, it is reassuring to me that the foregoing account is similar to published readings of the poem by Helen Vendler, Giorgio Melchiori, and Stephen Booth. When Booth says that "Sonnet 129, whose subject is unstoppable energy, is itself unstoppable," he gives a welcome anticipation of grammetrics, because he is not a metrist and his only wish is to make sense of the poem. "Of the sources of forward thrust in the sonnets," he writes, "the lure of an unfinished syntactical unit is the most important and the commonest."[8] Good grammetrical noticing is not necessarily reliant on the latest or most technical analytic terms. Probably all acts of ordinary reading, and also many published interpretations, will give evidences of a simultaneous processing of a poem's meter and syntax: evidences that of course need to be isolated, and judged. I do not see such evidence in the editorial choices of modern anthologies that forsake the 1609 Quarto edition and clean up the punctuation and meter of the sonnet, thus eliminating the ambiguities of sentencing and metering that are inseparable from the poem's cognitive density. I do not see such evidences, either, in the famous 1970 structuralist reading of the poem by Roman Jakobson, which finds intricate symmetries but provides hardly any footing in the poem's meaning why they should be there.[9] Jakobson tends to see this lyric as a simultaneity, a structure there all at once, but accepting this grammetrics insists also on the successiveness of poetry, the way it cuts a shape in time. Structuralism of Jakobson's sort used to encourage too much emphasis on the role of simultaneity, on form at the expense of meaning. But any strong poem is in itself an argument that simultaneity is only enhanced, only brought to the fore, by successiveness.

# Chapter 10

## Readings of an Array of Nonmetrical and Metrical Texts

Though my reading of Sonnet 129 is the most detailed given to any of my examples, it is not exhaustive. I have tried to show the places in the poem where interference of grammatical and metrical systems creates, and arcs over to the reader, cognitive energy. If poem and method seem to be made for each other, if the reading convinces, thanks are due to the faculties humans have for processing literary language: for *making simultaneous sense* of grammatical and prosodic information, of ordinary speech and art speech. This is no new reading or new way to read. Even after further examples, this book cannot keep its character of a prudent, expanded formalism and still claim that the grammetrical method permits, encourages, evokes, produces meanings or types of meaning hitherto unnoticed, inaccessible. The best commendation of the method is that it is in no respect original. Everybody reads this way. Some who do write analyses in a more or less grammetrical manner are Harai Golomb of Tel Aviv, Henri Meschonnic of Paris, Enikö Bollobás of Budapest; and more than a few Americans, including Josephine Miles, Eleanor Berry, John Hollander, Charles O. Hartman, Stephen Cushman. Why other readers do not talk this way about what they read is a wholly separate study, a sociology of scholarship.

It is time to surround the Shakespeare sonnet with the array from which I took it.[1] The reading of the sonnet has not been sufficient to confirm the ubiquity and centrality of grammetrical cognition; nor can the full array of fourteen poems constitute a final demonstration. What is here: fourteen poems, 330 lines in all, 110 nonmetrical and 220 metrical lines; a range of items from 1609 to yesterday, from intimate personal address to steely, noble impersonality, from the prose poem to the sonnet. The array is manageable yet various, with credible claim to wide representation of periods and types. Once the texts have been taken up singly, they can then be considered selectively for possible comparisons, and for their statistical properties as a population of data.

In this array, the nonmetrical poems have no meter, and the metrical poems have largely traditional usage. The exceptions are the polymetrical items by Pound and Peck, and the distinctively irregular (yet iambic, if we may use the term) poem by Emily Dickinson. The ratio of number of sentences to number of lines offers a rough guide to the grammetrical values of the poem, because the smaller the fraction, the more continuous and enjambed will be the utterance, sentences draped over line ends. Thus: Charles Tomlinson, 13/No Lines; W. C. Williams, 11?/22; George Oppen: 10?/33; Cid Corman: 4/12; Edward Dorn: 10?/30; Ezra Pound: 8/20; William Wordsworth: 6/38; Robert Lowell: 16/28; Emily Dickinson: 3?/12; John Peck: 8/40; Jonathan Swift: 13/32; Alfred Tennyson: 2/12; William Shakespeare: 1?/14; John Berryman: 2/14. Charles Tomlinson's poem has no lines, of course, but in order to reckon it in, if crudely, to the count, I have tallied the number of lines of type taken up by the poem in its published version. Unpunctuated poems by George Oppen and Emily Dickinson, and the archaic punctuation in the Shakespeare sonnet, put unusual pressure on naked grammar as the maker of sentence sense. The level of cognitive dissonance is increased when the little marks are missing, or when Dickinson uses only the dash. In several cases, namely those of Williams, Oppen, Dorn, Dickinson, and Shakespeare, it has proved impossible to get an accurate count of the number of sentences in the poem, and in all these I have determined that the ambiguity as to where one sentence ends and the next begins is functional, part of the text's obscuring the relations of thought for its own purpose. Usually that purpose is to prolong the thought or to interiorize it, to make grammar interfere in a less determinate way with the meter at points that are indistinguishably transition and break. Oppen's poem is a spectacular instance of a poem seeking a certain effect of brokenness by means of sentence fragments. The sequence principle of the array of fourteen is designed to increase the quantity of aesthetic information (in a neutral sense of the term: no judgment of merit involved), by stepping up slowly the number of conventions.

We begin with a prose poem composed of stanzalike versets, a poem without lineation or meter or rhymes; we end with a sonnet in a definite number of lines in a disposition of portioned-out beats and rhymes. The prose poem and free verse, the nonmetrical prosodies in the array, may be understood as versions that subtract certain sorts of possible beauty, in order to emphasize other sorts and phases. Thus chronologically the prose poem and free verse come later than the other poems. Logically, however, these nonmetrical texts come first, for in them cognition is more obviously represented by art-sentencing. The stepped-up addition of meter, rhyme, and stanzaic structure can follow on in later stages of the array; yet it is absolutely typical that rhyme (Dorn) and stanza structure

(Corman) can be heavily used within the nonmetrical group. It is an advantage of grammetrics to be able to put nonmetrical and metrical texts into the same array, and to be able to use the same descriptive language for both types of text.

Most of these poems are lyrics. Seven are in the iambic meter that has been the staple of English and American poetry since Shakespeare, and that continues in its centrality despite the polymetrical and nonmetrical developments of the past century. Several are poems of love and affection, several recount personal experience in a narrative mode, several engage in impersonal wisdom-writing, and two (Williams, Swift) use the measures and grammar of mockery. The nine metrical poems represent most period styles between the Renaissance and the present day. In Pound, Dickinson, and Peck the metrical set also contains whole poems that resist the received scansion.

The word *reading* occurs in the title of this book and chapter. How could anyone be unaware that this is, nowadays, a fighting term? As a professor of reading, I know most of the recent critical studies that have denied the possibility of objective interpretation, even as they have reinserted the reader in the poem and empowered the reader vis-à-vis the poem. I have here preferred to use the term *reading,* rather than *interpretation,* because the book must remain in the skills end of the spectrum; still, the spectrum is continuous all the way over to full-scale ideological interpretation, and the skills end is the sine qua non of the other end. As a reader, I aim to come forward here as one mind consciously limited, but at least conscious of itself and its interactions with the poems. As reader I am not that construct, the Superreader. My aim is to add to this subfield a practical suggestion as to how we might rescue metrics by a metrics of discourse—by resemanticizing the metrical code. My brief readings of the array of fourteen are an adjunct to this purpose: examples of how I construct a language of gram-metrical description. The best way to construct such a language convincingly is to describe actual whole poems in full view, beginning by remembering overall effect from the vantage of the end, and then reversing field and taking local effects more or less in sequence from the prolongational, projective, eventful vantage of the beginning. I go back and forth between overall and local meanings.

The purpose is not to contribute to Shakespeare scholarship, say, but rather to the emergent field of poetics that subsumes metrics. These days, poetics has little direct interest in interpretation as such, and indeed Jonathan Culler has argued "the importance of attacking interpretation" as a means of "loosening the grip which interpretation has on critical consciousness." For my project, Culler's admittedly tendentious view that we must go beyond the easy spate of readings—"we need a more sophisticated and apposite account of the role of literature in the psychological economies of both writers and readers"—is a challenge. Writing against Stanley Fish's attempt to keep formalization and ex- egesis together in the same book, Culler remarks that "to claim simultaneously that one is describing the experience of the reader and that one is producing valuable new interpretations is a difficult act to sustain."[2] That is an apt warning. If we are investigating the conventions that permit the production of meaning, if we hope to solve problems of processing and to show the infinitely difficult obvious, it is best not to make claims of originality. My readings are practical trials; they go "beyond interpretation" to the neglected, preinterpretive side of our practice. Call them, perhaps, the recapturings of first readings; interpretation proper involves second and later readings, and reckons in ideological-historical- institutional investments much more fully. So in the readings that follow, I shall be interpreting not in the sense of doing a hermeneutic unveiling of what is arcane and hidden, but in the sense of reminding ourselves of what we already know.

Traditionally, metrics has hoped to go in the other direction from interpre- tation: to desemanticize. Part of line and line have been the units for analysis. For a grammetrical analysis it becomes a matter of policy to quote and read whole poems. We are at least heading in the right direction, even if we cannot travel the whole distance in this vehicle.

## The Nonmetrical Prosodies

Sentences, I have argued, are the scissors of poetry, where meter is also and equally, and at the same time, the scissors of sentences. In the nonmetrical prosodies of the prose poem and free verse, we speak rather of measures than of meters. To speak thus is to describe, not to judge. Sentencing and measuring are in interference in the nonmetrical prosodies, and the structural principles of verbal art are thus fully at play, indefatigably dynamic.

### Charles Tomlinson, "Oppositions: Debate with Mallarmé"

Unlike the Russian tradition, which insists on a separation of essences between prose and poetry, in France, England, and America the prose poem is and has always been absolutely accepted as a poem. Because of the absence of line breaks, the prose poem offers a privileged context for the isolation of styles of sentenc- ing. The coincidence or noncoincidence of sentence and line is not a factor. The elements are deleted, distorted, or reweighted. For instance, in the Tomlinson poem, the verset functions as a longer than usual line that has equally the role of a stanza.

A reading of Tomlinson's texts in this hermaphrodite and avant-garde for-
mat must serve in the end to reinforce one's belief that he is after all a traditional
poet. He is traditional in the way of the painter Constable, whom he admires:
accepting the evidences of perception, loving the world's physical presences and
trusting that the artist's materials (word, pigment) can graph what is seen and felt.
The notation of the work of art would be, for him, accurate to the way of a
world, and also public; no accuracy but one that is communicable. The hygiene
of deconstruction is not unknown to him, with its privileging of ideas of ab-
sence, indeterminacy, the text as a "galaxy of signifiers" (Roland Barthes), but
Tomlinson is after all British, Midlands British—emphatically perception based,
an artist who watches climate and landscape with the kind of charged perception
that, he once said (quoting Kafka), catches a glimpse of things as they may have
been before they show themselves to the observer. Tomlinson's attraction to
notions of absence and change, to the dispersing tactics of the international
avant-garde, is always chastened by his fact-noticing Englishness.

For this reason we often see him in dialogue with Stéphane Mallarmé,
whose skepticism about language precedes by generations the philosophical
deconstruction of Martin Heidegger, Jacques Derrida, and Paul de Man. There is
a "Homage and Valediction" to Mallarmé, along with Laforgue and Eliot, in the
six-part poem "Antecedents" in *Seeing Is Believing* (1960); and the title of one of
Tomlinson's own drawings of a seashell, dated October 11, 1968, is "Débat avec
Mallarmé." More to the point, here is the first and to my mind the most
considerable of his prose poems in the "Processes" section of his book *The Way of
a World* (1969):

OPPOSITIONS
*debate with Mallarmé*
for Octavio Paz

The poet must rescue etymology from among the footnotes, thus
moving up into the body of the text, 'cipher': the Sanskrit word *sunya*
derived from the root *svi,* 'to swell.'

To cipher is to turn the thought word into flesh. And hence 'the body
of the text' derives its substance.

The master who disappeared, taking with him into the echo-chamber
the pyx which the Styx must replenish, has left the room so empty you
would take it for fullness.

Solitude charges the house. If all is mist beyond it, the island of daily
objects within becomes clarified.

Mistlines flow slowly in, filling the land's declivity that lay unseen until that indistinctness had acknowledged them.

If the skull is a memento mori, it is also a room, whose contained space is wordlessly resonant with the steps that might cross it, to command the vista out of its empty eyes.

Nakedness can appear as the vestment of space that separates four walls, the flesh as certain then and as transitory as the world it shares.

The mind is a hunter of forms, binding itself, in a world that must decay, to present substance.

Skull and shell, both are helmeted, both reconcile vacancy with its opposite. *Abolis bibelots d'inanité sonore.* Intimate presences of silent plenitude.

There are nine versets, six of them fully equivalent to a single sentence. The third and the ninth verset refer to Mallarmé, to whose sonnet "Ses purs ongles très haut dédiant leur onyx," Tomlinson's poem is a reply. Mallarmé there conjures an empty room (second quatrain):

>                               nul ptyx,
> Aboli bibelot d'inanité sonore
> (Car le Maître est allé puiser des pleurs au Styx
> Avec ce seul objet dont le Néant s'honore.)
>
>                               [no ptyx,
> Abolished bibelot of sounding inanity
> (For the Master is gone to draw tears from the Styx
> With this sole object which Nothingness honours.)][3]

For Tomlinson, who was drawing skulls and shells in profusion at just the time of his debate poem in 1968–69, such hollow objects are, and are occasions for, reconciliations of inner and outer, absence and presence. Tomlinson's lightly joking use of converging words, *ptyx* and *styx,* suggests another kind of reconciliation: rhyme forcing a strained semantic connection even in a prose poem, even when one of the terms seems to be a neologism.

The poem proceeds from a manifesto (versets 1–3) to instances of the union in the art object of absence and presence (4–7), to a generalizing statement (8) and a direct rebuttal of Mallarmé's sentence fragment in French by Tomlinson's in English (9). Tomlinson arranges this argument-by-juxtaposition so as to have the last word himself; but Mallarmé's assertion of a sounding inanity, a Nothingness, is not treated by Tomlinson with irony, merely contradicted with severe insistence. The mingling of assertion and example is Tomlinson's way to defend (by speaking) the silent plenitude of such natural yet artful objects.

His defense of presences in the final sentence is foreshadowed by a rhetoric of body and substance in all the earlier versets, but especially in the pun on *present* as both a transitive verb meaning "give" and as a adjective meaning "immediate" (verset 8). This doubling effect, putting into doubt etymology and phonology, would not function in a metered poem, where relative stress on first or second syllable would tell the reader how to sound and therefore definitely interpret the word. The prose poem preserves the several meanings.

Charles Tomlinson shows himself convinced, for this poem anyway, that the world means, means well, and means through a linguistic sign so thoroughly motivated that its cipher can "turn the thought word into flesh." What if we took Mallarmé's side in the debate, in order to resist Tomlinson's defiant Cratylism, his hope, with its emblem in the Sanskrit root, to charge the world with so much presence it actually protrudes toward the noticer? The poet seems positively to have encouraged such dissent by setting up the poem to make debating points—by pronouncing on the way of a world, his world. He does this often, too, in his line and rhyme poems, stating how the world is, but the prose poems seem to accept this argumentative, point-making approach somewhat more easily. For Tomlinson's purposes, the grammeasures of the prose poem have proved suitable, grouping instances into versets and regulating the proportion of image to declaration, encouraging several minor bursts of wordplay that support and diversify the argument, and then juxtaposing sentence fragments at the very end where the author's English caps Mallarmé's French. These are the grammeasures of assertion and persuasion, that seek to show the reader that perception is a profound and not altogether helpless form of moral cognition.

### William Carlos Williams, "Portrait of a Lady"

Your thighs are appletrees
whose blossoms touch the sky.
Which sky? The sky
where Watteau hung a lady's
slipper. Your knees
are a southern breeze—or
a gust of snow. Agh! what

sort of man was Fragonard?
—as if that answered
anything. Ah, yes—below
the knees, since the tune
drops that way, it is
one of those white summer days,
the tall grass of your ankles
flickers upon the shore—
Which shore?—
the sand clings to my lips—
Which shore?
Agh, petals maybe. How
should I know?
Which shore? Which shore?
I said petals from an appletree.

Williams's poem contains no quotation marks and so has the effect of obscuring its own speech orientation: tending to make into one textual voice what is actually two halves of a dialogue. The speaker addresses an unknown "you" who is a lovely woman, or more likely a projected image of a woman, for it is not she who replies to the metaphor he launches, "Your thighs are appletrees / whose blossoms touch the sky," but another of the speaker's voices, an alternative self whose questions are reprimands to the rhetoric of ideal love. The poem is a dialogue between the idealizing and the literalizing selves of the speaker. Sentence 2 answers sentence 1, sentence 5 answers sentences 3 and 4, and alternations continue throughout, though sometimes it takes two sentences and not just one between changes. Williams throws out a gorgeous erotic metaphor worthy of the idealizing of the painters Watteau or Fragonard, then disrupts it by fussy questions.

Averaging one sentence to two lines, the proportion of sentences to lines is very great, in itself suggesting extremes of disruption. There are six dashes, six questions, and three exclamations as signatures of the ironic breaks within the rhetoric of expansion. The switches and breaks create discontinuity and thus incoherence, until the reader discovers the principle of alternation that drives the poem. The instability begins to seem functional: sentences ending and beginning in midline (3, 5, 7, 10, 21), bits of grammar teetering at line end (3, 6, 7, 10, 19) create the desired effect of lurching as the expansive self seems in the middle of the poem to break down. The sixth and longest sentence is the major turning point, because this one condemns the rhetoric of metaphor from within its own boundaries. Irony has crept within the citadel of the ideal:

> Ah, yes—below
> the knees, since the tune
> drops that way, it is
> one of those white summer days,
> the tall grass of your ankles
> flickers upon the shore—
> Which shore?—
> the sand clings to my lips—
> Which shore?
>
> (10–18)

"The sand clings to my lips" is the representative line for the whole poem, because this speaker must slog through resistances every time he warms to his subject. The traditional "tune" he wants to sing gets raucous. "Those white summer days": the pseudoreference (which days? why white?) does provoke a challenge from any properly suspicious reader.

As the poem comes toward its ending, with three dashes and two question marks ending the lines quoted above, the speaker is put under an insistent pressure and seems to waver: "Agh, petals maybe. How / should I know?" His metaphors have been undercut by the literal, so much so that he can win the final comment in the last (emphatically unbroken) line only by a terrible overinsistence. He weakens, is pressed harder, and then responds angrily: "I said petals from an appletree." By this time, neither the expanding nor the reprimanding self is very appealing, but together they have made a careful little discourse that shows the absurdity of oversimple rhetorics. Both rhetorics are ironically diminished, though by intention the author does not give a hint of what might be a normative discourse or a normal description of a woman's body.

The irony is borne out to the end. Carefully the properties of every syllable and piece of punctuation are weighed. Quotation marks have been omitted to obscure the relation of the sentences one to another. Twelve lines in all are run-on, but these mostly come at the start when the utterance is opening out through lyrical flights. Of the last eleven lines of the poem, the second half, only three are run-on: by that time, the grammeasures have begun to line up. The poem's mocking self-deflation is controlled by the alternation of voices. The very high degrees of incoherence in the intonation and of unexpectedness in the rhythm must combine, exponentially, to step up the poem's intensity. What is produced as a result is a free-verse tone of sly humor.

### George Oppen, "Anniversary Poem"

The hope for a continually unsettling verbal texture, eventfulness everywhere, is shared by modern metrical and nonmetrical prosodies—which are, after all, equally heirs of the romantic discoveries about language and the relation to the reader.[4] So that the reader should get the next best thing to what Keats called the true voice of feeling, namely its simulacrum, postromantic prosodies emphasize or invent devices of verbal energy. Often, as in George Oppen, this means obscuring the relations of punctuation, grammar, syntax, voice, and narrative. The reader's interest and pleasure comes from following continuities through the disruptive breaks in the poem's verbal texture:

> 'the picturesque
> common lot' the unwarranted light
>
> Where everyone has been
>
> The very ground of the path
> And the litter grow ancient
> A shovel's scratched edge
> So like any other man's
>
> We are troubled by incredulity
> We are troubled by scratched things
>
> Becoming familiar
> Becoming extreme
>
> Let grief
> Be
> So it be ours
>
> Nor hide one's eyes
> As tides drop along the beaches in the thin wash of breakers
>
> And so desert each other
>
> —lest there be nothing
>
> The Indian girl walking across the desert, the
> sunfish under the boat
>
> How shall we say how this happened, these stories, our stories
>
> Scope, mere size, a kind of redemption

Exposed still and jagged on the San Francisco hills

Time and depth before us, paradise of the real, we
          know what it is

To find now depth, not time, since we cannot, but depth

To come out safe, to end well

We have begun to say good bye
To each other
And cannot say it

This kind of free verse differs from other kinds, and from traditional verse, by making it impossible for the reader to certify from the start a schema or formal contract. There is no carrying measure, no stanzaic structure, that would permit the reader to know from the first line how the second, or the last, would be constituted: every line must be taken as it comes. Though quotation marks, dash, and comma appear, this is essentially an unpunctuated poem, so the internal and external relations of sentences are not fully specified, or are given indirectly in the visual ellipse of white spacing either between or within the lines. (Maybe it is punctuated by phrase and by visual spaces, instead?) In a line like "Exposed *still* and jagged on the San Francisco *hills*," rhyme occurs, but here, as in the repetition of a key term like "depth," or the presence of a syntactic parallelism ("We are troubled . . . / We are troubled"), it is not easy to know if the effect of equivalencing is intended as a formal device.

The poem begins with an unattributed quotation in a voice other than the speaker's but assimilated to his, moves through injunction ("Let grief / Be"), the anecdotal flashes of the girl, the sunfish, and the San Francisco hills, to a personal statement to the woman who is the implied auditor; and although this plausibly represents what Coleridge might call a progressive transition, it is plainly not a discursive argument. Through hesitations, full stops, the glimpse of rudimentary narrative, occasional haste in the syntax of a line like "Time and depth before us, paradise of the real, we know what it is," George Oppen creates a sober voice, broken but urgent. Words form into little bursts of lines, as if unwillingly; and affirmations smuggle themselves into the middle of lines, as in the positional modesty of the only metaphysically daring phrase in the poem, "paradise of the real." The carefulness of this self-effacing speaking voice is revealed in its motives only at the end, where the poem's closure ("to end well") is associated with the end of life for these faithful lovers, who must treasure now their intensity because time is short.

We have begun to say good bye
To each other
And cannot say it

In a lesser poem, or elsewhere in the same poem, those lines would be inexcusably dull and flat; here, they engage the reader, as coauditor and cospeaker with the persons in the poem, in a curious reluctance to have the language act cease. That sort of weakened closure, which has the implicit injunction to the reader to feel and know his or her experience to the fullest, which sends the reader back to the self and out to the world, as well as resuming (summarizing, again beginning) the whole poem, is typical of most poetic structuring after Coleridge.

### Cid Corman, "The Tortoise"

Always to want to
go back, to correct
an error, ease a

guilt, see how a friend
is doing. And yet
one doesn't, except

in memory, in
dreams. The land remains
desolate. Always

the feeling is of
terrible slowness
overtaking haste.

A paraphrase does scant justice to the verbal art of Cid Corman's elegant miniature. The title is very much part of the poem's meaning. The poem is not about a tortoise but rather relies on our knowing the story of the creeping tortoise catching up with the fleet hare. The tortoise is the moral impulse to do right and to expiate guilt, especially the smaller guilts that are often overlooked. The speaker, in a poem about how conscience must always fail to catch up with our actions in the present, the prodigal haste of everyday living, is the elegist of small guilts.

Simple forms can have strong cohesion. Corman's stanzas of three short lines are highly stable blocks of type. To the eye, this might be a sculptured rhyme-and-meter poem by such as Théophile Gautier, but to the ear and the grammetrical attention it is something very different, a poem that plays against the stability of the stanza the changeability of sentencing. In the small parts this is a matter of words repeated but in different places:

Always *to* want *to*                    (middle-end-middle)
go back, *to* correct
    ★

       ease *a*
guilt, see how *a* friend             (end-of-line, not end)
    ★

*in* memory, *in*                          (beginning/end of same line)

It is also a matter of contradictory words at the same line-end position, one below the other:

the feeling is of
terrible *slowness*
overtaking *haste.*

This last stanza runs a tripping line, with a single stress for five syllables; and then runs four long words to take up two whole lines. There is emphatic speed, and then to change the pace a heavy rhythmic deliberation (balanced twos in the two last lines), and the most abstract diction in the thirty-eight words of the poem. The contrast of rhythms and lexicons makes for maximal closure.

In the larger parts of the poem, except for the final sentence just described, sentences extend past the end of the stanza blocks. Since no sentence coincides with a line or stanza, there are many tight turns. Sentence 1 is a listing of verbal actions: want, go back, correct, ease, see, is doing. It is three times broken with infinitive actions. It is the longest sentence in the poem and yet, grammatically, it is a fragment: catching the thought in passage as the initiation of the utterance. Sentence 2, beginning "And yet," qualifies the assertion of sentence 1, and then qualifies the qualification: memory and dreams as ineffectual ways of redeeming oneself. Sentence 3 is very different, a brief, subject-verb-subjective complement sentence that moves from midline to midline in the middle of a stanza. Line-locked, it complicates the poem by adding a metaphor for the ethical situation, desolate land for unfilled moral duties in life. After that expansion and confirmation by means of metaphor, sentence 4 connects back to the beginning with "Always": same word but now the last word in a line and not the first, now separated physically from the sentence it controls, and now controlling an intransitive verb ("is") rather than a series of infinitive constructions. There are no clauses to break the final sentence, no hesitations or reversals. Only the last line of the poem is end-stopped. New clots of phrase, new sentences begin in midline throughout, and thus help to make this a telling argument but not a propulsive one; the interference, or scissoring, is too bold for propulsion to be a dominant here. It begins to look like the fourth and last sentence will be similarly trapped by the line measures, like the middle two sentences, but the final period ends poem, sentence, line, and stanza.

Abstract terms and circuitous phrasing ("terrible slowness"; "the feeling is of") are used at the end, but they are made exact by our knowledge of the story of the tortoise and the hare. Our deeds are us; also our omissions. The tone is somber. The chiseled stanza shapes, requiring as they do the paring and turning of sentences, contribute to the sad inevitability of such an argument, such a tone. Very neat because very stable, like uncemented blocks in Incan architecture. However within the free-verse stanza the rule is a very high instability of sentencing: there too the unreconcilables of slowness and haste.

Eleanor Berry, reading the above, has asked: "Do you see the pacing of grammar and that of meter as functioning ironically here? And if so, which is the tortoise, which the hare? (I'm not sure any particular pacing can be ascribed to the stanza form alone—it seems spatial rather than temporal.)" Without knowing Berry's remark, Richard D. Cureton essays an answer when he remarks that "the poem is also beautiful at higher, rhetorical levels. The poem *falls* rhetorically. The poem is built on *appositions* that echo elegiacally. This is exactly appropriate."[5] So there exist at least three grammetrical readers of this little masterpiece; of course, my argument is that we are all grammetrical readers, though at varying degrees of consciousness of how we think against, along with, and by means of the poem.

### Edward Dorn, "The Rick of Green Wood"

In the woodyard were green and dry
woods fanning out, behind

                a valley to go.

Woodpile by the buzzsaw. I heard
the woodsman down in the thicket. I don't
want a rick of green wood, I told him
I want cherry or alder or something strong
and thin, or thick if dry, but I don't
want the green wood, my wife would die

Her back is slender
and the wood I get must not
bend her too much through the day.

Aye, the wood is some green
and some dry, the cherry thin of bark
cut in July.

My name is Burlingame
said the woodcutter.
My name is Dorn, I said.
I buzz on Friday if the weather cools
said Burlingame, enough of names.

   Out of the thicket my daughter was walking
singing—
      backtracking the horse hoof
gone in earlier this morning, the woodcutter's horse
pulling the alder, the fir, the hemlock
above the valley
       in the November
air, in the world, that was getting colder
as we stood there in the woodyard talking
pleasantly, of the green wood and the dry.

The world in Edward Dorn's poem is a place of exchanges, perceptual, vocal, monetary. It is pleasant enough—for now. Generally avoiding traditional end-rhymes, the first half of the poem nonetheless (before and during the passage of represented direct discourse) manages a good deal of tone leading, keyed to a small set of repeated vowels and consonants in recurring words. *Green* or *dry,* the choice the poem is built around, returns for the fifth time at the end (30), where the speaker is still talking to the woodcutter—but also now attending to the way of the world, whose climate is about to turn: "in the November / air . . ." In the poem, the speaker has a care for his wife's back and for his daughter's singing; he is led from "pleasure for the eye" at the beginning through the end's "talking / pleasantly," from the eye's evidence to a larger sense of the threat of climate, the context of our acts of attention. (*Rick* means a stack, but it also means a sprain, twist, wrench, or overstrain. Green wood waits to be seasoned like the participants in this poem's world.) The speaker also attends to his own form of singing: this poem's amazingly (for free verse) intricate structure of sound-recurrence is what principally conveys to the reader the pleasurable fragility of paying attention, of life and thought in and against "the world." The threat of the world is in this poem a mere suggestion, a hint of trouble; accordingly, the poem's qualities of tension and contentiousness are minimal, and the sign of this may be heard everywhere, especially at the beginning, in Dorn's obvious pleasure at the dense play of sound.

It might be argued that the extraordinary grounding in sound helps this poem make up for the absence of meter. But I have kept this poem for last in the progression of nonmetrical items in the array, precisely because it seems to advance on meter as well as on rhyme. Especially in the reported discourse (e.g., 7–9), but also in the narrative (21), the poem divides into ternary groups. Admittedly there is no norm, no consistency, and there is no point attempting a scansion; still, in its unpinnable, perhaps-Olson-inspired physiological rhythms, this might be at least as "regular" as the poems across the line by Pound and Peck. Saying as much, we seriously impugn the notion of regularity. Very likely Dorn's poem is transitional in this way between nonmetrical and metrical because the major theme is singing: as manifested by the daughter who is

walking

singing—
backtracking

("singing" is placed against the margin while the rest of the sentence is inset, as if the act of singing is frail and yet weighs against all the other forces); and as manifested in the remarkable incidence of like-sounding rhymes and near-rhymes on nearly every word, sounding upward and downward from any given point, so saturating as to be what Yurii Tynjanov calls a phonetic metaphor. For all his gnarliness and laconicism, the poet is led toward song as a declaration against the odds, against "the world," which evokes the singing but also gets colder. Just as Dorn is led toward song as a metaphor for mind, he is also attracted to the rhyme and meter that his chosen verse-form eschews.[6]

## The Metrical Prosodies

### *Ezra Pound, "The Return"*

See, they return; ah, see the tentative
Movements, and the slow feet,
The trouble in the pace and the uncertain
Wavering!

See, they return, one, and by one,
With fear, as half-awakened;
As if the snow should hesitate
And murmur in the wind,
              and half turn back;
These were the "Wing'd-with-Awe,"
              Inviolable.

Gods of the winged shoe!
With them the silver hounds,
              sniffing the trace of air!

Haie! Haie!
        These were the swift to harry;
These the keen-scented;
These were the souls of blood.

Slow on the leash,
        pallid the leash-men!

The images and the grammetrics carry a single theme: *these hunters are not what they were.* The poem concerns loss of powers, diminishment: how glorious the hunters used to be, and what they and their dogs are now. The overall tone as conveyed by sentencing and metering is one of praise, spoken against and through dismay. The speaker is an imagined observer from the same society, and the same precapitalist time in history, when hunting was an activity engaged by the powerful that conferred godlike charisma on the actors. To help the reader imagine that speaker's state of mind, Pound must use an archaism of diction, syntax, and meter.

That archaism as engaged by an avant-garde writer accounts for much of the oddity; for this is one of the most peculiar texts in the whole array. It is a transitional text between the nonmetrical and the metrical systems, but deformed toward the nonmetrical or the polymetrical from the side of meter. (Dorn's poem is lured toward the metrical from the other side.) "The Return" was written in 1912, when the existing traditional system was under attack, and by one of the attackers—who knew that system very well indeed. It is not a fluke but a careful experiment. The poem successfully resists a beat-offbeat and a traditional and a Halle-Keyser scansion because we cannot be sure if the meter is absent, multiple, or variable. The idea of a metrical contract must be a very loose idea if it applies to this poem.

I hope to show that there is scissoring across and within the lines, but (because there is no metrical contract) I am forced here to consider somewhat larger groupings than elsewhere in my readings of the array. It is better to document this attempt on the fiendish Pound example, than to substitute an example that is more easy, that is, regular.

The twenty lines are disposed in stanzas of unpredictable length, sense groupings that are not bound by rhyme or other obvious devices of equivalence. The lines are not heavily caesuraed, and not heavily broken by sentence phrasing. As if to initiate the sentence with heavy emphasis, the first line is the most broken of all:

> See, they return; ah, see the tentative . . .

Two imperative verbs, both obviously speech-stressed, separated by the heavy break of the semicolon-caesura; and an exclamation to redouble the emphasis on the imperative ("See . . . ah, see"). It is a syntax that gives a dodging rhythm. Just as "tentative" at the end of line 1 and "uncertain" at the end of line 3 manifest their meanings in their placement, so the heavily speech-stressed "slow feet" seems a deliberate thematizing of the formal material. In

> The trouble in the pace and the uncertain
> Wavering!

uncertainty manifests itself visually, but also in hovering of stress. We cannot know if the third "the" takes speech stress, for example, and thus we have two conflicting options of how to say the whole line aloud.

Fairly consistently in the second halves of lines there comes a formulaic use of phrases, to such an extent that the relationship between the group of phrases and the half-line is more significant, grammetrically speaking, than the relationship between sentence and line. I am thinking of the list of definite-article phrases:

> the tentative
> the slow feet
> the uncertain
> the "Winged-with-Awe"
> the winged shoe
> the silver hounds
> the trace of air

the swift to harry
the keen-scented
the souls of blood
the leash
the leash-men

By quantity of words, these take up more than a third of the poem, and Pound seems to notate them as special usages by placing them at line end, by indenting some of the lines in which they occur, and by putting in other line ends rather similar groupings of hyphenated or implied hyphenated constructions: *half-awakened, half turn back.*

The first halves of lines have their own rather formulaic opening gestures: "See, they return" (twice at lines 1, 5); "These were the" (four times, at lines 10, 16, 17, 18). The final sentence can be a sentence fragment because "These were the" is repeated so often as to be a pattern—a pattern so familiar it can be deleted and nonetheless understood.

Given the frequency of formulaic phrasing in first and second halves of lines, it is not surprising that the lines themselves have the stability of half-line block set against half-line block, and that seventeen of the poem's twenty lines are end-stopped by some kind of punctuation. These special proportions of syntactic expansion and deletion—blocks scissoring, and scissored by, a not-entirely-unpredictable stressing—are the grammetrical means Pound uses to create a texture of archaism, an uncanny voice. It is uncanny by comparison with the possible voice in traditional regular meter. The lexical means are more obvious: "Winged" appears twice, once in a formula with one stress, once two lines later with two stresses and an archaic pronunciation ("wingéd"); the exclamations "Haie! Haie!" just at the point the speaker is most taken by the memory of the hunters' former prowess; "one, and by one," as a way of extending a count into a dramatic description.

The speaker moves through three moments of understanding: the recognition of the hunters' return in the present (ll. 1–9); the evocation of their skill in the past (ll. 10–18), and a brief summary image of dogs and men in the diminished present, in a sentence fragment that omits the actors and gives only actions (ll. 19–20). In each of these sections of the poem the topic is pace, gait; and so too is the method, as the stress system disrupts itself and engages in dying-fall procedures ("tentative" in line 1 diverts the strong-stress opening into a falling rhythm that continues for three more lines). The gait of the hunters and dogs is uncertain, but so too is the gait of the poem's speaker, who is caught between the vivid image of the past ("Haie! Haie!") and the "slow-pallid" image of the present, unable to find a single response. As between the prosodic devices, the acoustic principles of arrangement, and the primary semantic functions, all the levels match.

### *William Wordsworth, Skating Episode from* The Prelude

| | |
|---|---|
| And in the frosty season, when the sun | /sentence 1 |
| Was set, and visible for many a mile | |
| The cottage windows through the twilight blazed, | |
| I heeded not the summons: happy time | |
| It was indeed for all of us—to me | (5) |
| It was a time of rapture! Clear and loud | /sentence 2 |
| The village clock tolled six,—I wheeled about, | |
| Proud and exulting like an untired horse | |
| That cares not for its home. All shod with steel, | /sentence 3 |
| We hissed along the polished ice in games | (10) |
| Confederate, imitative of the chase | |
| And woodland pleasures,—the resounding horn, | |
| The pack loud bellowing, and the hunted hare. | |
| So through the darkness and the cold we flew, | /sentence 4 |
| And not a voice was idle; with the din, | (15) |
| Meanwhile, the precipices rang aloud; | |
| The leafless trees and every icy crag | |
| Tinkled like iron; while the distant hills | |
| Into the tumult sent an alien sound | |
| Of melancholy not unnoticed, while the stars | (20) |
| Eastward were sparkling clear, and in the west | |
| The orange sky of evening died away. | |
| Not seldom from the uproar I retired | /sentence 5 |
| Into a silent bay, or sportively | |
| Glanced sideway, leaving the tumultuous throng, | (25) |
| To cut across the image of a star | |
| That gleamed upon the ice; and oftentimes, | |
| When we had given our bodies to the wind, | |
| And all the shadowy banks of either side | |
| Came sweeping through the darkness, spinning still | (30) |
| The rapid line of motion, then at once | |
| Have I reclining back upon my heels, | |
| Stopped short; yet still the solitary cliffs | |

Wheeled by me—even as if the earth had rolled
With visible motion her diurnal round!                    (35)
Behind me did they stretch in solemn train,        /sentence 6
Feebler and feebler, and I stood and watched
Till all was tranquil as a dreamless sleep.

This is one of the few passages of *The Prelude* published by the poet during his life. It appeared in Coleridge's journal, *The Friend,* in 1810, as an example of the influence of natural objects on childhood imagination. (The poet wrote this episode as lines 452–89 of Book I in the version of 1805.) For our purposes it is sufficiently self-contained to be separated from its setting in a long auto-biographical poem; and it shows Wordsworth as a master of blank verse, impressing on his chosen medium (the medium of Shakespeare and Milton) his own themes and stylistic habits.

This is a narrative that may stand for those others in *The Prelude* where the poet describes how he has been shocked into a perception. The early sentences prepare for the assertion in sentence 5, that the cliffs went circling "even as if the earth had rolled / With visible motion her diurnal round." That recognition is the imaginative outcome of the ice-skating experience for the child. To tell this story of the access of imaginative power, the poet uses sentences progressively, showing shifts of attention whereby the outer can dart inside, the internal can invest outside objects. The passage moves from the pack of skating children, with the loud din of social activity, to the one child's private activity of skating across the image of a star, his wheeling and abrupt stopping-short. Then after the vision of the cliffs wheeling, an optical illusion that leads to a genuine flooding-in of imaginative power, the poet shows how a vision dissipates; the turning of the cliffs is "feebler and feebler." The exalted vision is presented by stages, progressive alternations of social and individual being, scene and agent, sound and then sight in the foreground of the perceptual field. Finally, for a moment, the child's wheeling helps him to match with the revolutions of the earth, and there comes visible a motion beyond the threshold of human perception.

In a phrase like "even as if," the adult Wordsworth knows the physiology of such experiences of vertigo, and yet he would respect the imaginative gift he received as a child. A mistake about the world nonetheless leads to a real emotion that is formative and cannot be devalued by taking thought about it. There might even be a written language that aspires to reimagine and evoke the emotion.

Let us resist doing a traditional scansion of these thirty-eight lines of blank verse, remarking only that seven lines begin with the permissible variant of first-syllable stress; and that in nine places Wordsworth elides a syllable in order to fit three sounds into two spaces. There are ten caesuras, fairly well distributed throughout; and twenty-one run-on lines, making rather higher than 40 percent of enjambment. There are two uses each of *while* and *then* as coordinative adverbs, four dash constructions used as additional extensions and not parenthetically; and six uses of *and* as syntactic connective (including the first word of the passage, which points back to the narrative context in earlier lines of book 1). Defining sentences in terms of punctuation not grammar, there are six sentences for thirty-eight lines, ending at lines 6, 9, 13, 22, 35, 38; so on average each sentence is over six lines long, though in fact sentences 4 and 5, the emotional center, take up twenty-two lines, more than half the passage.

Under constraint of the meter, including Miltonic and Augustan conventions for the iamb, Wordsworth occasionally permits himself to elide a phrase ("man-ya" for "many a" in 2), or to invert the normal word order (two inversions in 4–5: "I *heeded not* the summons: *happy time / It was*"). Clearer examples of grammetrical two-way scissoring are the sentences (numbers 1, 2, 3, 5) that use the dash construction, beginning by description of the scene and then abruptly turning to agent or moral in emphatic midline shifts of the center of attention. Wordsworth in several of these instances pivots a sentence on itself, in the pattern

*clause in apposition +  ,— + I + extended hierarchical predicate*

The dash or comma + dash is the notational sign of a continuity that rushes across a break, picking up new energy as it loads detail into the predicate end of the sentence. There is a reordering of sentence features, principally to get a delay from a left-branching apposition before the subject is brought in, and this is possibly influenced by the necessities of keeping blank verse correct—as well as by the poet's wish to get long sentences by filling up every possible place before during and after the subject. Not coincidentally, this serves to foreground scene and climate first, and agent and events later: every sentence imitates the whole passage's feinting between ground and figure, the whole passage's arrival at agency, consciousness. Extension is the principle of syntactic structure in the passage, with effects heightened by the way sentences are draped over lines. Usually, the enjambments point propulsively ahead, not recursively back.

Some clauses are the length of a line, such as the amazing "When we had given our bodies to the wind" that foreshadows and prepares the boy's abandonment to vertigo below in the same sentence. When a line is not interrupted by shorter-than-clause segments, as for example the last line of the passage,

Till all was tranquil as a dreamless sleep,

there is a more emphatic certainty. The last lines of sentences in the verse period are usually resolving lines, unbroken by punctuation and working toward the final knitting of sense. By that line, the relations of the sentence have clarified themselves. However, the early and middle parts of sentences (except for sentence 2) are usually very involved, usually breaking at syllable number 6, 7, or 8 in the line (e.g., "The village clock tolled six,—I wheeled about").

The first three sentences, we have said, turn on dashes and end with actual or implied exclamations. They have some inversions and stock phrasings—"the frosty season," "many a mile"—and yet they urgently describe the wintry twilight scene, even down to the precise hour of six o'clock and the kind of time ("It was a time of rapture"), the child transformed into an *untired horse* or one of a *pack* of dogs in the chase for game. In sentence 4 Wordsworth dwells on the voices of the children as agents, returning the resonance of the scene as a response to the skaters' noises: the precipices *rang* and the trees and crags *tinkled* in reverberation; but the distant hills seemed to go further, to initiate "an alien sound / Of melancholy not unnoticed." The negative affirmation, as often in Wordsworth, brings special emphasis: even the child can make out the feeling tone of horizons, their odd sounds and the symmetries of the death of the sun in the west and the birth of stars in the east; even the child knows about melancholy and about death.

And the child knows of the need to set against clock time and the death of the day another kind of time, "a time of rapture." That is the whole purpose of Wordsworth's fifth sentence, which begins with the backward phrasing of another negative affirmation, "Not seldom." He here brings in the less important events of the skating scene, as a further deferral and preparation. He multiplies descriptive clauses, only one of which is equal to a line (28), and thus achieves an insistent plunging forward to get to the grammetrical event of stopping short:

> then at once
> Have I, reclining back upon my heels,
> Stopped short; yet still the solitary cliffs
> Wheeled by me—even as if the earth had rolled
> With visible motion her diurnal round!
>
> (ll. 32–36)

The crucial turn and break is well prepared by syntactic delay and has emphasis from the equal double stress on "Stopped short"; after a heavy caesura, the sentence then presses on to show the wheeling cliffs, and further still to venture a metaphysical meaning ("even as if . . ."). The sinuous syntax brings to the foreground the markers of time: "Not seldom . . . oftentimes, / When . . .

spinning still . . . then at once . . .; yet still . . ."; but the time of rapture is outside this tissue of overlapping sequences so carefully calibrated. Sacramental time is when the boy's life coordinates with the earth's diurnal round; it takes place between "Stopped short" and "yet still" because it cannot be shown, can be known only in the differential between the stopped solitary skater and the wheeling *solitary cliffs*. The child "heeded not the summons" of the cottage lamps, he was "Proud and exulting like an untired horse / That cares not for its home," because his truest home was shown to exist in the rolling of the earth in *her diurnal round*. That home outside ordinary time occurs in the grammetrical gap that fissures line 34.

### Robert Lowell, "Man and Wife"

Tamed by Miltown, we lie on Mother's bed;
the rising sun in war paint dyes us red;
in broad daylight her gilded bed-posts shine,
abandoned, almost Dionysian.
At last the trees are green on Marlborough Street,
blossoms on our magnolia ignite
the morning with their murderous five days' white.
All night I've held your hand,
as if you had
a fourth time faced the kingdom of the mad—
its hackneyed speech, its homicidal eye—
and dragged me home alive. . . . Oh my Petite,
clearest of all God's creatures, still all air and nerve;
you were in your twenties, and I,
once hand on glass
and heart in mouth,
outdrank the Rahvs in the heat
of Greenwich Village, fainting at your feet—
too boiled and shy
and poker-faced to make a pass,
while the shrill verve
of your invective scorched the traditional South.

Now twelve years later, you turn your back.
Sleepless, you hold your pillow to your hollows like a child;
your old-fashioned tirade—

loving, rapid, merciless—
breaks like the Atlantic Ocean on my head.

The opening is dazzling: an arresting first line, the weird image of the tranquilized lovers, the bed and the blossoms giving a malign setting for a malign event, impeccable rhyming and metering in seven lines where a classical iambic pentameter contains jagged personal details. The discourse of a husband at fault, unable to change, possibly crazy: we have his view of a wife made of *invective* and *tirade,* whose loving tongue-lashings cannot make him change. Her bravura and his irresolution are the same as they were when they met: there is continuity in their relationship in the three times of the poem, from the now of the opening (1–12), to the single long sentence that evokes their meeting in the past (12–22), back to the bed again in the present (23–28). In this verbal family portrait of stasis, their marriage is predictable, but the discourse that describes it is not. Especially in the last four of the six sentences, a variegation of line length and rhyme patterns is matched by an unpredictability of sentencing. (By traditional scansion there are about 110 feet in the poem, 95 of which are iambic, and all lines but line 26 have at least one foot iambic. By rough count there are eight trochees, four anapests, two spondees, one dactyl. Fifteen of twenty-eight lines are iambic pentameter. One does not engage in this kind of counting without some sense that the poem's irregularity quotient has a bearing on meaning.) The meters are more irregular at the close of the two verse paragraphs, where Lowell switches toward his ending in alternative rhythms, different line-lengths, more insistent (because closer together) rhymes. Beginning at line 5, the rhymes are interlaced across sentence boundaries, even across verse paragraphs (e.g., "Marlborough Street" in 5 with "Oh my Petite," 12; "pass" in 20 with "merciless" in 27). Somewhere between meter and grammar is the effect of using lowercase letters to begin lines, except where new sentences begin lines. That imports a convention of free verse into a rhyme-and-meter poem, tending to deemphasize the metrical and to foreground and speed up the grammatical side of the interference.

The major break in the poem occurs in the middle of line 12, between sentences 3 and 4, at

and dragged me home alive. . . . Oh my Petite,

for here begins the memory of the past, the direct apostrophe that is really a tribute to his wife's eloquence (with emphasis given here by suspension dots, caesura, a word in French; below by anapests to give a lilt to "to the traditional

South"). After the longest sentence in the poem, the next and shortest (and the only line and sentence without a rhyme, "Now twelve years later . . .") marks the transition back to the present and Marlborough Street's unhappy opulence.

The ending of the poem is not as stunning as the beginning, but its purpose is to restate the theme of the marriage struggle, the speaker's helpless self-knowledge and his love even of her exasperation, especially of her invective. As the manuscript shows, and as we should determine anyway from the off-rhyme with the end of the last line, "tirade" is pronounced with the accent on syllable 2 in the French manner.[7] Along with several metrical irregularities (26 doesn't scan; 24, 27, and 28 begin with other than iambs), the oddity of two concluding similes one of which ("like the Atlantic Ocean") is a wild hyperbole, and also with the heaping of three adjectives after their noun ("loving, rapid, merciless") taking up a whole line, the puzzle of pronunciation over "tirade" helps to signal an ending. Lowell piles it on; maybe he piles on too much, or in too graceless a way, though it is true that he is intending to speak here in a voice that is more than a little unhinged, dangerous to itself if not to another person, struggling for sanity, it may seem, even by means of the formal utterance that is the poem.

### Emily Dickinson, "The Soul Selects Her Own Society"

The Soul selects her own Society—
Then—shuts the Door—
To her divine Majority—
Present no more—

Unmoved—she notes the Chariots—pausing—
At her low Gate—
Unmoved—an Emperor be kneeling
Upon her Mat—

I've known her—from an ample nation—
Choose One—
Then—close the Valves of her attention—
Like Stone—

Dickinson comes clear, eventually, but the grammetrics of "The Soul selects" is a style of very pronounced oddity, lurching into wisdom with the most unpromising materials and techniques. Amazing! Her thought, on the exclusivity of friendship (or soulship), is in no way daring except for its intensity and obscurity. From the beginning the Soul is personified as a woman, whose "divine Majority" or special society is uninfluenced by the numbers or rank of suppliants, and once a friend is taken the soul's attention is exclusive, in a terrible objective closing-off of all the others. This is friendship taken with the force of religion, religion described in the metaphor of friendship. Predestination; election. (However, much of the language is political rather than theological: Emperors at Amherst!)

Dickinson works to obscure the internal relations of sentences, and to be emphatic about the prosodic sorts of relations. The peculiar interferences between the obscuring of the insides of sentences and the prominence making in other parts of the poem, the symmetries and breaking of symmetries, the exaggerated stoppage and scissoring, makes the style of this poem. It is rather like the effect one finds in Oppen's poem in this array, but Oppen uses spacing and sentence fragments in place of the dashes that make the bursts of phrase in Dickinson.

To take up briefly the prosodic emphasis first, plainly this works by establishing schemas and by heavily violating them: instead of her usual 4-3-4-3 scheme of metrical feet per line, she in these three quatrains measures out 5-5-4-2, 5-2-5-2, 5-1-5-1 (a traditional metrist looking at this would say the lines are, still, fourteeners buckled: common measure at 7 + 7). More than half but considerably less than all the feet in the poem, if we count that way, are iambs. The rhyming is various: end-syllable exact (2 and 4), unstressed final syllable (ll. 1 and 3, 5 and 7, 9 and 11), long and short vowel differential (6 and 8), short and long vowel differential (10 and 12).

Against and within those forms, the grammar divides the poem into five sentences, all of which end at line end (ll. 2, 4, 6, 8, 12), all of which are complete thoughts and recognizable as sentences despite the lack of periods in the poem's punctuation by dashes. A minor grammetrical crux comes in sentence 2, at "Present" in line 4, where the correct meaning and sounding of the imperative verb is isolated by the iambic meter (exactly the opposite effect from the one we noticed in the Tomlinson prose poem). Another scissoring of some importance comes at the next line's "pausing," a word broken from other words by dashes and its line-end position, a turning-point word that is both transition and break, and where placement and meaning coincide. Is it she that pauses, or the chariots? We cannot say. The following sentence is more indeterminate still, and to get its sense we have to rewrite it in an expanded way as: "[She is] unmoved-[even though] an Emperor [may] be kneeling / Upon her Mat-." This is a subjectless sentence, with the subject implied from the previous sentence, "she"; "Unmoved," the adjective modifying the subject, "notes" the transitive verb that takes the action; it is not a subject at all, really. As Dora Sue Besser has said of this crux: "In the third line, we take the subject 'she' from line one and put it with an 'understood' intransitive verb, of which 'Unmoved' now becomes the object. A neat double twist."[8] So "Unmoved + dash" has two different grammatical functions in lines 5 and 7; this suggests that the dash may have more than one operation, even in midline, as well as different operations at midline (caesura and word or phrase marker), and at end line (line and phrase marker). If Dickinson uses no other marking than the dash, then the dash is any and all punctuation; we see the grammetrical results.

In the last stanza, there are nearly as many vocal stops and pauses, but the syntax is not in need of expansion to get the sense, and indeed the second-to-the-last line repeats the same "Then + dash + transitive verb" construction that occurred in a mirror-image position in the second line of the poem. Here at the end, Emily Dickinson turns for emphasis to the prosodic level of the poem, using back-to-back stresses in lines 10 and 12 for emphasis, and using heavy rhyme sounds in unexpected places, especially in the second syllable of each of four lines taken vertically: "known-One-close-Stone," a very unusual paradigm of sound, and a far denser one than earlier in the poem. The sounds signal closure, but so too does the allusion in "close the Valves" and possibly too the image of physical heaviness in "Like Stone" and the capital letters on the stress words in lines 10 and 12, unusual emphasis on monosyllabic words. The last of the poem is the dash of open continuation, but (here Dickinson's last unplayful irony) the line and sentence and poem are very emphatically over.

### John Peck, "Fog Burning Off at Cape May"

Vaguely at first, then firmly,
The beach extended west
Of our sandspit. That point, then,
Was not the last.

A mile more and we found
The broken blockhouse wall
From nineteen-forty, arm-thick
Firing cable

Shredding into surf.
Oddly archaic, those
Batteries untested,
Greenish fuzz

Bearding the rifle platforms

Offshore, concrete stripped
And draining rhythmically
In the tide's beat

While the line floated one daub
Of zinc white over slate,
The Cape Lewes Ferry sliding
Cleanly from sight.

It was our idleness
Slow as that widening day
That held us. But through haze
Burning away,

A fat man being tugged
By his paunchy dog, and tanning
Women finding sleep,
And our girl running,

These held through more than distance,
For that shore was a shore
No one can now extend
To any future,

The margin that had gone
Unfired on, the last edge
Behind which houses waited
Without damage—

World to which men returned.
Archaic, it cleared through air
And we walked into it,
Whole. We were there.

This is a recent example of the long-lived genre that Paul Fussell has called the American Shore Ode: a narrative at and on the margins, descriptive and speculative, personal and national. The speaker is walking with his young family on an Atlantic beach, and the fog of the title is the obscuring and revealing medium, representing memory, and the obliterations of time. The word used twice (10, 38) is "archaic," but really this is the archaeology of the recent past, of the post–World War II history that has permitted the speaker's generation to live and work. There could have been "damage" (36), but there was not, and the soldiers returned from the other world of war that our speaker tries to imagine from war's remnant, the broken blockhouse wall, the rifle platforms. The family walks the beach and comes to see and know more as the fog burns off, and thus the progressive revelation hinted in the title. The broken wall, by the end, is John Peck's emblem of the world, an alternative history demanding a life neither he nor his fellows had to live. So he is one who comes after, spells out a history that permits him to live, have a family, walk on the beach, write.

Peck writes a stanzaic poem rhyming *abcb,* with a short fourth line in each quatrain. The scansion is extraordinarily difficult, more so even than the Ezra Pound "Return," with a porous metrical contract, violable everywhere. In fact, let us abandon the notion of a metrical contract here, since if we were to scan the poem we would find a majority of iambs, but also a heavy scattering of trochees, nine spondees with two in the last line, several anapests, and a couple of dactyls. About a third of the lines, fourteen of forty, end in an uncompleted or dangling partial foot. But let us also abandon the notion of a metrical foot, too, since we mention it only as a partial, approximative attempt to show this poem's extremely high degree of irregularity by any measure. To these metrical approximations must be added a remark on the unemphatic rhyming on only the second and fourth lines of each stanza, with sounds as distant from each other as "wall-cable," "stripped-beat," "shore-future," rhymes neither to the eye nor the ear but plainly intended as minor chimes. Oddly enough, the mixture of stress patterns (withholding the term *meters,* now), and the lack of attention to prudent rhyming, do not seem peculiar in this poem, and these show up only on inspection.

The uninsistent, recessive nature of the stress pattern seems to encourage a ruminative kind of sentencing that pays very little attention to the lines or to the stanzas, so that, for example, seven of the ten stanzas (excluding only stanzas 1, 5, and 10) fail to conclude a sentence at a stanza end. Lengths of sentences vary, with the most interesting effect at the end, a diminuendo with the third-from-the-last sentence very long indeed with detail and speculation, the next-to-last sentence the length of two lines plus one word, and the last sentence three little words: "We were there." This structure certainly does isolate that last sentence as a closural gesture, and the more emphatic stressing that comes from stop-and-start short sentences heaps further emphasis on to a final rhyme ("air-there") that is one of the few perfect rhymes in the poem.

We walked past the edge, and yet were still alive. We were at the margin. The land is the homely personable place of ordinary time, the ocean is the war and the violence history can throw up, and the battery is to defend the one from the other and exists in the place of transition. This is the interest of the poem, its argument about a contingency that did not become a reality, a wrecked place that speaks of history for those who can read the signs, penetrate past the fog. Appropriate to the argument is a certain looseness of prosodic pattern and of sentences strung out by long clause-making, by adversative "but" phrases, and by a rhetoric of apposition and dashes, expansive, almost a demonstration of the precious idleness that the speaker comes to be thankful for.

Admirable that John Peck registers the threat in the distance, and understands his domesticity and idleness in relation to it. However, it is not perverse to be wary of the relaxed convention of this poem of all those in the array. The poem comes after Dickinson in the sequence because it is a variant of the Dickinson stanza, but it does other, ultimately more tame, things with the relationship of sentence to line, stanza, poem. The lack of insistence in the prosody permits the descriptive sentences to gabble somewhat ("A fat man being tugged / By his paunchy dog"), the meditative sentences become heavily prophetic ("Archaic, it cleared through air"), and the result is that the sentencing somewhat reduces the meter to material, diminishing thereby the quotient of cognitive-aesthetic interference. In Peck's need to get straight the meaning of his broken blockhouse wall, he has allowed the sentencing partly to win out. The interference of sentence and meter is thus not full or tight, and this yields an increase in predictability, coherence, and lack of intensity. These forms of meaning would be harmful to the poem, if not for the functional and full interference between sentencing and lineation/line grouping, in lines already short, which offsets the metrical fault by making it less noticeable.

### Jonathan Swift, "A Satirical Elegy on the Death of a Late Famous General"

His Grace! impossible! what, dead!
Of old age, too, and in his bed!
And could that Mighty Warrior fall?
And so inglorious, after all!
Well, since he's gone, no matter how,
The last loud trump must wake him now:
And, trust me, as the noise grows stronger,
He'd wish to sleep a little longer.
And could he be indeed so old
As by the news-papers we're told?
Threescore, I think, is pretty high;
'Twas time in conscience he should die.

This world he cumber'd long enough;
He burnt his candle to the snuff;
And that's the reason, some folks think,
He left behind so great a s—k.
Behold his funeral appears,
Nor widow's sighs, nor orphan's tears,
Wont at such times each heart to pierce,
Attend the progress of his herse.
But what of that, his friends may say,
He had those honours in his day.
True to his profit and his pride,
He made them weep before he dy'd.

    Come hither, all ye empty things,
Ye bubbles rais'd by breath of Kings;
Who float upon the tide of state,
Come hither, and behold your fate.
Let pride be taught by this rebuke,
How very mean a thing's a duke;
From all his ill-got honours flung,
Turn'd to that dirt from whence he sprung.

Jonathan Swift tells the genre and tone in his title, even before the poem begins, but he does not give the name of his victim. Everyone would know of the demise of Marlborough, just as everyone reading the poem would be able to fill in the middle letters of the word s—k in line 16. Swift's modern editor Harold Williams speaks of it as an "ungenerous attack," but I should rather call outrageous this reviling of a corpse. This elegy will not be a eulogy. The lines

Threescore, I think, is pretty high;
'Twas time in conscience he should die

are astounding in their violence, even worse (better) because of the mock-concessive "I think" and "pretty." Swift is here trading in images of "stink" and "dirt" and in his day these were barely euphemisms for ordure. In the second verse paragraph he generalizes the attack by apostrophe to all those like the duke, "Ye bubbles rais'd by breath of Kings," and, speaking to them, he truly speaks beyond them to the reader of good sense who must condemn royalty's bought creatures.

Swift is the Augustan master of the short couplet with every rhyme a joke. Tetrameter is more than pentameter a comic medium, perhaps, because one gets to the rhymes more quickly. The regularity of these lines is the greatest of any lines in our array, and inseparable from the satiric meanings. Swift sounds and values every syllable, using few long words, continually fitting feet to sense-units, employing syncope ("in/glor/ious" as three syllables not four) to get the count right, measuring out four stresses to every line, giving perfect rhymes and avoiding two-syllable rhymes except for a rare effect. Usually, too, he contrives a couplet so as to rhyme one part of grammar with another, usually noun with verb:

> True to his profit and his pride,
> He made them weep before he died.

Thus does the rhyme attack the great dead extortionist, linking back *pride* alliteratively with *profit,* linking *profit* with *before* to get the insult. Prosodically speaking, the interest is in how these lines can be divided internally by minimal shifts of caesura and juncture (there the syntax comes in), and how the flashing of rhyme's semantic changes can be used for insult, the same-sounding words with the same or different meanings. The syntax, also a phenomenon of *control,* is allocated to get the rhymes, working back from line ends to make the full line. It means many tight turns. The first four lines end on mock exclamations or mock questions, and nearly all the other lines end on a phrase break or a sentence end, so that (with but one run-on at line 9) lines are heavily coincident with sentences or other major sentence-elements. The *couplets themselves* are often coincident with sentences. Thus the insult is divided into many smaller insults and squibs that consume a line or a rhyme-mated pair of lines, exactly sixteen syllables. Swift's violent insult is richly rule-bound, and the deviations from the rules are themselves rule-bound. The poem's speech orientation is what distinguishes Swift's tight couplets from those of lesser poets of his era: I would mention the arresting opening line's onslaught of oddities, and the way those exclamations segment the reader's attention; and the little concessive touches that are themselves humorous because so transparent:

> "And, | trust me" (7)
> "Threescore, | I think" (11)
> "that's the reason, | some folks think" (15)

Those caesuras, scissoring the line with such well-bred good sense, call attention to their own attempts to be fair in such a way as to deflate what's said. They are confidence-building tricks, mock concessions, thus jokes. The poem as a whole is a joke on a grand scale. The animus is conveyed by those gestures to the honest reader by the honest speaker, by diction ("How very *mean* a *thing*'s a Duke"), by the interest raised by where the junctures will fall, and by oddities of frequency like the piling up of exclamations at the start—not by metrical rule-breaking. The speaker is beyond decorum in his utterances, though very controlled in his claims and his format. That is the differential that makes for Swift's style of satire, coolness of the framing elements with and within the white heat of innuendo.

### Alfred Tennyson, In Memoriam, section 7

Dark house, by which once more I stand
  Here in the long unlovely street,
  Doors, where my heart was used to beat
So quickly, waiting for a hand,

A hand that can be clasped no more—
  Behold me, for I cannot sleep,
  And like a guilty thing I creep
At earliest morning to the door.

He is not here; but far away
  The noise of life begins again,
  And ghastly thro' the drizzling rain
On the bald street breaks the blank day.

*In Memoriam* as a whole in its 131 sections is an elegy for Arthur Henry Hallam; section 7 is also a type of minor genre in classical poetry called paraclausithyron, the song of a lover who stands outside his mistress' door and holds the door responsible for his exclusion. The speaker is describing things, and through the form and sound of the description and the feelings mentioned ("ghastly"; "blank") he is conveying the truth of an inner state wherein nothing can be valued. But more than description is involved, because the speaker engages in direct address to the dark house and its doors. House, door, and hand are metonymies of the absent one who was life itself, presence and meaning: so how can life and day begin when he is gone? Such is the poem's question, which is asked through its statements. We know where the poem's grammetrics put most pressure on this agent in the scene, and on his statements: markedly in the last stanza. But how?

As in Swift we have iambic tetrameter, but immensely different in handling and intent. The *abba* stanza of *In Memoriam,* with the two middle lines rhyming and indented, uses the couplet in the center to join and separate the first and last lines. Traditional scansion by feet shows a high degree of regularity; the exceptional places are spondees beginning lines 2, 3, and the first two "feet" in line 9; and then to end the poem a very striking line that scans, probably, to use the outmoded terms: pyrrhic, spondee, trochee, spondee. That is the hearable meter of line 12, which cuts across the expected line of four iambs, substituting in each case a two-beat foot for another type of two-beat foot. Noticing this in my regularity scan, I now, once again, abjure foot reading.

Often this versatile *In Memoriam* stanza equals a sentence, or a large constituent part of a sentence. Robert Dilligan's splendid study of *In Memoriam* verse periods has shown the variety of sentence-line interaction in the whole long text, and he has given tables to show where, typically, caesuras fall, and where in the line the form classes of grammar tend to cluster (nouns, for example, on the stressed even syllables especially at ends of lines). Here in section 7, there are two sentences, drawn out over twelve lines by both linear and recursive structures of syntax.

"Dark house, by which" (l. 1) and "Doors, where" (l. 3) are equally pointing gestures and apostrophes, and parallel in syntax, but there is a tapering as the sentence goes on in its formal frame, a shortening that differently cuts line 3. These additive structures early in the poem seem to suggest the movement of the speaker's mind: anger, excitement. Later on he keeps the anger but becomes more composed. Between lines 4 and 5 is a huge apposition that also has prosodic implications:

                              a hand,

        A hand

Tennyson continues the sentence and the poem, but he makes the spacing between stanzas perceptible because of the way it is spanned with the same sentence, which gains extension—repetition and recoil of a possible new clause. The same sentence is taken further by the dash at the end of line 5, charging it with new energy to its end at the end of stanza 2. "Behold me" in line 5, referring back to the compound subject of *house* and *doors* and addressing those objects directly, is both a command and a descriptive verb (with the agent uncertain as to *you* or *they*). So what seemed an apostrophe may not be, as the poet seems to hint the taking back of a possible overstatement. Both this sentence and the other go to their conclusion, in the last two lines, with an "And" in paratactic addition. Now in stanza 2, a pattern seems to be emerging by which the third line of each stanza will be enjambed onto the fourth line, an effect of driving forward.

The next stanza and sentence begin with "He is not here," the most decisive scissoring moment in the poem. This occurs exactly at midline, plainly a way to prepare the major turn to the ending:

> but far away
> The noise of life begins again,
> And ghastly through the drizzling rain
> On the bald street breaks the blank day.

The drastic multiplication of modifiers, four in the last two lines, is the most insistent thing here. The last two lines make an independent clause with its own subject and verb, but the subject comes last in order. A more usual order would have "The blank day breaks ghastly through the drizzling rain on the bald street," but Tennyson wants deferral of full sense until the final words, wants separation of adverb from verb ("ghastly" from "breaks"), of adjective from noun ("ghastly" from "day"), and the interposition of modifiers in the form of the double-barreled phrase:

>     | through the drizzling rain |
> | On the bald street. . . .

Four separate segments are produced by these embeddings, but the lines are scissored only by the one line ending. Deferral of sense creates expectation. Thus syntax; these two lines at the same time cut across the rhyming of the stanza, unrhymed themselves so looking backward for their mated pairs. The heavy connecting alliteration that ("b" in l. 12) moves across the midline cut to connect the stressed words, *bald-breaks-blank*. Uncertainty and incoherence give way to pattern in the meter, too, as the heavy and unusual stress-sounds of the last line supplant but take up no more space than four iambs, and so hint while they contravene the presence of the standard *In Memoriam* line. Displacement creates emphasis: such meters force apart the lobes of the line. This hierarchy of orders of recursiveness, this interference of systems, intensifies the tone of elegiac loss, by verging on incoherence, miming the speaker's distraction.

### William Shakespeare, Sonnet 129

This analysis occurs in chapter 9, above.

### John Berryman, Sonnet 13

*Berryman's Sonnets [Now First Imprinted]* (1967), the poet's title for his sequence of 115 poems about a doomed love affair, surely contains a self-mocking allusion to the love sonnets of Shakespeare. Always implicit is the question: can the modern, late-coming lyric of marital infidelity have serious claim to enter the tradition of the early masters? That question applies not only to generic choice, but also to the metrical and syntactic contracts of Sonnet 13, which everywhere strains but does not break its recognizable forms. (One strain: Berryman writes an Italian, not Shakespearean, rhyme scheme.) Here the poet is out of town, and his lady has suggested that they drink a toast at the same hour:

I lift—lift you five States away your glass,
Wide of this bar you never graced, where none
Ever I know came, where what work is done
Even by these men I know not, where a brass
Police-car sign peers in, wet strange cars pass,
Soiled hangs the rag of day out over this town,
A juke-box brains air where I drink alone,
The spruce barkeep sports a toupee alas—

My glass I lift at six o'clock, my darling,
As you plotted . . . Chinese couples shift in bed,
We shared today not even filthy weather,
Beasts in the hills their tigerish love are snarling,
Suddenly they clash, I blow my short ash red,
Grey eyes light! and we have our drink together.

A witty voice: breathless, everywhere concerned to suppress all hints of Shakespearean magniloquence. Except for the last words of the last line, the utterance seems curiously skewed; it seems a difficult poem, even though it is not especially complex in argument, or in diction or pattern of images or sound. Indeed, there is no argument at all, in any strict sense; rather the imagined performance of an action, the toast, which staples the poem to an outer event at beginning, middle, end. In the spaces between this statement (1), restatement (9), and final explanation (14) come two lists: the attending circumstances of the toast, first (2–8) of physical setting and then of speaker's psychology (10–14). The same toast is shown first in relation to outer scene, then, darting inward, in relation to thoughts; so the poem is strongly static, a selected instant replayed twice for the reader. Thus the movement from the "I" of the first line to the "we" of the last is illusory, for there is no connection between the lovers but the symbolic one of a shared toast. To a speaker intent on physical love, the gesture is violently inadequate.

What explains the wry tone, the irony that soaks the details and rhythms? The jukebox that "brains air," conveying a sense that the speaker is assaulted by the setting of this bar, is but the most striking item in a list of sensations all tainted by frustrated lust: an apparently random sequence of things noticed, often expressed in line-long strips of language, yet withal saving the good detail of the barkeep's toupee for the last note of the octave. In the sestet the lovers' separation is compared with the coupling of Chinese and of beasts. "Suddenly they clash, I blow my short ash red, / Grey eyes light!": the exotic or "tigerish" lovemaking is connected to the lover in the bar by the stringing syntax of the final lines, and by the rhyme ("clash-ash"), and yet he has invoked these images as extreme, disjunctive opposites to his own situation. The toast is symbol of love and must suffice. So the final words, "and we have our drink together," banish self-pity and fantasy, and mark an acceptance of limitation: this phrase is the least skewed in syntax and meter and ends the poem with a turn to regularity, the reassurance of rhyme.

It is time to relate these findings to the poem's metrical contract. I would look first at those places where breaks in the metrical contract overlap with breaks in the syntactic contract—occupying, with their different types of disturbance, the very same string of words. But I may discuss those places only after affirming that this poem, after all, does credit traditional iambic meter, sonnet structure, and the normal subject-verb-object structure of the English sentence. I say "after all," because the sheer quantity of irregularity in Berryman's poem is so great as almost to put into question the norms of regularity. An iambic pentameter sonnet contains seventy positions of stress, five in each line, and in this case considerably more than half of these positions are filled by Berryman's stresses: that is sufficient to sketch in the poem's major structure, but the actual lines themselves suffer very great distortion. Nearly every line violates the abstract meter in a very pronounced way. Eight of fourteen lines begin with a stressed syllable (2, 3, 4, 6, 10, 12, 13, 14), an unusual number of displacements of iambic stress, significantly grouped at beginning and end of the poem: places of greater intensity, as we shall see. There are two twelve-syllable lines (4, 10), possibly three (13?). There are also several metrical cruxes or stutters, none more dramatic than those that begin the first and last lines:

I lift—lift you five States away your glass

. . . . . . . . . . . . . . . . . . . . . . . . . . . . . . .

Grey eyes light! and we have our drink together.

The lines can be scanned and solved by the iambic system, but perhaps at a cost of losing the anomalous way syllables 2–5 in both lines have an insistent stress.

These clusters of equal stresses make for emphasis, metrical pounces, either to launch the utterance or to bring it down to and beyond the exclamation that is the poem's one intense recreated moment. The sonnet has eight caesuras, including lines self-divided by dash, three suspension dots, and exclamation point; and ten of the first thirteen lines are end-braked by the punctuation of either comma or dash. The prosody of the poem integrates every line into the movement, but nearly every line is separately marked by internal division or deviation. We get the curiously contradictory effect of adherence to the husk of the metrical contract, with tenacious resistance to every particular pattern at the molecular level. In the sphere of prosody, this is Berryman's special way of being both archaist and innovator.

In an era of rhythm study and the search for larger structures in the poem, generative metrics looks played out; but its terminology might still have some role to play in our reading. Generative metrics gauges the "complexity" of the iambic line by the number and pattern of displaced stress-maxima. In my reading of Berryman, seven lines have a high degree of complexity in this sense. If I am right, half the sonnet's lines are unusual, and their distribution (1, 3, 4, 6, 10, 13, and 14) follows the pattern of emphasis already noticed: a gathering of irregularities at beginning and end of poem, which is the expression in the poem's technique of the speaker's self-mocking introspection. I would also note that line openings displace their stress maxima more often than the other parts of the line. Line endings, leading up to the rhymes, are much more stable in Berryman, as indeed in nearly all traditional rhyming poets; apparently the stability of the rhymed ending is one aspect of the general syntactic stability of the last half of the line. Berryman also seems unusual in the way he gives even-numbered line position to major form-classes of syntax. By my count twenty-four nouns, seventeen verbs, and eight adjectives are thus dignified with the even-numbered, or stress-maximum, position in the line. Implied in what has already been noticed, we have already seen how the emphatic verbs "lift" and "light" are promoted to stress maxima even though they are in the odd-numbered positions in the line. Conversely, one might remark how, in the last line, a word from a minor form-class, the coordinator "and," is promoted to stress-maximum position to make it a ligature between the exclamation "Grey eyes light!" and the dying-fall coda of line and poem. Much more detail of this sort might be adduced, but my purpose is only to suggest that, noting such variations from the usual positioning of syntactic classes, we build up metrical theory to take account of syntax.

The point is that sentencing, like stressing, is in traditional English poems determined by being allocated to places according to the chosen meter and rhyme scheme. Thus does the long sentence that is Berryman's sonnet meet a number of diversions; juncture, caesura, line break, the dash and other punctuation, coordinate clauses, and lists of things seen or thought all pleasurably delay the ending. Berryman, sometimes to keep and sometimes to break the meter, disposes of English syntax as a set of movable blocks of different sizes: of course all poets do this, but the persistent sense of oddity in this poem derives from the many unexpected switches from normal runs of language. For instance, "where none / Ever I know came" could be rewritten with the same or slightly different words, perhaps most normally as *where no one I knew ever came;* but Berryman has connived the compression of this denial of the usual order. Systematically used, such wrenching becomes a principle of eventfulness and a stylistic signature. Simple inversion is the most easily recognized technique of this sort: "Soiled hangs the rag of day," "My glass I left," "Beasts in the hills their tigerish love are snarling." Another way of wrenching is to exceed the norm by redundancy: "I *lift—lift you* five States away *your* glass"; the list of "where" clauses; specifying the "you" of line 1 as "my darling" in line 9; repeating the toast in lines 1, 9, 14. Reinforcing this overlayering of syntax is a host of other kinds of repetitions, as for instance in the heaping of adjectives in "wet strange cars," the alliteration of the middle lines of the poem ("box brains . . . spruce barkeep sports . . . shift in bed / We shared"), the internal rhymes of lines 7 and 13 (both coming just before major structural breaks).

Perhaps the most interesting and characteristic of these methods, though, is the method of deletion that turns a fairly direct if prolix statement like *I lift my glass to match your glass as you lift it five states away* into the arresting puzzle that is line 1. That line, which we have already identified as a prosodic minefield, hardly reassures the reader with unambiguous "contracts" of meter and syntax. The "where" that coordinates clauses in lines 2–4 is deleted and assumed in the clauses of lines 5–8. "Grey eyes light!" omits to specify a pronoun: it is left unexplained just whose eyes are flashing, so that in this image the passions of the speaker and Lise, the Chinese, and the beasts are briefly identified. Here, too, the syntactic and the metrical disturbances coincide.

To move from such technical description to the meaning of a poem is to draw an analogy. The probative value of analogy is notoriously weak, and yet this is an inference the writer, on the showing of the details noticed here, clearly wants us to make. The frustration of the speaker is presented by metrical and syntactic means in the poem and is especially strong, we may surmise, in the opening and closing lines, where the several patterns are the most wrenched. This is to say neither more nor less than that the structural and semantic patterns are mutually reinforcing. For this poet in this poem, structural disturbances are a sign of intense feeling.

Of this convergence and smashing of patterns I would mention one more example, in the wonderful line,

The spruce barkeep sports a toupee alas—

The eventfulness of that rhyme on "alas" is carefully prepared by syntactic, metrical, and rhyme-scheme forethought that can be traced back into the first line of the poem, but of special concern to me is the way the rhyme word works in the syntax of its own line. The toupee is to the barkeep as the toast is to the separated lovers, a bogus substitute for the real thing; "alas" is the commentary on this, a tag on the line end that proclaims itself, while judging, a joke. The joke is one of sound, Byronic; but also of placement, coming before the dash at the major structural articulation of the sonnet. With just that sound and meaning, at just that place, the word may be taken, without undue reduction, as the epitome of the whole poem. Berryman exercised much premeditation to achieve such an effect of surprise. He has been able to achieve a very high degree of irregularity and still to write a conventional poem. His personal relation to the conventions of sanctified marriage, of literary love and sonnets, of the iambic pentameter line, of ordinary English syntax, turns out to be the same relation: the need to keep the forms but to rearrange them without mercy. We arrive at such hybrid statements more quickly and completely, the more conscious we are of the way our reading is already, and inevitably, a grammetrical practice.

## Chapter 11

# On the Array of Fourteen, Considered as a Group

Our model for representing the phenomena of verbal art has been that of an interference between grammar and meter. The intention has been to bring rather more than the usual into the ranges of observation and comprehension. The readings of the previous two chapters have been successful only so far as I, as the representative reader, have been able to develop my own capacities for recording and retaining many simultaneous observations.

It might be argued that I should have begun with a triangular model, using the system of stylistics (words and their meanings, especially their levels of meaning; lexis; metaphorical study; genre) as another element to put into the interference. To some small extent I have done this, without proclaiming the extension of my method. All these matters have been smuggled into my readings, in the opening paragraphs of each commentary, as information I knew before or learned during my readings. Essentially, though, I have tried to remain close to the curve of cognition: simultaneous, scissoring cognition of meter against grammar. The other leg of the triangle must be added after this book's main work is completed: adding interpretation to reading. (It is already there, of course. But being more strenuously conscious of the historical-ideological dimension of reading must come at the next stage of the analysis, and is beyond the modest work of the present study.)

Working with a triangular model runs counter to the principle of parsimony, in this particular attempt to read merely for cognitive practices. For my purposes here, I would argue that a capacious idea of sentencing, taking grammar and syntax in a larger context, will bring us sufficiently within the realm of discourse. Let us try to build up sentencing so that it can include genre and other determinants, speech orientation, and historical styles of writing. For these purposes, a sufficient inclusion is a pertinent hint and guess: brief but hitting the mark. The danger in this experiment, as I have admitted, has always been not excessive narrowness but indefeasibility. To protect the argument, my method has been to load the terms of the system of interference. If I have succeeded, the rules of cognitive-aesthetic interference will parallel the relational propositions in my description. I have at least shown a scissoring both ways, meter grammar and grammar meter in a contextual cutting and shaping; and I have described grammetrical scissoring in a discursive rather than deductive form.

The present chapter intends to corroborate. Having looked at the member units, the verse periods in single poems, I now inquire whether grammetrics finds any support in the aggregate behavior of the array.

In order to give the force of example to my exposition of grammetrics, I have in the previous two chapters bracketed certain difficulties that may now, if briefly, be faced. I have interpreted my array of fourteen as though those poems had rhetorical and moral weight, and as though meanings could be discussed in a commonsense way. In this I have not been different from those deconstructionists who, in the process of showing how the structure of a text has already dismantled itself, write their analysis as if the texts were—in some sense—there. In fact, my analyses, most especially that of Shakespeare's Sonnet 129, have emulated notions of indeterminacy learned from deconstruction. But I am not myself a deconstructionist and will argue that one who would consciously do grammetrics cannot also be a fully fledged cognitive atheist about texts and their reading. Grammetrics as a method, seeking to redeem metrics by a metrics of discourse, must by its very nature resist, while appreciating the reasons for, the thesis of the work as a self-reflexive verbal system. (Reading for tone, I have also pursued here the speech orientation of verbal art, but not with any systematic design.) Grammetrics is about contextual shaping, the influence of everything on everything else, and only in its historical phase (really, its superseding: not addressed in this book) is also about the work's social and literary conditions of possibility. As a method of describing texts, grammetrics can absorb and maybe surpass some of the leading insights of deconstruction. As another method of describing texts, deconstruction is by program incapable of using to the full the powerful habits of attention that grammetrics uses. Because deconstruction's selective spatializing mostly limits itself to the equivalence named metaphor, deconstruction underrates the many modes of human literary intelligence that permit one to be a deconstructionist in the first place—the determinate skills and meanings that enable us to argue for the indeterminacy of all reading. However, habits of attention need not remain below the threshold of knowledge. When we know them consciously we know that they are us, our very power.

Writing in tactful reproach to certain ideas of poetic structure in Roman Jakobson, Edward Stankiewicz has cogently said: "What makes all poetry an art of 'difficult reading' . . . is precisely the fact that the principle of succession is at every step complicated and resisted by the principle of simultaneity, which compels attention to the structure as a whole."[1] Grammetrics would likewise insist that the two principles of succession and simultaneity need to be integrated, and would agree with Stankiewicz that modern poetry and criticism have placed an increased emphasis on the role of simultaneity at the expense of contiguity. Two categories of structure have received equal, if not always simultaneous, attention in the readings that make up my array of fourteen:

> The Structure of Articulation (Sequential)
>> line-length and division of lines within themselves
>> stanzas
>>> unrepeated or progressive sentence structure, all
>>>> sentences new and different

> The Structure of Redundancy (Recursive)
>> repetition of the ground patterns of measure, meter, rhyme
>> repeated images, words, forms and places of punctuation
>> repeated sentence structure (parallelism)

This distinction immediately and usefully breaks down, because lines and stanzas, as units of equivalence, are plainly as much part of a structure of redundancy as of a sequential structure; and sentencing appears in both categories. Meaning is motion as well as shape or stasis; sense making is progressive as well as rear regarding. In a famous statement about similarity and contiguity as the two axes of poetry, Roman Jakobson would seem to be saying the same thing, but in his own studies in poetics the tendency is to focus on parallelism and paronomasia and to foreshorten or spatialize the linear. The major American representative of deconstruction in its heyday, Paul de Man, stated that for him the figure may be taken as the type of all literary language: rhetoric as figure without persuasion, poetic as figure without succession. Against such limiting positions, the role of grammetrics might be to remind criticism of the necessary equality and integration of the two principles of succession and simultaneity, and to proselytize the neglected functions of linear sequence.[2]

In the making and the reading of a poem, the formal structure may determine the operational process, and conversely process may determine structure. This, some have argued, is more generally the way the mind works when it stores and deploys language. Gregory Bateson's *Mind and Nature: A Necessary Unity* (1979), a book that bears on problems of formalization in the language arts though its subject is biology, speaks of the world of mental process as "both tautological and ecological," taking tautology as an aggregation of linked propositions in which the validity of the links cannot be doubted. Mind is "a slowly self-healing tautology." Analysis of the mind's works, preeminently poems though Bateson does not discuss poems, must be engaged by going through a hierarchy of orders of recursiveness, instead of a hierarchy of classes—it involves a zigzag analytical sequence from form to process and back again, from calibration to feedback. Grammetrics is this kind of tautology, philosophically and psychologically speaking. Inevitably, grammetrics consists of a tentative explanation because the metrical and grammatical terms with which it is loaded are, as yet, still probationary, still only partly defined.

Several of my readings in the array use phrases of description and praise, as for example "the nonclarification of the relations of the sentence," "the nonclarification of the relations between sentences." And several readings also speak in a neutral way of polymetrism so pronounced, as in the Pound and Peck examples, that no certain metrical contract is possible between poem and reader. Grammetrics in this definition makes a good deal of such instabilities as part of poetic intention. To meet with a high degree of irresolution is one of the cognitive pleasures of the experience of lyric. (The exception is the poem by Swift, which is not a lyric and derives from historical, psychological, and stylistic conditions of possibility that eschew instabilities at every level.) From working through texts in the array it is possible to learn what deconstructionists have learned by another route, namely that there can be productive indeterminacies in texts—whether global or local, these must be preserved and understood, sometimes by resisting disambiguations that later interpreters would foist upon the text. From working through the array it is also possible to have some assurance in making two statements about interpretation: there are better readings and less good readings, and the better ones are based on the better editions; the better readings allow the multiplicities of the text to play, and do this by foregrounding the several sorts of irresolution that a scholarly edition allows.

Grammetrics, aided by the inherent indeterminacy of its governing notion of the interference of systems, has to decide where we cannot and should not decide as between alternative readings. The possibilities of meaning are multiple, but not infinite. For grammetrics, the indeterminacy is contained by larger structures of determinacy. Grammetrical habits of attention, as practiced by all competent readers, would seem actively to resist the ideas of infinite freeplay of signifiers, unlimited semiosis, even as they make those ideas possible.

In judging their revisions on early drafts, poets themselves have sometimes worked to comprehend more meaning by dropping what is univocal, and adding

what is not easily resolved. (This is spectacularly true of Keats's revisions of "The
Eve of St. Agnes," and usually untrue of Wordsworth's recension of *The Prelude*.)
An author's revisions would either challenge or validate a meaning already there
in the diction, syntax, or disposition of materials. In developing a meaning by
increasing the indeterminacy of poetic language, the author must also, if slightly,
change the voice of the text, bring it closer to the desired mode of address—
making it a closer approximation to a "speech which afters and oftens its in-
scape," in G. M. Hopkins's definition of poetry. It happens that we have evidence
of authorial revisions for a few of the poems in the array of fourteen. If we can
show the authors themselves displaying grammetrical habits of attention as they
realign and compress meanings, we can win for grammetrical theory an at least
partial falsifiability.

There are three versions of Wordsworth's ice-skating passage, the third
somewhat different from the earlier two.

From the two-part *Prelude* of 1799:

> Not seldom from the uproar I retired
> Into a silent bay, or sportively
> Glanced sideway, leaving the tumultuous throng,
> To cut across the shadow of a star
> That gleamed upon the ice. And oftentimes . . .

From book 1 of the 1805 version:

> Not seldom from the uproar I retired
> Into a silent bay, or sportively
> Glanced sideway, leaving the tumultuous throng,
> To cut across the image of a star
> That gleamed upon the ice. And oftentimes . . .

From book 1 of the 1850 version:

> Not seldom from the uproar I retired
> Into a silent bay, or sportively
> Glanced sideway, leaving the tumultuous throng,
> To cut across the reflex of a star
> That fled, and, flying still before me, gleamed
> Upon the glassy plain; and oftentimes . . .[3]

1799's "shadow" has become "image" in 1805 and "reflex" in 1850, becoming
progressively metaphorical and metaphysical, but also more exact in scientific-

literal meaning. Though all three words mean "reflection," the final choice has the least to do with perception and the most to do with consciousness or imagination. The 1850 version's other major change of vocabulary is to substitute "the glassy plain" for "ice," an artificial item for a natural one and a contravention of Wordsworth's own policy against poetic diction. And yet "the glassy plain," while not especially accurate as an Augustan periphrasis, is not objectionable; it might even be considered on balance more descriptive. It picks up a sound from "gleamed," the word Wordsworth had moved back up to the end of the line above; and it fills out its own line to the point where the poet can hook onto his continuation, "and oftentimes. . . ."

The line with "gleamed" in the 1850 version is a new addition, except for that very verb. The line is well tailored to the iambic format but breaks the sense across the meter at odd junctures (positions 2, 3, and 9 in the line): adding more play with sounds, a progressive verb-paradigm "fled-flying," a displacement of one predicate clause from another ("fled . . . gleamed") by a participial clause. This change serves to intensify the action and to emphasize (before the scissoring at "Stopped short") its quality of continuousness. That quality is also given emphasis by interposing here a foreshadowing usage of the time concept "still," which will be picked up in "spinning still / The rapid line of motion," four lines below; and by the lack of indentation as well as the special punctuation (not a period, but a semicolon). It all goes to make the sentence and its meter more demanding to the reader, more difficult because more eventful. On consideration, a good bargain; the poet sacrifices "glassy plain" to Augustan diction, in order to purchase the slight increase of unexpectedness, incoherence, and intensity given by the new line.

The draft version of Robert Lowell's "Man and Wife," printed for the first time in Ian Hamilton's 1982 biography of the poet, has forty-five lines, including the material on the magnolia blossoms and on the poet's wife at the Rahvs, and including two longish verse paragraphs mostly not used, one of these on "Boston's negro culture" as heard out the windows, the other a first-person outcry of the wife herself that was used in another poem, "To Speak of Woe That Is in Marriage." To make the final version in twenty-eight lines, Lowell dropped the voices out the window and the wife's speech, put his already-written lines on the Racinian *tirade* at the end, and added four new lines on "Mother's bed" at the beginning. Since the first four lines are detachable in the sense of being rhymed among themselves *(aabb)*, and not rhymed down into the rest of the poem, I omit them in order to compare the most-changed short segment, the part on the magnolias that leads to the direct address, "Oh my Petite."

The first version, titled "Holy Matrimony," lines 1–6:

At last the trees are green on Marlborough Street,
Blossoms on our Saucer Magnolia ignite
For their feverish five days white. . . .
Last night I held your hands, *Petite,*
Subtlest of all God's creatures, still pure nerve
Still purer nerve than I. . . .[4]

The published version, "Man and Wife," lines 5–13:

At last the trees are green on Marlborough Street,
blossoms on our magnolia ignite
the morning with their murderous five days' white.
All night I've held your hand,
as if you had
a fourth time faced the kingdom of the mad—
its hackneyed speech, its homicidal eye—
and dragged me home alive. . . . Oh my Petite,
clearest of all God's creatures, still all air and nerve . . .

Only the first line is kept intact; three and a half lines are added on the wife's reaction to the speaker's madness; beginning-line capitals are dropped and "Petite" loses its italics; useless words are dropped, such as the specification of "Saucer" for the magnolia and the weakly redundant "still pure nerve, / Still purer nerve." "Last night I've held your hand" becomes "All night I've held your hand" to give the utterance immediacy, an image of touching while speaking; "feverish" becomes "murderous" to give an even more violent image in nature for the speaker's state of mind, and to pick up more "m" sounds from the first two lines ("the morning with their murderous"); and "subtlest" becomes "clearest" to catch onto the "c" of "creatures" and to prepare for sound and sense in "still all *air* and nerve." Most significant grammetrically is the change in "ignite": still a line-end verb, but moved from intransitive to transitive—with the discovery that it *is* transitive, and that the preceding line was enjambed, coming only in the *rejet*.[5]

There are further and more exploratory exploitations of the language material. Lowell removes the suspension dots from the end of the third line of the earlier draft, following "white," and expands the context of the hand holding so that the ellipse can then come below as a marked break in midline, thus:

and dragged me home alive. . . . Oh, my Petite

This makes the address to her—coming after the short line "as if you had" and after two lines that end in dashes and the suspension dots of heavy implication— the major break in the poem. It is as if what is unsaid in the ellipse can now be given as a sigh of affection and tribute. The line is perfect iambic pentameter, but wrenched fundamentally in its structure because of the weight of that caesura after the sixth syllable. There is also the effect of knitting the line's rhyme word "Petite" back further into the line's syntax, not leaving it isolated (and italicized) as in the first version.

The longest line of the poem, line 13, takes meanings and phrasings from lines 5–6 of the draft, with an effect of lyric abandon:

clearest of all God's creatures, still all air and nerve

Perhaps the line swings well because it ends in a recognizably iambic way after opening so variously. Perhaps it does because, by seven to five, the beats outnumber the offbeat syllables. There is more unstressing and then more stressing than the earlier lines of this poem have led the reader to expect. In such cases, the stress is more of a stress, and that starts the swing. If the second "all" is stressed like the first, the line is even less regular, and a scansion by traditional feet becomes doubtful, forcing more importance upon the caesura and the grammetrical break between "creatures" and "still," where there occurs a breathing place created by an undoubted gap. Lowell uses this moment of grammetrical wobbling to suggest the pressure of feeling behind his tribute. Certainly this sets into motion the poem's longest sentence, its most speedy prosodies and bravura rhyming. (As Eleanor Berry has suggested in a note to me, this is probably one of those cases where analysis at the rhythmic phrase and tone unit levels would come closer to suggesting why the line swings well; she writes: "traditional feet do not afford an adequate analysis of the constraints observed and freedoms exercised in traditional iambic lines.")

Tennyson's manuscript draft of section 7 of *In Memoriam* was recast in far less drastic fashion, due to the limits forced on him by the poem's stanza form. However, even tiny deflections are of interest if they are Tennyson's and can change the tone as much as his brilliant "drizzling" for "dripping" at the end— "ghastly thro' the drizzling rain."[6] In the final version, lines 3–6 read

Doors, where my heart was used to beat
So quickly, waiting for a hand,
A hand that can be clasp'd no more—

but the first draft has

So quickly waiting for the hand,
The hand. . . .

Tennyson has forced apart "quickly" and "waiting" in order to keep the gram-
matical relationships straight, and he has changed the "the" to "a" in order to
keep mystery about who the other might be and how distant. In the lines

Behold me, for I cannot sleep,
And like a guilty thing I creep

he has changed the original "But" to "And" so as to produce the same two-line
"And" clause ending to both the poem's sentences, both the last two stanzas.
These are all highly constrained lexical substitutions; grammar and metrics are
the constraints upon the fine-tuning. Tennyson makes absolutely the right cor-
rections, and no others.

Would that could be said of editors after the poet's work has been done! Too
often the editor's idea of meaning is more pinched than the poet's. All of Emily
Dickinson's poems printed before 1955 dropped her dash punctuation and en-
forced another system of sentencing (and even after the 1955 edition there have
remained reasons for worry).[7] Pace and meaning were inevitably changed in the
previous editions, and the experience of reading the poet was less violent and
uncertain a thing than it should have been. She was still striking—but on her
editors' terms. The 1890 edition altered Dickinson's line,

Unmoved—she notes the Chariots—pausing—

by making "Chariots" a possessive, thus severely diminishing the line's beautiful
ambiguities (they may be pausing; so may the Soul; so may Dickinson), the
wrenching oddity of the position of "pausing" at line end. The same edition
changed the verb "be" to "is" in the line "Unmoved—an Emperor be kneel-
ing": thus mistakenly clarifying the sly implied syntax of the stanza. There is no
warrant in the manuscript for such alterations.

Very likely the modern editor of an anthology that contains Shakespeare's
sonnets will hope to lead students, by means of enjoyment, to some of the
intricacies of form and theme. However, such a pedagogical aim may serve to
justify editorial practices that give considerably less than the full meaning of
Sonnet 129. *The Oxford Anthology of English Literature* (1973) modernizes spell-
ing, supplies heavy semicolon and colon punctuation, keeps the diacritical sign
over "despised" but gives "murdrous" as "murderous," and tries a period at the

end of line 12 rather than at the end of line 8.[8] But if my grammetrical analysis of the Elizabethan printer's text of the poem has some claim to being a strong reading, there can be no justification for editions that overspecify meter, grammar, and meaning.

If the rationale for grammetrics is correct, it should hold for any and all languages including inflected languages and those, like Chinese, that have ideograms rather than letters of an alphabet. Only the rhythm will obviously be different as between the five-character line in Chinese, with its word-syllable blocks of equal length and differential tones, and the profusion of little words in a noninflected alphabetic language like English. The containment of pauses between units will most certainly vary between Chinese and English; generally speaking, the pauses will be more plentiful and less emphatic in English. But in either case one task of grammetrics will be to plot where the cuts come and with what intensity. These telltale places, which may not always be pausing places, are absences that always occur between two presences within the poem; they space out the presences, redistributing emphasis. Even when they do not occur, as when Shakespeare (or his printer) puts no comma after "blouddy" in "blouddy full of blame," the tale is both acoustic and semantic. Punctuation often is a notation of the intensity of a pause: a dash at line end (as in Lowell or Dickinson) will be different from a dash at midline, and a period at line or poem end is different from a period elsewhere. (There is still no consensus as to how to reflect these marks in performance; and will not be until we achieve a more complete grammetrics.)

Also part of the minor form of grammetrics are the shorter grammetrical segments, longer than a word but less than a clause, such as the hyphenated adjectives Pound loves, doubled adjectives like Tennyson's "long unlovely street," the repetition of a noun or verb like Tennyson's "a hand, / A hand" or Berryman's "I lift—lift you," sequences of participles in Peck, doublet nouns ("all air and nerve" in Lowell, "his profit and his pride" in Swift), anaphora, appositives, asides. Making somewhat longer sequences are the

the + *adjective* + *noun*

or

the + *adjective* + of + *noun*

formulas that, when tripled, make so memorably dense the end of Tennyson's poem and the beginning of Shakespeare's.

Obviously, short sentences and lines make for a more predictable length of the language elements, whereas long sentences and lines have less clumping, less predictable length of elements. Short lines with long sentences, their structure out of phase with the lineation, maximize perceptibility of interference: maximize unpredictability. A syntax of listing or a profusion of sentence fragments (both, in the Oppen poem) must scissor into smaller nuggetlike lengths of language. Polysyndeton permits and asyndeton discourages continuities. Alternation of short and long sentences, or sentences and fragments, makes for abrupt changes of tone and theme at the end of poems by Tomlinson, Peck, and Shakespeare. A whole taxonomy of such effects could be worked out; John Sinclair has made a contribution to this taxonomy.[9] We could, to glance at the array, compare Swift's couplet-length sentences, that play half-line against line, line against line in the couplet, one couplet against the next, with Wordsworth's unrhymed blank verse. The latter's driving, exploratory, confessional enthusiasm pushes past the small effects that make up precisionist irony in Swift—seeking unbalanced, nonironic phrasing in sentences as long as eight lines that seem as if they could go on almost forever or end anywhere.

To build a taxonomy and get beyond impressionism in the study of the array as an aggregate, we may conduct a computer-assisted investigation. This will yield no more and no less than sophisticated bookkeeping, in a study that will help to verify assertions made in separate readings. The evidences are weak, not only because merely corroborative, but mainly because the very nature of the array prevents some types of comparisons that might be productive. An unexpected benefit, deriving from even a minor foray into computer-assisted study of prosody, is our recognition of the computer's inability to do the kind of contextual shaping that the human mind does normally, every day, in every reading of texts. Increased knowledge of what computers do leads to increased knowledge of the reach of mind.[10]

So far as grammetrics is concerned, the work of Robert Dilligan is perhaps the most useful contribution to computational metrics. In the early 1970s, Dilligan and Todd K. Bender saw the advantages of the Halle-Keyser description of iambic pentameter for the purposes of turning the metrical line into an algorithm. To develop a scanning algorithm, they used the Halle-Keyser definition of the line as a sequence of ten positions, in which syllables theoretically strong (not in speech stress) occupy the even-numbered positions, and there are two optional "weak" syllables permitted at line end. They tested this on 840 lines of iambic verse from G. M. Hopkins, and determined, for example, "that in the poems Hopkins wrote before 1876, the fourth position (the ictal position of the second foot in traditional terminology) is the most likely to receive stress maximum."[11] The method is perfected on a massive scale in Dilligan's 1980 article on the prosody of *In Memoriam,* where he begins by arguing that since prosody is the most common example of repetition in the poem, "a computer is a much more appropriate instrument for prosodic study than a sound spectrograph."[12] Using his scanning algorithm on an immense sequence-poem that is written in one line length and has one recurring rhyme scheme, Dilligan marks the position of theoretical strong syllables and of grammatical form-classes within Tennyson's line. He shows how "major form classes fall into odd-numbered or even-numbered positions," and how in reading *In Memoriam* we need to be very careful to note variations from the usual position of syntactic classes; this is because displaced norms are for Tennyson a device for emphasis. (For example, in the last line of Tennyson's section 7 in our array, "On the bald street breaks the blank day," there is a "strikingly effective use of displaced verbs in position 5." Exactly so.) Nouns as subjects occur near the beginning of lines, whereas nouns in prepositional phrases occur near the end. There is a great stability of line endings, which is an aspect of the general syntactic stability of the last half of the line throughout the poem. Phonological patterns are even more regular in the long poem than syntactic ones—phonological regularity in the poem is, Dilligan shows, "obsessive." A verse period this measured, with all the recurrent sound features and recurrent devices of rhetoric and image, helps the poet "to make his own voice into the voice he seeks," the sad and magical voice of elegy. Elegy as genre penetrates down all the way, with absolute particular scissoring of each syllable, to an obsessive grammetrics.

My computer study of the array, with results in the form of graphs and histograms, proved well worth attempting but not worth printing in full. The trouble has been the unreliability of the count: possible incomparability of some items counted both in the meter and the grammar track; and excessive space needed to reproduce results. The computer study taught something about the contents of particular poems and of the aggregate, but its use has mainly been to show the limits of the machine as we try to make it account for the reading of poems.

Let me briefly describe how the study was performed, and offer comments on the types and merits of the evidences that came from counting. Following Dilligan's method, for each poem in the array, every word was tagged for form class in grammar; and, for the nine metrical poems, every syllable was tagged for stress or nonstress. For each poem in the array, a count was done to get number of lines, sentences, sentence fragments, words, and twelve different form classes in grammar (for example, Tennyson's section 7 has eighty-one words, including sixteen nouns, thirteen adjectives, and eight verbs; this gets interesting only when we plot where such items fall along the line.) Using the metrical set only, poems 6-14, and treating the numbered positions in the line as vertical columns, a run was made to reckon how many times a given grammatical class fell into a given numbered position. Then taking the iambic or largely iambic poems as a subset, with the computer's help I counted how many "complete pattern" lines there were against "broken pattern" or caesuraed lines, and determined the percentages of each for comparison. The last and perhaps the most productive operation was to plot on histograms the number of occurrences there were of words, caesuras, and twelve grammatical form-classes, against the number of lines in all fourteen poems in the array. (For example, Berryman had by far the highest average of nouns, with 2.07 nouns per line).

The limitations of this study by comparison with Dilligan's are obvious. He had a relatively large corpus of similars from one writer, one artistic intent, one genre; I had a relatively small corpus of dissimilars, explicitly chosen to contain a very wide variety of formal means by many writers, with many intents and genres. The changeability of the array was its merit in the deployment of the array but its difficulty when I came to computation. The difference between the nonmetrical set (poems 1–5) and the metrical set (poems 6–14) has not proved very significant for statistical purposes; however, *that in itself* suggests these two methods of writing are less distinct, formally speaking, than we may have imagined. The figures for Tomlinson's prose poem, number 1 in the array, are all inevitably skewed because I have gone ahead to count a line of type as a poetic line; that is of course inexcusable, but the unbalanced results are themselves of some interest. (For example, on average there are far more prepositions per line in the Shakespeare sonnet, and as many in Wordsworth's blank verse, even though Tomlinson's "lines" are longer than theirs.) The reader will make the appropriate adjustments when these drawbacks of the study are understood.

I will give one of the histograms as an example of the kind of information the computer elicits, using Dilligan's algorithm (see fig. 9). For the Wordsworth passage (number 7 in the array), the position in the line is the horizontal axis and the number of occurrences of nouns (in increments of two) is in the vertical axis. Even after repeated readings, it is unlikely we would have noticed this grouping of nouns at the end of Wordsworth's lines, at even (stressed) positions 4 and 6 and especially at the last syllable in the blank verse line. There are eighteen nouns at line-end out of 38 lines, with not a single noun in the first position.

Lowell's "Man and Wife," as it turns out, has on average most nouns at the fourth position—so too Swift, while Shakespeare has most at the second position. Swift has as many as eleven pronouns at the third position, and many others distributed in all positions, whereas Shakespeare has not a single pronoun: there

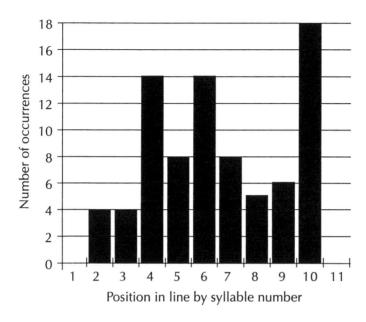

*Figure 9. Positions of nouns in Wordsworth*

are obvious causes for this difference in the dominants, and the speech orienta-
tions, of the two poems. Verbs tend to be much more evenly distributed across all
the positions in the line than nouns or pronouns, with one major exception
being the Swift poem's heavy end-line rhyming on verbs, as I have already
noticed in my reading (eight lines end with verbs in the eighth or last position).
Infinitive, imperative, and auxiliary verbs show little significant pattern in their
distribution. Adjectives in Lowell and Peck tend to cluster heavily at line begin-
nings, and the histogram for adjectives goes down by increments to next to
nothing, in the last positions in their line. Wordsworth's blank verse shows an
extremely high frequency of adjectives (seventeen) in the eighth position, a fact
that correlates with the fact above on nouns in the tenth or last position. To this
may also be correlated the high incidence, in Wordsworth, of conjunctions in the
sixth position and of articles in the seventh. The connective or transitional
midline in the Shakespeare sonnet, discussed in my reading, shows up on the
histogram as a grouping of conjunctions in positions 4 through 7 in the line. All
these statistics on frequency confirm what I have discursively shown in the
grammetrical readings.

For purposes of tallying complete as against broken-pattern lines, poems 7
and 9–14 were the iambic database. (Lowell's "Man and Wife" should have been

included, but was not.) The results might have been predicted, for Peck's poly-metric and syntactically busy poem had the fewest complete lines (lines un-broken by caesura), 27.5 percent; while Swift's compulsively regular poem had by far the most complete lines, 96.88 percent. Figures for the other poems move modestly in the middle of the range between those two extremes.

The graphs that plot the poems (horizontal) against the attributes-per-line (vertical) have given the most new information in the array. Berryman's sonnet stands out in a number of ways, by this method of counting. As I have pointed out, deletion is a dominant feature in Berryman's style; hence the high propor-tion of lexical items. Berryman has most nouns per line, most pronouns per line, most verbs per line (1.64; the nearest was Shakespeare with 1.14), most adjectives and adverbs per line, and, as might be guessed by now, most words per line. Shakespeare's lack of pronouns shows up again by a pronounced dip in the graph; but Shakespeare and especially Dorn lead in the number of infinitive verbs per line. Wordsworth and Lowell almost match Berryman in the number of adjec-tives per line, while Oppen and the free-verse poets generally use adjectives and adverbs with extreme sparing caution, almost a programmatic avoidance, shared also by Dickinson though in a less marked degree. Williams, Oppen, Corman, Lowell, Peck, Swift, and Berryman eschew articles, but Wordsworth uses them in comparative profusion. Pound leads in the number of interjections, with Williams and Berryman nearby. Shakespeare and Berryman have the greatest number of caesuras, perhaps because the sonnet form calls for more midline grammetrical scissoring to ruffle its continuities.

Even this modest brush with computer metrics may serve to confirm Hubert Dreyfus's well-founded skepticism, in *What Computers Still Can't Do: The Limits of Artificial Reason* (MIT, 1992), on the subject of artificial intelligence. More pertinent than the hard confirmatory facts we have found by such study is this skepticism, which is the opposed face of a trust in the meaning-making, interpretive abilities of the competent reader. We can teach the computer to imitate certain types of perception (for example, to scan beat-offbeat after we have already programmed beat-offbeat), to make certain sophisticated connections—but never (at least not yet) to perform multiple, simultaneous processing on several levels. And what else is reading?

## Chapter 12

# On Explanatory Adequacy

For grammetrics, uncertainty gives way to conviction, but the way we read preserves full knowledge of original indeterminacy. For these purposes, what is chancy and entropic does not constitute a full interpretation and yet is not diminished or denatured in the interpretive process. With and through the uncertainty, we are led to postulate that the mind has a significant bias toward harmony, toward sense making. If this is so, then perhaps the gestaltist Law of Prägnanz formalizes all apprehension, aesthetic and other. This is the law that says the field of sense qualities will organize itself as economically as the conditions will allow, according to such criteria as simplicity, regularity, and symmetry. Thus the arc of a circle develops into a true circle: one instance of the gestalt concept of "good continuation," which says a line tends to be completed in accordance with its own rule. By applying a cognitive as well as sociolinguistic register to mediate between single text and period style, I would say that the moment of Augustan form was the one, of all English literary history, that most required cognitive harmony according to this law. The continuous tension of expectation and fulfillment in Augustan language is reduced so far as possible to local effects within the line or half-line, and to the emphatic symmetries of maximal closure. By contrast, Romantic form "as proceeding" requires an active unsettling, the massive arrest of the tendency to respond, so that extreme violations of the Law of Prägnanz may be said to be the deliberate method of prosodic avant-gardism. George Oppen's poem in our array shows how postromantic prevention of the coincidence of formal and syntactic elements has the effect of strengthening the reader's expectation of continuation. Lexical, punctuational, syntactical, and structural irresolutions that prevent stable shapes become norms of this period style. These are all techniques that multiply and prolong the text's moments of ambiguity and prevent the reader from collecting and understanding it from an additive point of view. The more the reader is pleasurably disrupted in this way, the more he or she becomes producer rather than consumer of the poem.

From the standpoint of prosodic technique, Oppen's love poem is not, in these respects, very different from John Berryman's. A quite similar descriptive language may be used to account for a metered and a nonmetered poem of the same historical period. This is, we know, open to debate: in one of the most telling statements ever made against free verse as a method of writing, Yvor Winters said that with no metrical principle of norm and variation, the free-verse line has little intrinsic interest, tends to blur into the same arbitrary and monotonous tone. To my mind, Oppen's poem is one indication that this is not necessarily so, if the writer knows how to segment, enjamb, halt, and sing his or her lines, how to make a whole poem through the management of a credible voice that supervises all the minor effects of prosody. Oppen's virtual absence of punctuation has the same intention as that curious Coleridgean-Wordsworthian usage, the combined semicolon and dash (;—): a decisive break that is just as decisively a continuation. Such smaller effects are the indices not of cognitive harmony but of extreme energy. It is the larger form of the poem that shows a bias toward harmony, and the larger form preserves and extends, while it contradicts, these effects of smaller form.

Just in this way, it may be, one begins to generate a narrative of the way the poem's grammar cuts across the rhymes (if there are rhymes) and the breaks of the lines, from the start making assumptions about the aptness of prosodic choices to the poem's developing meaning. If, with such a method, we can integrate the semantic level with the others, we make prosody possible and attain concepts that do justice to a variety of cases, both traditional and innovative.

Yet explanation in this field must always have less adequacy, less probative value than we desire, because conjectures can so rarely be set up to cover a variety of cases, while at the same time narrowed to make them testable, refutable. The challenge to theory, thus, is that adequacy of explanation in prosody is judged not only or primarily by the precision of codes of formalization; it is judged by the degree to which the field may usefully be opened to history, linguistics, and human emotional logics. A truly hermeneutical prosody will not be dissolved into these studies, or confused with them. Books in the last generation by Henri Meschonnic, Derek Attridge, and Richard D. Cureton have brought us closer, but we still await examples of prosody in this strong sense; perhaps Meschonnic and Cureton are right, and when we arrive, rhythm and not metrics will be the focus of our inquiries. Meanwhile, the best policy is to keep a skeptical willingness to build bridges of theory to the related disciplines.

Here I have suggested that the sentence is our broadest, nearest bridge. I have already quoted Roland Barthes's quip that the writer is the one who thinks sentences. Linguistics as a discipline analyzes the sentence as the domain of grammatical structures and of meaning, but apparently cannot go beyond the sentence to formulate a satisfactory text grammar. (Text grammar studies in the 1970s and 1980s went on outside linguistics in Departments of Rhetoric and in journals of the emergent field known as composition theory.) On the other hand, literary hermeneutics has not come down to study the sentence as a primary meaning-making unit in the text. The rank of the sentence has been bypassed in favor of the sentence's constituent words, especially words that make revealing puns or metaphors; or bypassed in favor of the larger structures in which the sentence participates, such as articulation of sections, structures of utterance and argument. Grammetrics, especially as it focuses on the relation of sentence and line, proposes a look at the rather friable middle ground between the linguistic and the hermeneutical disciplines.

The intent of most metrical theory is to make the study objective by excluding cognitive elements and studying patterns. The explicit intent is to desemanticize meter. That is not my intent. In proposing that we add a loop of grammatical-structural information to (to be precise: against) the circuit of meter, I would like to give metrical theory the beginnings of an interpretive basis. It would be foolish to propose that meter as a system has specific semantic importance; it does not, except in the sense that different meters have been associated with specific genres and certain kinds of emotional effect. Meter is an arbitrariness that is naturalized, over centuries and through habit, into an influence, a "form" and a format. Meter's usable-recognizable quality is what it needs to perform its function; from the writer's point of view it must be a detachable mold, which is bent to individual purposes. (Free verse by abreaction defines itself as free because it abandons such a mold, so free verse needs the memory and copresence of the mold.) Nonetheless, meter and meaning do intricately influence each other, and not just at points of "irregularity." Structuralists do not claim to interpret meaning but rather to investigate the regularities that may be observed in a text. My own study is not a structuralist one because I take the risk of interpreting, while admitting that the results are weak and partial. Formalists privilege the aesthetic over the cognitive, by stating that literary rhetoric is a surplus beyond meaning that can never be read back into meaning. My own study is not a formalist one because it takes the aesthetic and cognitive on the same level, as necessary to each other in the text, and as mutually interfering.

Grammetrics shows that literary texts gain their special ontological status and their intensity in no small measure by inserting, deleting, blurring, fragmenting, and otherwise distorting English sentences. Metrical texts are different from others only in being more obviously rule-bound, in putting more constraints on the allocation of places to parts of the sentence. The sentence is no longer only expressive, once it comes within the sphere of the text. Whenever a sentence ends, some type of metrical unit breaks or is disturbed. The reverse is just as true; caesura and line are the great examples of meter scissoring sentences. But we always knew that. What we have not analyzed is why and where the scissoring is mutual.

Can the syntax and style of sentencing of a poem be taken as a notation? How does one move from the verse period to an interpretive text-grammar? From grammetrics to interpretive hypotheses? At least we have arrived at the right questions.

Onto what surface shall a theory be mapped? My answer has been: *Onto human cognition as represented in the poem by the grammar of the sentencing.* The decision to try this answer—to crank down the level of generality, to increase the theory's tolerance for empiricism, to concern ourselves with process rather than with calibration—has three implications.

First, since grammetrics deals with cognitive psychology of the reader, it calls for a more complete working out of a concept of plot in poetry. We are dealing here with questions of the intersection of systems, of sequencing of items, rhythms of phrasing, proactive and retroactive memory, foreshadowing, reinforcement, repetition-with-change, frustration and fulfillment of expectation. Plot as a narrative of consciousness and of sentences—of straight paths and false leads grammatical rather than in the larger structure of events—is a notion especially well adapted to the study of lyric modes. Eventfulness in the torsion of the verse period is perhaps the plot of lyric as a type; if it does not actually differentiate the lyric from more extended and more obviously narrative types of writing, the peripeteia of sentencing should at least be more consciously reckoned in as a primary feature of lyric.

Second, since prosody is the most common example of repetition in the literary work of art, the computer, I have quoted Robert Dilligan saying, "is a much more appropriate instrument for prosodic study than a sound spectrograph."[1]

My own attempt to imitate Dilligan's method in his study of Tennyson's *In Memoriam,* on a far more unwieldy corpus, 330 lines including poems ranging from a prose poem and four free-verse poems to nine metered poems in varying degrees of conventionality, is more an amateur trial, even a toy. Even if the results are inconclusive, it is instructive to see how the computer is programmed to do something more unlike than like reading. Poems put into the memory of the machine are stored as a single block, rather like the ancient manuscript inscription of Greek or Anglo-Saxon poetry, with markers for carriage returns that signal line ends. Other markers in this packed array indicate the syllable number in the line, whether strong or weak, where caesuras occur between syllables, and what form class in grammar a word belongs to. Metrical and grammatical information must be stored separately, retrieved separately. The computer cannot remember that a word like *present* can be either a noun or an infinitive verb, and it must be programmed with one or the other meaning, one or the other syllable-stress. To store the Shakespeare sonnet in memory along with all the grammetrical control characters takes over three thousand bytes of memory, and a byte is eight bits of information, or in other words answers to a yes/no question. It takes, thus, an enormous amount of machine memory.

The computer can tell us things that it would be tedious to count out manually. However the project, if we ever had it, of using the computer as a model of reading may be doomed. The machine is an inadequate metaphor for mind, because it cannot limit from the abstractly possible to the probable. The computer is helpless when it comes to making sense of the interference of systems. It cannot process different types of information at the same time. By contrast mind, especially literary mind, is economical.

Third, W. K. Wimsatt, speaking of "the ever-present, the ever-different disparities between formal meter and the linguistic totality," affirmed that "You can't write a grammar of the meter's interaction with the sense." Paul de Man, speaking for a more recent era but phrasing the same objection, questioned the legitimacy of criticism's reduction of rhetoric from figure to grammar—and in the process of his argument de Man said he would not hesitate to equate the figural potentiality of language "with literature itself." Grammetrics answers both Wimsatt and de Man by showing the interference of the aesthetic metrical-figural principle, which they treasure, with the cognitive principle, which they diminish. Grammetrics does not demolish but rather subsumes most of the traditional metrical categories. It does not brush away but rather complements those read-ings that exclusively emphasize the undecidability of figures. The difficulty of finding stable meanings, and the subversion of grammar and logic—these are attributes of texts and especially of the figures they carry. Emphasis on lack of resources, undecidability of the figural in language, strict impossibility of inter-pretation, is not misplaced. Shakespeare's lyric should be example enough, for now, that literary language perplexes and disables the meanings it has enabled. But it would not do to reduce the text to its figures and omit study of the grammar *that spaces the figures out;* it would not do to omit study of the many convergent cognitive processes that get us to the point of appreciating the lyric's beautiful difficulties in the first place.

Literary theory can face the issue of unwelcome complexity by ruling out of bounds certain sectors such as the notions of grammar and cognitive process. In traditional metrical theory, the issue has been handled by reduction of the domain of study—hiving off meter from grammar and style. Perhaps complexity of the discipline has been increased and not reduced thereby. Grammetrics broadens the scope of study by moving into the forbidden zones, investigating meter and sentencing together. Thus grammetrics faces the possible logical difficulties of theories that deal simultaneously with collective and member units. Ecological correlations are not valid substitutes for individual correlations. There is no denying that grammetrics is in this sense an ecological metrics. That is inevitable given its aim to be perception-oriented, interpretive, and fully historical. The danger of the proposal comes in basing its observational phase on currently available accounts of meter and syntax; this has been inescapable, and we can only plot to bend and correct these theories as we find the fit between rules of interference in the system and relational propositions in the description.

Can the broader scope lead to a decrease in the complexity of our theories and models? Through the theory of cognitive-aesthetic interference and the theory of a parallel morphology of two systems as wholes, grammetrics proposes to return a more complete text to the reader. The hypothesis is still largely untried but gains some force by enlisting as part of its notation the powerful processes of human cognition and expression.

My unfolding of the hypothesis of grammetrics has been literary in emphasis, discursive in method. Having watched structuralist and generative metrics fail in the late 1970s, because they were not sufficiently literary and discursive, I respect that rigor but opt for something multidimensional, even messy. Grammetrics is closer, now, to certain new agendas, preeminently an increased emphasis on rhythmic phrasing brought in by linguists Henri Meschonnic and Richard D. Cureton. In Meschonnic, this work is a full-scale (714 pages!) philosophy of rhythm; in Cureton, a full-scale (441 pages) cognitive psychology of rhythm. Just now there is also an affiliated exploration of nonmetrical prosodic devices, particularly in the work of John Hollander, who hears chimes and perceives symmetries in large designs and tiny corners of texts; a renewed interest in visual poetry, and a related entirely new interest in the space-loving prosodies of disposition on the page or screen in hypertext. Also new on the scene, and also largely started by Richard D. Cureton, is a belief that meter as a field must be teachable to children from the sixth grade onward, and thus must have a clear notation and a model exposition. This request would not invalidate advanced work on the edge of scholarship, but rather attempts to make our studies responsible to reading. Admirable in this regard is Charles O. Hartman's hypertext tutorial and reference for college students, *An Introduction to English Metrics* (1992).

Through emphasis on the sentence I have tried to bring discourse back into our consideration of the poem's formal structures. Sturdy yet protean, the sentence is a necessary, recognizable, and bounded element of discourse. Grammetrics explains why, how, and where explosive eventfulness is of supreme importance in lyric poetry. Midlevel study of the way grammar and meter scissor each other, along the divisible ground of the poetic line, and within the infinitely various length of the verse period, will always have pertinence. Midlevel study is where the action is, the energy of cognition. The elements are large enough to be within the boundaries of discourse, but small enough to be within the boundaries of short-term memory.

In *Rhythmic Phrasing in English Verse,* Richard D. Cureton's "hierarchical, componential, and preferentially based theory of verse rhythm" (441) is magnificent as a linguistics-informed theory that eliminates earlier myths and muddles, accounts for all elements in the text and in the reader's cognition, takes meter out of the center stage and makes it one more component, and defines a poetic-musical time sense that is rhythm's major function. His stated and implied critique of grammetrics—the inability to trace statements about point of view and tone of voice back to something in the notation—is one this theory will have to struggle with. Will Cureton's comprehensive theory manage to subsume grammetrics by developing a more powerful notation? I admire Cureton's handling of the levels of phrasing from the lowest on up (he finds twelve levels in all), but I am more convinced by his rhythmic alternations of weak and strong at the low and mid and high-mid levels, in his diagrams and analyses, than by his claim that the reader is able to perceive alternation and opposition in the overall frame of the poem. Through loyalty to grammetrics, I continue to hover at the midlevel inspection of sentence and line.

Richard D. Cureton's grouping well-formedness rules and grouping preference rules, summarized in his powerful tree and bracket diagrams, achieve a tight fit between an armamentarium of rules, and analyses of widely different texts. By contrast, my account of sentencing as a notation, in the form of suggestions on how to recognize scissoring points, has not a perfect fit with my retellings of my readings of the fourteen poems in the array. My version of grammetrics has at least this merit: no suggestion that the reading experience as experience can be in any way matched, reproduced, squared away in description; the reading experience can only be reinvented as a narrative, in this case a story of remembered grammetrical scissorings and remembered guesses toward coherent context. Those scissorings and guesses do move us into hypotheses about local and overall meaning.

By showing that syntax scissors not only meter—it also scissors grouping—Cureton's theory of phrasing helps the argument for grammetrics. When meter achieves a more rigorous formalization, this will also strengthen my grammetrical claims. What if meter is itself not static but dynamic, like syntax? Perhaps Cureton is right to think that a breakthrough in this field will come with a new philosophy of time.

The subtitle of this study was "Grammetrics and Interpretation," but I decided that I do not want to dignify what I have written with that term, though my readings head that way. A single term carries and intends the whole range from *reading* as a process (a skill) to *a reading* as a product (a positioned analysis that is biased, ideological, hermeneutic). Interpretation, as a more capacious criticism than I can fully claim here, relies on and uses grammetrical reading. Plainly, though, I have engaged in interpretation in gross and obvious ways in the construction of the example set: this is the choice of a straight white male with a certain literary training in the United States and United Kingdom during the 1950s and 1960s; probably too the actual analysis has its own bias, as it resists an inclination to formalism. By using the term *reading,* I intend the whole range implied in it, because that is inescapable; all reading is ideological; and yet I have wished to remain toward the skills end of the range.

There is some possibility that standard literary interpretation is no longer as experimental, no longer as much a discovery procedure as basic work on how we think and read; perhaps formalization, not exegesis, is where the news is about to be made. In any event, *reading* signals a less ambitious claim and accords better with what has actually been done. Also it places this book within a tradition of reader-response criticism, in the line from I. A. Richards's protocols in *Principles of Literary Criticism* (1924) through Jonathan Culler's call for fewer interpretations and more reports on conditions that permit reading, to Stanley Fish's affective poetics. As Elizabeth Freund has argued, each of these predecessors has the usual trouble of reader-response criticism, in finding answers to the "nagging dualism of literary object and reading subject."[2] But each at certain points in his career is either calling for or performing something like grammetrics. Richards's critique of his students' protocols was an example of how to use examples and raised tricky questions for theory; Culler's scorn for the endless "procession of atomistic readings bequeathed us by New Criticism" (Freund, 71), his belief that "to engage in the study of literature is . . . to advance one's understanding of the conventions and operations of an institution, a mode of discourse" (quoted in Freund, 71) cleared a space for study of the skills end of the range; and Fish's follow-the-text-for-amazement readings in *Surprised by Sin* (1967) and *Self-Consuming Artifacts* (1972) was a model of ground-level attention to fluctuations of logic and feeling. Alas, as Elizabeth Freund has shown in her flinty yet admiring critique of reader-response theory, Richards in his distinction between technical remarks and critical remarks authorized a separation between the literary object and the reading subject; Culler also avoided the issue of reading by separating conventions from understanding, for "structuralism and semiotics treat literature as an already constituted and closed system" (Freund, 71); and Fish in his affective stylistics posited a docile reader, with no resistance, and could not settle what is the proper object for study: "When the reader's experience is the object of analysis, the integrity of the text is threatened; when the text becomes the focus, Fish's program reverts to a closet formalism, in which the concept of the reader is only an extension of textual constraints or authorial intention" (Freund, 103). By development away from these positions later in their careers, both Culler and Fish, according to Freund, overinvest in the public and institutional role in reading. Still, in practice and program these are forerunners.

There are other reader-response traditions that grammetrics refuses: the heroic superreader in Michael Riffaterre, the antiheroic reader manipulated by an uncanny text in J. Hillis Miller and Paul de Man, the student of inner psychology in Norman Holland and David Bleich, the wishy-washy interact-with-the-text implied reader of Wolfgang Iser. Freund's grim survey in *The Return of the Reader* shows how "inconclusiveness is intrinsic" to these projects: "Reader response criticisms are . . . both generated and destroyed in the dialectical interplay between the monism of theory and the dualism of practice" (154). The reader has been returned as an active participant, after being eschewed in the text-based New Criticism, which had contempt for the critic's cognition and personality; but the history of reader-response theories, self-contradictory and self-consuming, suggests to Freund that the project "has a past rather than a future" (10). From our small window onto the history, this movement may be described as the generation begun by Harvey Gross's anti–New Critical first chapter on "Prosody as Rhythmic Cognition" in his *Sound and Form in Modern Poetry* (1964).

The author had its heyday in the nineteenth century. The text had its heyday in the era of New Criticism. The reader had its heyday in the era of reader response, now drawing to a close. We are now in the curious moment of *The Death and Return of the Author* (Seán Burke, 1992) and of *The Return of the Reader* (Elizabeth Freund, 1987). Entering the interminable dialogue between work and reader-interpreter, grammetrics comes forward in the 1990s as a skills theory making small claims but warranting to motivate and justify every act of attention. Invented by Peter Wexler and others in the 1960s, early in the era of reader response, grammetrics will not be constrained by New Criticism's devaluing of cognition. Achieving its first book in an era when reader-response is on the wane, but when the text is no longer separate from our response to it, grammetrics participates in a paradigm when rhythm and not meter is the focus of scholarly study. With these origins and limits, grammetrics will be influenced by and respond to the indeterminacies of deconstruction, without affiliating with that critical mode; meaning is multiple, not infinite, not impossible. It will marvel at the symmetries structuralist readings turn up, but will not accept that the evidences Roman Jakobson produces from Sonnet 129 have much to do with literary meaning. I speak of "it" as a thing or movement with a will of its own, by conventional exaggeration, but grammetrics remains a hypothesis. Its purpose is to do work. Its work is to reduce the gaps between the poetic text, our experience of it, and the narratives we make of our experience. Grammetrical reading is neither textuality nor self-indulgence. The scissors of meter divides the reader's attention, and yet it is the reader's attention that divides meter. After every division except the poem's final period, the mind resutures itself.

# Notes

## Chapter 1

1. A correlative issue, not addressed here, is the relation of rhyme to meter in the constitution and reading of line and poem. Modern metrical theory usually treats rhyme as the stub or shoe of the line, and so neglects the interanimation of rhyme and meter. The issue is touched on briefly in my reading of John Berryman's sonnet in chapter 10, and I have discussed it in *The Chances of Rhyme: Device and Modernity* (Berkeley and Los Angles: University of California Press, 1980). A fully coordinated description of these two devices remains an assignment for criticism.

2. Craig La Drière, "The Comparative Method in the Study of Prosody," in *Comparative Literature,* Proceedings of the Second Congress of the International Comparative Literature Association (Chapel Hill: University of North Carolina Press, 1959), 1:161.

3. Robert Bridges, "A Letter to a Musician on English Prosody," in *The Structure of Verse: Modern Essays on Prosody,* ed. Harvey Gross (New York: Fawcett Premier, 1966), 101.

4. This is T. B. Rudmose-Brown, reviewing Paul Verrier's *Essai sur les principes de la métrique anglais* (1911), in *Modern Language Review* 6 (April 1911): 231.

5. Both Shapiro and the sentences on *PMLA* are quoted in Richard W. Bailey and Dolores M. Burton, *English Stylistics: A Bibliography* (Cambridge, Mass.: MIT Press, 1968), xiv.

6. Seymour Chatman, "New Directions in Metrics," in *The Concise Encyclopedia of English and American Poets and Poetry,* ed. Stephen Spender and Donald Hall, 2d ed. (London: Hutchinson, 1970), 233, 229.

7. Tzvetan Todorov and Oswald Ducrot, "Versification," in their *Dictionnaire encyclopédique des sciences du langage* (Paris: Seuil, 1972), 241; my translation.

8. Patmore's essay was written in 1856; it is most conveniently available as the appendix to Patmore's *Collected Poems* (London: Bell and Sons, 1878).

9. I quote here Richard D. Cureton's March 19, 1985 letter to me concerning the draft of this book.

10. W. K. Wimsatt Jr., "A Note on the Terms Versification, Verse, Meter, Prosody," in *Versification: Major Language Types,* ed. W. K. Wimsatt Jr. (New York: Modern Language Association/NYU Press, 1972), xix.

**Chapter 2**

1. "The Concept of Meter: An Exercise in Abstraction," *PMLA* 74 (December 1959): 585–98; also published in Seymour Chatman and Samuel R. Levin, eds., *Essays on the Language of Literature* (Boston: Houghton Mifflin, 1967): my quotation from this version, 112.

2. I owe points and phrasing in this sentence to David Crystal's excellent summary: see "Past Work on Prosodic Features," *Prosodic Systems and Intonation in English* (Cambridge: Cambridge University Press, 1969), 26.

3. See Paul Fussell Jr., *Theory of Prosody in Eighteenth-Century England* (1954; rpt. Hamden, Conn.: Archon Books, 1966). Fussell has described how several modern prosodists have tended to understand the highly constrained, numerical metrics of the Augustan era by categories developed largely out of Tennyson's practice, a clear case of retrospective reasoning. Bysshe (1702), not Saintsbury (1910), is the theorist of this Augustan moment, with its architectural sense of form and its need to shackle the reader's attention. Bysshe's *Art of English Poetry* went through nine editions between 1702 and 1762; it has been reprinted by the Augustan Reprint Society in the 1708 text, with an introduction by A. Dwight Culler (Los Angeles: William Andrews Clark Memorial Library, UCLA, publication no. 40, 1953). The excellent introduction to this reprint draws on the fuller discussion in A. Dwight Culler's "Edward Bysshe and the Poet's Handbook," *PMLA* 63 (September 1948): 858–85. See also, for a valuable general account of Augustan metrical arguments, Alicia Ostriker, *Vision and Verse in William Blake* (Madison: University of Wisconsin Press, 1965), esp. chaps. 1 and 2.

4. Quoted from Thomas Taig, *Rhythm and Metre* (Cardiff: University of Wales, 1929), 137.

5. W. K. Wimsatt, "Rhetoric and Poems: The Example of Swift," paper read in New York at the annual meeting of the Modern Language Association, December 1974; thanks are due to Mrs. William Kurtz Wimsatt for permission to print this passage.

6. For further accounts of the achievement of Say, see T. S. Omond, *English Metrists* (1921; rpt. New York: Phaeton Press, 1968), 50; and especially Fussell, *Theory of Prosody,* 111ff.

7. Omond, *English Metrists,* 88.

8. Hollander is excellent on Joshua Steele: see *Vision and Resonance: Two Senses of Poetic Form* (New York: Oxford University Press, 1975), 18–19. See also Omond, *English Metrists,* 86–95; and David Abercrombie, "Steele, Monboddo, and Garrick," in *Studies in Phonetics and Linguistics* (London: Oxford University Press, 1965).

9. *Collected Letters of Samuel Taylor Coleridge,* ed. Earl Leslie Griggs (Oxford: Oxford University Press, 1959), 4:603. Coleridge in this passage makes no distinction between stress (Beat) and accents, and in this usage reflects the "welter of variation" T. V. F. Brogan finds in modern scholarship, in his article on "Accent" in *The New Princeton Encyclopedia of Poetry and Poetics,* ed. T. V. F. Brogan and Alex Preminger (Princeton: Princeton University Press, 1993): 3–6. Brogan's article clarifies the distinction, especially when he takes up "confusions about the nature of 'quantity' and 'accent,' deeply interrelated acoustic phenomena" (4). Specifically on the issue of stress and accent: "In nontechnical usage, the simplest thing to say is that accent in the sense of emphasis is the more general term, stress the more precise, and that stress can denote intensity as opposed to pitch or length" (4).

The Princeton *Encyclopedia* contains no entry on stress; if I make much of it here, despite the Princeton volume and despite the usual term for Engish verse in my chapter-title (accentual-syllabic), this is because of the post-Coleridgean emotional content in the term, where we take stress as intensity of feeling. This is a historical artifact and has nothing to do with technical questions in linguistics.

10. Crystal, *Prosodic Systems,* 27.

11. See Robert Dilligan's sophisticated computer analysis: "*Ibant Obscvri:* Robert Bridges' Experiment in Quantitative Verse," *Style* 6, no. 1 (winter 1972): 38–65.

12. I refer to John Sparrow in his introduction to *Robert Bridges: Poetry and Prose* (Oxford: Oxford University Press, 1955) and in *Robert Bridges* (London: Longman, 1962); Yvor Winters in *Forms of Discovery* (Denver: Alan Swallow, 1967); and especially Albert J. Guerard Jr., *Robert Bridges: A Study of Traditionalism in Poetry* (Cambridge, Mass.: Harvard University Press, 1942; rpt. New York: Russell and Russell, 1965).

13. George Saintsbury, *A History of English Prosody, from the Twelfth Century to the Present Day* (1910; rpt. New York: Russell and Russell, 1961). Quotations from Saintsbury in this paragraph, all from vol. 3, in order from 490, 391, 509.

14. Omond, *English Metrists,* both quotations from 250.

15. A passage from Saintsbury's vol. 1 has been reprinted in Gross, *The Structure of Verse.* Harvey Gross has also reprinted, with his own introduction, Saintsbury's *Historical Manual of English Prosody* (London: Macmillan, 1910; rpt. New York: Schocken Books, 1966). The special double issue on rhythm of *Agenda* (London) appeared in 10, no. 4, and 11, no. 1 (autumn-winter 1972–73).

16. Saintsbury, *History of English Prosody,* 3:393.

17. Omond, *English Metrists,* 266.

18. See John Crowe Ransom, "Wanted: An Ontological Critic," originally published in *The New Criticism* (1941), and in part reprinted in Chatman and Levin, *Language of Literature.*

19. Wimsatt and Beardsley, "The Concept of Meter," 100.

20. Wimsatt and Beardsley, "The Concept of Meter," 110.

21. Wimsatt and Beardsley, "The Concept of Meter," 110–11.

22. Barbara Herrnstein Smith, *Poetic Closure: A Study of How Poems End* (Chicago: University of Chicago Press, 1968), 87.

23. W. K. Wimsatt in the discussion of metrics that makes up the comments to part 5 in T. A. Sebeok, *Style in Language* (Cambridge, Mass.: MIT Press, 1960), 205.

24. Wimsatt in the discussion in Sebeok, *Style in Language,* 201.

25. W. K. Wimsatt, "On Scanning English Meters," a review of Harvey Gross's *Sound and Form in Modern Poetry,* in *Michigan Quarterly Review* 5 (fall 1966): 291.

26. Quotations in the previous two sentences come from Wimsatt's forward to *Versification,* viii.

27. Paul Fussell Jr., *Poetic Meter and Poetic Form* (New York: Random House, 1965); Robert Beum and Karl Shapiro, *A Prosody Handbook* (New York: Harper and Row, 1965); James Macaulay, *Versification: A Short Introduction* (East Lansing: Michigan State University Press, 1966); Joseph Malof, *A Manual of English Meters* (Bloomington: Indiana University Press, 1970). The most recent in this series is also the best, because the most interactive: *An Introduction to English Metrics: Hypertext Tutorial and Reference,* written and published in

the form of disks by Charles O. Hartman, Connecticut College, New London, Connecticut.

28. Roy Fuller, *Professors and Gods: Last Oxford Lectures on Poetry* (London: Andre Deutsch, 1973), 63. One other example, from Kingsley Amis: "For me . . . a regular metrical or rhythmical beat is one first essential. Rhyme is optional. . . . These days . . . it's the traditional type of poet who takes the risks: his rhythms can be seen to be slack or broken, his rhymes forced, his meaning trivial, inane, humdrum, pretentious. Gibberish is a safe option. Formal restraints like meter are not just desirable in themselves, or as a kind of certificate showing that the poet is serious. They are helpful to the poet in that they give him something to push against, a series of recognizable problems to solve. Writing verse with no such restraints strikes me as like cheating at patience." ("Why Poetry?" *Observer,* September 30, 1973, 39.)

29. Yvor Winters, "The Influence of Meter on Poetic Convention," in *In Defense of Reason* (London: Routledge and Kegan Paul, 1960), 129; quoted and extended in a slightly different context by Winters himself, 551.

30. Harvey Gross, *Sound and Form in Modern Poetry* (Ann Arbor: University of Michigan Press, 1964), 12.

31. Smith, *Poetic Closure.* For other works mentioned, Gay Wilson Allen, *American Prosody* (New York: American Book Company, 1935); Karl Shapiro, *Essay on Rime* (New York: Reynal and Hitchcock, 1945), and *English Prosody and Modern Poetry* (Baltimore: Johns Hopkins University Press, 1947); Yurii Lotman, *La structure du texte artistique*, trans. Henri Meschonnic (Moscow, 1970; Paris: Seuil, 1972), and *Analysis of the Poetic Text*, ed. and trans. by D. Barton Johnson (Ann Arbor, Mich.: Ardis, 1976); Walter Sutton, *American Free Verse* (New York: New Directions, 1972); Hollander, *Vision and Resonance;* Enikö Bollobás, *Tradition and Innovation in American Free Verse: Whitman to Duncan* (Budapest: Akadémiai Kiadó, 1986). I have reviewed Sutton in "Thoroughly Modern Measures," *boundary 2* 3, no. 2 (winter 1975): 455–71; and Hollander in *Chicago Review* 28, no. 1 (summer 1976): 141–46.

32. Quotations in this portmanteau sentence are from, in order, Terence Hawkes, "The Matter of Metre" (reviewing John Thompson's *Founding of English Metre*), *Essays in Criticism* 12 (1962): 416; Chatman, "New Directions in Metrics," 231; and John Thompson, *The Founding of English Metre* (New York: Columbia University Press, 1961), 156.

33. La Drière, "Comparative Method," 1:169.

34. Thompson, *Founding of English Metre,* 9.

35. The phrasing is Jonathan Culler's from *Structuralist Poetics: Structuralism, Linguistics, and the Study of Literature* (Ithaca, N.Y.: Cornell University Press, 1975), 65.

36. This definition of the "ultimate aim of metrics" comes from A. Walter Bernhart, "Complexity and Metricality," *Poetics* 12, Generative Metrics issue edited by J. C. Beaver and Jens F. Ihwe (Amsterdam: North-Holland, 1975), 140.

37. Seymour Chatman and Samuel R. Levin, introduction to the metrics section of Chatman and Levin, *Language of Literature,* 69.

38. Bernhart, "Complexity and Metricality," 113.

39. The phrasing of Chatman and Levin is concise: Jespersen "recognized that the stress system of English was more complex than the metrical system, and asserted an

essential principle—the relativity of an ictus; that is, whether a syllable carries ictus is determined not intrinsically but by its environment" (*Language of Literature,* 69).

40. Otto Jespersen, "Notes on Metre (1900)" in Chatman and Levin, *Language of Literature,* 90.

41. Jespersen, "Notes on Metre (1900)," 81.

42. Fred W. Householder, "Phonemes and Distinctive Features: I," in *Linguistic Speculations* (Cambridge: Cambridge University Press, 1971), 167.

43. Many of Roman Jakobson's studies of versification are collected in *Questions de poétique* (Paris: Seuil, 1973), but see also: "Linguistics and Poetics," in Sebeok, *Style in Language,* and in Chatman and Levin, *Language of Literature,* "The Structure of Chinese Modular Verse," in *Echanges et communications: Mélanges offert à Claude Lévi-Strauss* (The Hague: Mouton, 1970), and *Selected Writings,* 2d ed. (The Hague: Mouton, 1971–), esp. vol. 3. Michael Riffaterre: "Criteria for Style Analysis," *Word* 15 (1959): 154–74, "Stylistic Context, *Word* 16 (1960): 207–18, "Problèmes d'analyse du style littéraire," *Romance Philology* 14 (1961): 216–27. Samuel R. Levin: *Linguistic Structures in Poetry* (The Hague: Mouton, 1962). Pierre Guiraud: article on French prosody in *Le langage,* sous la direction d'André Martinet (Paris: Gallimard, 1968), *Essais de stylistique* (Paris: Klincksieck, 1969), esp. parts 1 and 4.

44. Culler, *Structuralist Poetics,* 74.

45. Michael Shapiro, *Asymmetry: An Inquiry into the Linguistic Structure of Poetry* (Amsterdam: North-Holland, 1976): see esp. on Jakobson, 79–82.

46. Harold Whitehall, "From Linguistics to Criticism," a review of Trager and Smith in *Kenyon Review* 18, no. 3 (summer 1956): 413.

47. George L. Trager and Henry Lee Smith Jr., *An Outline of English Structure,* Studies in Linguistics, Occasional Papers 3 (Norman, Okla: Battenberg Press, 1951).

48. Whitehall, "From Linguistics to Criticism," 413.

49. Edmund L. Epstein and Terence Hawkes, *Linguistics and English Prosody,* Studies in Linguistics, Occasional Papers 7 (Buffalo: University of Buffalo Department of Anthropology and Linguistics, 1959), 21. See also Henry Lee Smith Jr., "Toward Redefining English Prosody," *Studies in Linguistics* 14, nos. 3–4 (1960): 68–76; and Terence Hawkes, "The Problems of Prosody," *Review of English Literature* 3 (1962): 32–49, and "The Matter of Metre," 413–21.

50. "The intonation patterns of stress, pitch, and juncture, together with those features of sound we call vowels and consonants, provide the signals of sound that are our language. . . . Metre is made by abstracting from speech one of these essential features and ordering this into a pattern. The pattern is an imitation of the patterns that the feature makes in speech": this explanation, adequate as far as it goes, is the one given in Thompson's introduction to *Founding of English Metre,* 11. Hawkes's "The Matter of Metre" is a review of Thompson, from within the Trager-Smith paradigm, but nonetheless adversary.

51. W. K. Wimsatt reviewing Thompson in *Renaissance News* 16 (1963): 131, 133.

52. Seymour Chatman, *A Theory of Meter* (The Hague: Mouton, 1965), both quotations from 14.

53. See Spender and Hall, *Concise Encyclopedia,* 233.

54. Morris Halle and Samuel Jay Keyser, "Chaucer and the Study of Prosody" appeared in *College English* 28 (1966): 187–219, and is reprinted in *Linguistics and Literary*

*Style,* ed. Donald C. Freeman (New York: Holt, Rinehart and Winston, 1970). See also, for the initial theory: Samuel J. Keyser, "The Linguistic Basis of English Prosody," in *Modern Studies in English,* ed. David A. Reibel and Sanford A. Schane (Englewood Cliffs, N.J.: Prentice-Hall, 1969), 379–94; Keyser, "Old English Prosody," *College English* 30 (1969): 331–56, with "A Reply," *College English* 31 (1969): 74–80; Joseph C. Beaver, "A Grammar of Prosody," *College English* 29 (1968): 310–21, reprinted in Freeman, *Linguistics and Literary Style;* Joseph C. Beaver, "Contrastive Stress and Metered Verse, *Language and Style* 2 (1969): 257–71.

    55. A useful account of the essential revised theory was condensed by R. J. Dilligan and T. K. Bender, as they prepared to take it as the basis of a verse-scanning algorithm in their "The Lapses of Time: A Computer-Assisted Investigation of English Prosody," in *The Computer and Literary Studies* (Edinburgh: Edinburgh University Press, 1973):

> [The Halle-Keyser] description of iambic pentameter regards it as a sequence of ten positions in which syllables receiving primary stress occupy even numbered positions. Two optional unstressed syllables are permitted at the end of the line, and position one may be unoccupied. Schematically this can be represented as
>
> (w) s w s w s w s w s (x) (x)
>
> where s represents a position with primary stress, w a position with any level of stress less than primary, x an unstressed syllable, and parenthesized positions are optional. A position may be composed of a single syllable or at most two vowels immediately adjoining or separated by a single sonorant consonant. There are three possible combinations which constitute a metrical line:
>
> 1. Fully stressed syllables occur in s positions only and in all s positions.
> 2. Fully stressed syllables occur in s positions only but not in all s positions.
> 3. Stress maxima occur in s positions but not in all s positions.
>
> A stress maximum is defined as a fully stressed syllable occurring between two unstressed syllables in the same syntactic constituent in a line of verse.
>
>     To scan a line according to this theory, one assigns syllables or sonorant sequences to positions numbered one through ten omitting from the numbering extra-metrical syllables in verse final and verse medial positions. If the third condition is violated and stress maxima occur in odd numbered positions, the line is judged unmetrical. The number of exceptions to conditions 1 and 2 contained in the line determine the degree of metrical complexity of a line. (See *The Computer and Literary Studies* [Edinburgh: Edinburgh University Press, 1973], 188.)

With other linguistic metrics, this assumes that an extralinguistic pattern may be, as Halle and Keyser say, "perfectly compatible with the linguistic givens of the spoken language" ("Chaucer," 188). Dilligan and Bender have shown the empirical value of this scheme by basing their FORTRAN program on its assignment of metrical stress to even positions in the line; they are able to pinpoint the "frequency of stress maximum in ictal positions for [Gerard Manley] Hopkins's early iambic verse," as well as other information such as the distribution of assonance and alliteration across all ten positions in the iambic pentameter line. Thus they are able to show "metricality" by the Halle-Keyser definition: convincing, indeed indisputable proof that Hopkins is a more conventional technician, in poems 1–27, than anyone had previously imagined, but also precise earmarking of all points where he strains against metrical convention.

56. The Halle-Keyser defense, revision, and extension of their theory took place in this sequence: Morris Halle, "On Meter and Prosody," in *Progress in Linguistics,* ed. Manfred Bierwisch and K. E. Heidolph (The Hague: Mouton, 1970), 64–80; Morris Halle and Samuel J. Keyser, *English Stress: Its Norm, Its Growth, and Its Role in Verse* (New York: Harper and Row, 1971), "Illustration and Defense of a Theory of the Iambic Pentameter," *College English* 33 (1971): 154–76, and "The Iambic Pentameter," in Wimsatt, *Versification.* The initial theory was extended and applied by Donald C. Freeman in "On the Primes of Metrical Style," *Language and Style* 1 (1968): 63–101, reprinted in Freeman, *Linguistics and Literary Style;* and by Dudley L. Hascall, "Trochaic Meter," *College English* 33 (1971): 217–27. The initial theory was attacked by W. K. Wimsatt Jr., "The Rule and the Norm: Halle and Keyser on Chaucer's Meter," *College English* 31 (1970): 774–88; by Karl Magnuson and Frank G. Ryder, "The Study of English Prosody: An Alternative Proposal," *College English* 31 (1970): 789–820, and "Second Thoughts on English Prosody, *College English* 33 (1971): 198–216; and by David H. Chisholm, "Lexicality and German Derivational Suffixes: A Contribution to the Magnuson-Ryder Theory of Prosody," *Language and Style* 6 (1973): 27–38. The revised theory was extended by Joseph C. Beaver in two articles: "Current Metrical Issues," *College English* 33 (1971): 177–97, and "The Rules of Stress in English Verse," *Language* 47 (1973): 606–11; by Paul Kiparsky in "Stress, Syntax, and Meter," *Language* 51, no. 3 (1975): 576–616, and in "The Rhythmic Structure of English Verse," *Linguistic Inquiry* 8 (1977): 189–247); by Bernhart, "Complexity and Metricality"; and by Gilbert Youmans in "Generative Tests for Generative Meter," *Language* 59 (1983): 67–92. The flurry was more or less over by 1984 when a conference on metrics at Stanford was held: conference papers were collected five years later in *Rhythm and Meter,* ed. Paul Kiparsky and Gilbert Youmans (San Diego: Academic Press/Harcourt Brace Jovanovich, 1989). The most philosophical and skeptical account of all the issues involved is Jens F. Ihwe's "On the Foundations of 'Generative Metrics'" from *Poetics* (Amsterdam: North Holland, 1975), 367–400.

57. The most useful result of the generative-metrics era was Derek Attridge's development of the beat-offbeat notation, in his book *The Rhythms of English Poetry* (London: Longman, 1982.) Attridge's notation is the one I recommend and employ in the Shakespeare analysis below.

58. Donald C. Freeman, "On the Primes of Metrical Style," in Freeman, *Linguistics and Literary Style,* 479.

59. Jacques Roubaud, "Quelque thèses sur la poétique, I," *Change* 6 [La Poétique La Mémoire], 20–21; my translation.

60. Paul Kiparsky in *Language* 51, no. 3 (1975): 576–616.

61. Ihwe, "Foundations."

62. T. V. F. Brogan, *English Versification, 1570–1980: A Reference Guide with a Global Appendix* (Baltimore: Johns Hopkins University Press, 1981), xii, and "Meter" and "Prosody," in *The New Princeton Encyclopedia of Poetry and Poetics,* ed. T. V. F. Brogan and Alex Preminger (Princeton, N.J.: Princeton University Press, 1993).

63. Richard D. Cureton, "Traditional Scansion: Myths and Muddles," *Journal of Literary Semantics* 15 (1986): 171–208, and *Rhythmic Phrasing in English Verse* (London: Longman, 1992).

## Chapter 3

1. George Steiner, *After Babel* (New York: Oxford University Press, 1975), esp. 110–15.

2. Roman Jakobson and Morris Halle, *Fundamentals of Language* (The Hague: Mouton, 1956), 13–14.

3. Phrasing from B. O. Unbegaun, *Russian Versification* (Oxford: Oxford University Press, 1956), 13.

4. Jan M. Meijer, "Verbal Art as Interference between a Cognitive and an Aesthetic Structure," in *Structure of Texts and Semiotics of Culture*, ed. Jan van Eng and Mojmir Grygar (The Hague: Mouton, 1973), 316.

5. Pallister Barkas, *A Critique of Modern English Prosody (1880–1930)* (Halle: Saale, 1934), 11.

6. Paul de Man, "Literary History and Literary Modernity," in *Blindness and Insight: Essays in the Rhetoric of Contemporary Criticism* (New York: Oxford University Press, 1971), 164.

7. I first worked out some of these ideas in a 1971 article on free verse; only later did I think to pursue them with metered verse. That provenance seems to be important for this theory. The 1971 article is slightly rewritten as my chapter "The Prosodies of Free Verse," in *The New Poetries: Poetic Form since Coleridge and Wordsworth* (Lewisburg, Pa.: Bucknell University Press, 1985). Also relevant: the entry on free verse that I wrote with Enikö Bollobás for *The New Princeton Encyclopedia of Poetry and Poetics*, ed. Brogan and Preminger.

## Chapter 4

1. Marjorie Perloff, for example, concludes that Olson's projective-verse manifesto is "hardly a break-through in literary theory it is reputed to be. It is essentially a scissors-and-paste job, a clever but confused collage." See her article "Charles Olson and the 'Inferior Predecessors': 'Projective Verse' Revisited," *English Literary History* 40 (1973): 285–306.

2. For Ginsberg, see *Allen Verbatim: Lectures on Poetry, Politics, Consciousness*, ed. Gordon Ball (New York: McGraw Hill, 1974), 106 and 150 for quotations used here; also see the lecture "Poetic Breath, and Pound's Usura," esp. pp. 161–73. For David Antin see "Notes for an Ultimate Prosody," *Stonybrook* 1–2 (1968); and "Modernism and Postmodernism: Approaching the Present in American Poetry," *boundary 2* 1, no. 1 (fall 1972): 98–133. I would like to acknowledge a general debt in this chapter to Eric Mottram's lecture on open-form poetry, which I heard in London at the National Poetry Centre, May 13, 1974.

3. Williams's complaint against complicated ritualistic forms may be found in *Spring and All*, written 1923, and collected in *Imaginations*, ed. Webster Schott (New York:

New Directions, 1970), 102. The Blake sentences are quoted as fathering concepts in the headnote to Donald M. Allen and Warren Tallman, eds., *The Poetics of the New American Poetry* (New York: Grove Press, 1973), viii.

4. Karl Shapiro, *The Bourgeois Poet* (New York: Random House, 1964), 112. Shapiro also writes, pertinently (98–99): "Why am I happy writing this textbook? What sublime idiocy! What a waste of time! A textbook on prosody at that. . . . And I dream, like others, of writing a textbook that is not a textbook, a book that not even a student would part with, a book that makes even prosody shine."

5. Oliver Wendell Holmes's "The Physiology of Versification" is in *Pages from an Old Volume of Life* (Boston, 1892): see esp. 316. For the others, see: Chatman, *A Theory of Meter* (The Hague: Mouton, 1965); Robert de Souza, *Du rhythme en français* (Paris: Librarie Universitaire, 1912); Henry Lanz, *The Physical Basis of Rime* (Stanford: Stanford University Press, 1931); Stanley Burnshaw, *André Spire and His Poetry* (Philadelphia: Centaur Press, 1933); André Spire, *Plaisir poétique et plaisir musculaire* (Paris, 1939; new ed. Paris: J. Corti, 1986); Stanley Burnshaw, *The Seamless Web: Language-Thinking, Creature-Knowledge, Art-Experience* (New York: George Braziller, 1970); Charles Olson, "Projective Verse" (1950), in *Selected Writings of Charles Olson*, ed. Robert Creeley (New York: New Directions, 1966); David Abercrombie, "A Phonetician's View of Verse-Structure," in *Studies in Phonetics and Linguistics* (London: Oxford University Press, 1965).

6. Robert Duncan in *Poets on Poetry*, ed. Howard Nemerov (New York: Basic Books, 1966), 134–35.

7. Duncan speaking, in *Allen Verbatim* (1974), 107.

8. This sentence relies on the idea and phrasing of David Antin, in "Modernism and Postmodernism."

9. W. C. Williams, statement in notes on contributors, *Poetry* 93, no. 6 (March 1959): 416.

10. Williams quotations in this paragraph: "It is in the minutiae," *Selected Essays of William Carlos Williams* (New York: Random House, 1954), 109; "Vers libre is finished": from an early typescript, "Speech Rhythm," quoted by Mike Weaver, *William Carlos Williams: The American Background* (Cambridge: Cambridge University Press, 1971), 82–83; "up to us": quoted by Sutton, *American Free Verse*, 141; "sequestration" and "all the advantageous jumps": *Selected Essays*, 109.

11. Quotations in this paragraph: "metrical table of values" in "The Poem as a Field of Action," *Selected Essays*, 286; "relatively stable foot" from "On Measure" (1954), printed in *The William Carlos Williams Reader*, ed. M. L. Rosenthal (New York: New Directions, 1966); "our concept of musical time": *Selected Essays*, 286.

12. The title of Robert Duncan's first major book, *The Opening of the Field* (1960), makes allusion to the new poetics.

13. For an elaborate exploration of the issues in this sentence see Bram Dijkstra, *The Hieroglyphics of a New Speech* (Princeton, N.J.: Princeton University Press, 1969); and Wai-lim Yip, *Ezra Pound's Cathay* (Princeton, N.J.: Princeton University Press, 1969).

14. Olson, "Projective Verse," 18, 16.

15. The most prominent and influential anthologies have been *The New American Poetry*, ed. Donald M. Allen (New York: Grove Press, 1960); and Stephen Berg and Robert Mezey, eds. *Naked Poetry* (Indianapolis: Bobbs-Merrill, 1969) and *The New Naked Poetry* (Indianapolis: Bobbs-Merrill, 1976). Speaking of success, I will give here the titles

of three magnificent poems in open forms: poems that bear comparison in range and skill with the finest writing in traditional forms: Charles Olson, "The Kingfishers"; Robert Duncan, "Poem Beginning with a line by Pindar"; Paul Blackburn, "The Watchers." Since the time of these 1950s–1960s poems, essentially the time of late modernism, postmodern work absolutely assumes the breakthrough into open form and eschews not only rhyme and meter but usually, too, the line and the denomination *poem,* and sometimes also the English sentence and the categories of logic. See Ron Silliman's collection of Language poets: *In the American Tree* (Orono, Maine: National Poetry Foundation, University of Maine, 1986); and Paul Hoover's anthology of *Postmodern American Poetry* (New York: Norton, 1994).

## Chapter 5

1. Any account of this growth industry—poets on poetry—will be selective. I am thinking of the published letters of Frost and Stevens, and the interviews in *Paris Review* and *Contemporary Literature,* the Oxford Poetry Lectures of Graves, Auden, Fuller, and Levi, and the Norton Lectures at Harvard by Guillèn, Day Lewis, Paz. There is also the Poets on Poetry series at University of Michigan Press, including books of essays by (for example) Donald Davie, Donald Hall, Galway Kinnell. Other sources of technical comment: statements on form in Allen, *The New American Poetry,* and in Berg and Mezey, *Naked Poetry* and *The New Naked Poetry;* Howard Nemerov, ed., *Poets on Poetry* (New York: Basic Books, 1966); Gregory Orr, ed., *The Poet Speaks: Interviews with Contemporary Poets* (New York: Barnes and Noble, 1966); *Agenda* (London) issues on rhythm (autumn–winter 1972–73) and on American rhythm (spring–summer 1973); William Packard, ed., *The Craft of Poetry: Interviews from the New York Quarterly* (Garden City, N.Y.: Doubleday, 1974); William Heyen, ed., *American Poets in 1976* (Indianapolis: Bobbs-Merrill, 1976). The Language poets have been tireless, prosody-fixated polemicists, in journals like *This* and *Roof* and *L=A=N=G=U=A=G=E* and *Poetics Journal;* in books like Charles Bernstein's *Content's Dream* (Los Angeles: Sun & Moon, 1986), Steve McCaffery's *North of Intention* (New York: Roof Books, 1986), Ron Silliman's *The New Sentence* (New York: Roof Books 1987); and in the poetics statements that make the final quarter of their group anthology, *In the American Tree,* ed. Silliman. One final UK item: Seamus Heaney, *The Government of the Tongue,* the 1986 T. S. Eliot Memorial Lectures and Other Critical Writings (London: Faber and Faber, 1988).

2. Auden is interviewed in Packard, *The Craft of Poetry,* 7–8.

3. Roy Fuller in Orr, *The Poet Speaks,* 63–64.

4. Richard Wilbur in Nemerov, *Poets on Poetry,* 168.

5. W. S. Merwin, in Berg and Mezey, *Naked Poetry,* 271–72.

6. Lotman, *Structure du texte artistique,* 229; my translation.

## Chapter 6

1. Lotman, *Analysis of the Poetic Text,* 3.

2. Peter Wexler's two studies are: "On the Grammetrics of the Classical Alexandrine," *Cahiers de Lexicologie* 4 (1964): 61–72; and "Distich and Sentence in Corneille

and Racine," in *Essays on Style and Language,* ed. Roger Fowler (London: Routledge & Kegan Paul, 1966), 100–117. The passage here quoted is from the first, but since I quote from PW's typescript, not the published version, I omit page number. The neologism *grammetrics* originates with Wexler, but he says that there are hints of the idea in Richner, de Lage, and Guiraud and in French versification treatises.

3. From Robert Dilligan's letter to me, dated October 19, 1976.

4. M. A. K. Halliday, "Categories of the Theory of Grammar," *Word* 16 (December 1961): 241-92.

5. Richard Ohmann, "Literature as Sentences," *College English* 27 (January 1966); rpt. in Chatman and Levin, *Language of Literature.*

6. Roland Barthes, *Le plaisir du texte* (Paris: Seuil, 1973), 80; my translation.

7. One example of many: Vincent B. Leitch, *Cultural Criticism, Literary Theory, Poststructuralism* (New York: Columbia University Press, 1992). This is an excellent book; perhaps my phrase "simply assuming the cognitive . . . and dissolving the aesthetic" is unfair.

## Chapter 7

1. Wimsatt and Beardsley, "The Concept of Meter," 110–11.

2. Wimsatt, *Versification,* xix; and in "On Scanning English Meters," 291.

3. Gérard Genette, "Valéry and the Poetics of Language," in *Textual Strategies: Perspectives in Post-Structuralist Criticism,* ed. Josué V. Harari (Ithaca, N.Y.: Cornell University Press, 1979), 360. Genette is quoting Roland Barthes, but Genette is himself the major student of this phenomenon. See his *Mimologiques: Voyage en cratylie* (Paris: Seuil, 1976).

4. Meijer, "Verbal Art as Interference," esp. 216, 313, 327, for materials dealt with here.

5. Craig La Drière, "Structure, Sound, and Meaning," in *Sound and Poetry,* ed. Northrop Frye (New York: Columbia University Press, 1957), 85–108.

6. "Tall Nettles," *Collected Poems of Edward Thomas,* ed. R. George Thomas (Oxford: Oxford University Press, 1978), 307.

## Chapter 8

1. This book is the late-born triplet of my earlier, historical studies: *The Chances of Rhyme* and *The New Poetries.* Also pertinent: Jacques Roubaud's study of the history of our preoccupation with form, *La veillesse d'Alexandre* (Paris: F. Maspero, 1978), esp. 106–7.

2. All fourteen poems used in the analyses below are judged, if not transcendent masterpieces, at least successful, so the issue of evaluation is not directly raised in this inquiry. It is raised implicitly in the comments on one of the poems, and in the concluding pages on authorial revisions and editorial tampering, but a fully fledged grammetrics would need to confront the issue directly and exhaustively.

3. Roman Jakobson, "Poetry of Grammar and Grammar of Poetry," in *Verbal Art, Verbal Sign, Verbal Time,* ed. Krystyna Pomorska and Stephen Rudy (Minneapolis: University of Minnesota Press, 1985); Mac Hammond, "Poetic Syntax," *Poetics 1,* ed. Donald Davie et al. (Warsaw: Polish Scientific Publishers, 1961): 475–82.

4. Jiří Levý, "The Meanings of Form and the Forms of Meaning," *Poetics* 2 (Warsaw: Polish Scientific Publishers, 1966), 45–59. This virtually unknown article is, I believe, one of the foundations of any poetics aspiring to relate form to meaning.

5. See Annie Finch, *The Ghost of Meter: Culture and Prosody in American Free Verse* (Ann Arbor: University of Michigan Press, 1993).

## Chapter 9

1. *The Sonnets of Shakespeare,* from the Quarto of 1609 with variorum readings and commentary, edited by Raymond Macdonald Alden (Boston: Houghton Mifflin, 1916), 309. This puts the sonnets into modern typefaces with no changes in spelling or punctuation. Stephen Booth's more recent edition, *Shakespeare's Sonnets* (New Haven: Yale University Press, 1977), prints the original in facsimile and on facing pages the modern versions of each sonnet: Booth's changes are slight, are always for clarity as he defines it in his useful preface, but do add up to hundreds of deviations from the Quarto. He aims for a midpoint between the Quarto text and modern "directive" spelling and punctuation. He is aware of the sacrifice of energy this involves.

2. Helen Vendler, "Jakobson, Richards, and Shakespeare's Sonnet CXXIX," in *I. A. Richards: Essays in His Honor,* ed. Reuben Brower, Helen Vendler, and John Hollander (New York: Oxford University Press, 1973).

3. Randolph Quirk et al., *A Grammar of Contemporary English* (London: Longman, 1972), 792.

4. The confusion or seeming confusion of hellish lust is compounded by these factors: three of the terms involved, *expence, Spirit,* and *waste* are puns; the four operating terms in line 1 are all of a highly general quality, and seem to be related by parallel construction (Spirit/shame, expence/waste); then to these four related items two more, *lust* and *action,* are added. Are these terms inter-related, and if so, how? The reader cannot work this out—on first reading, perhaps ever.

5. Georgio Melchiori's account of the time frames of the sonnet is splendid; see esp. his diagram of the poem's time scheme in *Shakespeare's Dramatic Meditations: An Experiment in Criticism* (Oxford: Oxford University Press, 1976), 147.

6. Vendler, "Jakobson, Richards," 196.

7. The point is brought out well in Melchiori, *Shakespeare's Dramatic Meditations,* 142–43, from whom I take the idea itself and the quotation from Puttenham.

8. Stephen Booth, *An Essay on Shakespeare's Sonnets* (New Haven: Yale University Press, 1969): see 148–51 for a reading of the sonnet's propulsiveness, which everywhere verges on grammetrics without ever making the premises of grammetrics explicit.

9. Roman Jakobson and Lawrence G. Jones, *Shakespeare's Verbal Art in Th' Expence of Spirit* (The Hague: Mouton, 1970). In addition to Helen Vendler's article mentioned above, there were two distinguished responses to the Jakobson-Jones monograph: I. A. Richards, "Jakobson's Shakespeare: The Subliminal Structures of a Sonnet," *Times Literary Supplement,* 28 May 1970, 589–90; Charles Rosen, "Art Has Its Reasons," *New York Review of Books,* June 17, 1971, 32–38. A sustained argument against Jakobson's preference for symmetries is Michael Shapiro's *Asymmetry.*

**Chapter 10**

1. Here I would list the editions from which I have drawn the fourteen texts in my array:

> Charles Tomlinson, "Oppositions: Debate with Mallarmé," *The Way of a World* (Oxford: Oxford University Press, 1969), 49.
>
> William Carlos Williams, "Portrait of a Lady," *Selected Poems of William Carlos Williams* (New York: New Directions, 1969), 35.
>
> George Oppen, "Anniversary Poem," *Collected Poems* (New York: New Directions, 1975), 219–20.
>
> Cid Corman, "The Tortoise," *Root Song* (Elmwood, Conn.: Potes and Poets Press, 1986), no pagination, but this is poem 15 in Part II..
>
> Edward Dorn, "The Rick of Green Wood," *Collected Poems of Edward Dorn, 1956–1974* (Bolinas, Calif.: Four Seasons Foundation, 1975), 3–4.
>
> Ezra Pound, "The Return," *Selected Poems,* ed. T. S. Eliot (London: Faber and Faber, 1959), 85.
>
> William Wordsworth, from book 1 of the 1805 version, *The Prelude: 1799, 1805, 1850,* ed. Jonathan Wordsworth, M. H. Abrams, and Stephen Gill (New York: Norton, 1979).
>
> Robert Lowell, "Man and Wife," *Life Studies* (New York: Farrar, Straus and Giroux, 1959), 87.
>
> Emily Dickinson, "The Soul Selects Her Own Society," poem 303 in *The Poems of Emily Dickinson,* ed. Thomas H. Johnson (Cambridge, Mass.: Harvard University Press, 1955), 1:225.
>
> John Peck, "Fog Burning Off at Cape May," in *The Broken Blockhouse Wall* (Boston: David R. Godine, 1978), 21–22.
>
> Jonathan Swift, "A Satirical Elegy on the Death of a Late Famous General," in *The Poems of Jonathan Swift,* ed. Harold Williams (Oxford: Oxford University Press, 1958), 1:296–97.
>
> Alfred Tennyson, section 7, *In Memoriam,* ed. Susan Shatto and Marian Shaw (Oxford: Oxford University Press), 43.
>
> William Shakespeare, Sonnet 129, *The Sonnets of Shakespeare,* from the Quarto of 1609 with variorum readings and commentary, ed. Raymond Macdonald Alden (Boston: Houghton Mifflin, 1916), 309.
>
> John Berryman, Sonnet 13, *Berryman's Sonnets [Now First Imprinted]* (New York: Farrar, Straus and Giroux, 1969), 13.

2. Jonathan Culler, "Beyond Interpretation," in *The Pursuit of Signs* (Ithaca, N.Y.: Cornell University Press, 1981), esp. 7, 5, 6, 11. I return to Culler and to Stanley Fish in the final pages of this book.

3. Both the Mallarmé quatrain and its translation are quoted from the text Tomlinson seems to have used, *Stéphane Mallarmé: Poems,* trans. Roger Fry, with commentaries by Charles Mauron (New York: New Directions, by arrangement with Chatto and Windus, London, 1951), 104–5.

4. See on romanticism and reading: my own *The New Poetries;* and especially Tilottama Rajan, *The Supplement of Reading: Figures of Understanding in Romantic Theory and Practice* (Ithaca, NY: Cornell University Press, 1990).

5. Eleanor Berry and Richard D. Cureton commented here in the margins of my manuscript.

6. For more on Edward Dorn, see *Internal Resistances: The Poetry of Edward Dorn,* ed. and with a chapter by Donald Wesling (Berkeley and Los Angeles: University of California Press, 1985).

7. The manuscript of "Man and Wife" is printed in Ian Hamilton, *Robert Lowell: A Biography* (New York: Random House, 1982), 265–66.

8. Dora Sue Besser, "A Prosodic Analysis of Nine Poems by Emily Dickinson, with Special Attention to Last Lines," M.A. thesis, University of California, San Diego, 1981, 68. Also I want to mention Susan Howe's great book, *My Emily Dickinson* (Berkeley, Calif.: North Atlantic Books, 1985). Howe returns us to the manuscript books, as printed in R. W. Franklin, ed., *The Manuscript Books of Emily Dickinson* (Cambridge, Mass.: Harvard University Press, 1981). Here (on 1:450) we find, to the discomfiture of editors and grammetrists, that "pausing" is the first word in the following line, not a line-end event at all for Dickinson at the moment she wrote. Edwin Fussell, in a comment on this page of my manuscript, wrote wisely: "E. D. is so sure in her ear how these poems sound (all the same) that she is completely indifferent how they look on the page—lines end when she comes to the right-hand edge of the paper, and often for no other reason than that." Plainly, when the manuscript books are printed as Dickinson's poems, in wide circulation, we may expect changes in reading.

## Chapter 11

1. From Edward Stankiewicz, "Poetic and Non-Poetic Language in Their Inter-relation," in Davie et al., *Poetics 1,* 11–24.

2. Paul de Man, "Semiology and Rhetoric," *Diacritics* 3 (fall 1973): 30; rpt. in *Allegories of Reading* (New Haven: Yale University Press, 1979). For a largely negative account of de Man's position on tropes and undecidability, see Frank Lentricchia, *After the New Criticism* (Chicago: University of Chicago Press, 1980), esp. 314–17.

3. Wordsworth, *The Prelude,* 5, 52, 53.

4. From the draft printed in Hamilton, *Robert Lowell,* 265–66.

5. The point in this sentence comes directly from Eleanor Berry's comment in the margin of my manuscript.

6. Tennyson, *In Memoriam,* 43, for the variants from the 1850A manuscript.

7. Howe's *My Emily Dickinson* (1985) finds imaginativeness in the chinks of manuscript pages. This is the first book to see on Dickinson's page prosody.

8. *The Oxford Anthology of English Literature,* ed. Frank Kermode and John Hollander (New York: Oxford University Press, 1973), 1:635–36.

9. John McH. Sinclair, "Lines about 'Lines,' " in *Current Trends in Stylistics,* ed. Braj B. Kachru and Herbert F. W. Stahlke (Edmonton, Alberta: Linguistic Research, 1972), 251–62.

10. "Only perception," writes Rudolph Arnheim, "can solve organizational problems through sufficiently free interaction among all the field forces that constitute the patterns to be manipulated": *Visual Thinking* (Berkeley and Los Angeles: University of California Press, 1969), 78. "Discovery, like surprise, favors the well-prepared mind," writes Jerome Brunner: "Needless to say, children who employ constraint location as a

technique preliminary to the formulation of hypotheses tend to be far more organized in their harvesting of information. . . . [Cumulative constructionism] is characterized by sensitivity to constraint, by connective maneuvers, and by organized persistence": *On Knowing: Essays for the Left Hand* (Cambridge, Mass.: Harvard University Press, 1962) 82, 86.

11. Dilligan and Bender, "The Lapses of Time."

12. Robert Dilligan, "Computers and Style: The Prosody of *In Memoriam*," in *Victorian Poetry* 16 (1980): 179–96.

## Chapter 12

1. Dilligan, "Computers and Style."

2. Elizabeth Freund, *The Return of the Reader: Reader-response criticism* (London and New York: Methuen, 1987). Below I mention Seán Burke's related and similarly titled book, *The Death and Return of the Author* (Edinburgh: Edinburgh University Press, 1992).

# Index